India in Translation, Translation in India

India in Translation, Translation in India

Edited by

G.J.V. Prasad

BLOOMSBURY
NEW DELHI • LONDON • OXFORD • NEW YORK • SYDNEY

BLOOMSBURY INDIA
Bloomsbury Publishing India Pvt. Ltd
Second Floor, LSC Building No. 4, DDA Complex, Pocket C – 6 & 7,
Vasant Kunj New Delhi 110070

BLOOMSBURY, BLOOMSBURY ACADEMIC INDIA and the Diana logo are trademarks of Bloomsbury Publishing Plc

First published in India 2019
This edition published 2019

Bloomsbury Academic
An imprint of Bloomsbury Publishing Plc

ISBN: HB: 978-93-88414-19-7; eBook: 978-93-88414-21-0

2 4 6 8 10 9 7 5 3 1

Typeset in Minion Pro by Manipal Digital Systems
Printed and bound in India by Replika Press Pvt. Ltd.

For

the translators of my life,

Kamala and Shubha

Contents

Acknowledgements

I must acknowledge the help I have received from my colleagues at the Centre for English Studies, and thank them for the DSA funds made available under the Special Assistance Programme of the UGC, and to the Research Fellows Rupali and Fuzail A. Siddiqi for their unstinting support. I must thank Fuzail specifically for his great help in putting this book together.

Introduction

India is a nation of translations. India is not a name given by Indians to India, nor did the majority of the population call themselves Hindu. These are the names given by others, names in other languages that they used to speak of people who lived on the banks of the river Sindhu, called Indus by the outsiders. One can see that the name India is derived from the river Indus. The river was called 'Hindu' in Old Persian, derived from the Sanskrit word 'Sindhu'. The Hindus were people who lived near the Indus. Herodotus, the so-called father of history, was perhaps the first one to call the people Indians. Thus, what the country is called today is because of how the name of a river was translated in other languages and how this translation was used further to refer to the people and a community. This naming is a political issue even today, since other countries in the subcontinent may ask what India refers to. This was a question raised during the partition—Pakistan had been a part of India, but India was not an independent nation then. After independence, shouldn't the name India be used for the pre-independent subcontinent? Shouldn't the two new nations be given different names? Obviously, Indian politicians thought otherwise, most of them did not even support the creation of Pakistan. However, while 'India' would ensure the breakaway status of Pakistan, wouldn't it actually make the country an invention of the British? Shouldn't the nation take a name that would refer to our civilisational past? The Constitution has visible traces of such a debate.

> Having proudly declared in the preamble to the Constitution of India on 26 November 1949 that, 'WE, THE PEOPLE OF INDIA, having solemnly resolved to constitute India into a [SOVEREIGN

> SOCIALIST SECULAR DEMOCRATIC REPUBLIC] and to secure to all its citizens: JUSTICE, LIBERTY and EQUALITY', the members of the constituent assembly went on to say in Part I of the Constitution, which delineates the Union and its Territories, that 'India, that is Bharat, shall be a Union of States'. (1.1)

The Constitution of India thus immediately points attention to the problematic issue of naming, that is, the translation—'India, that is Bharat'. We the people of India are also we the people of Bharat. Why did the constitution makers do this? Did they think of our country as India or Bharat or both? Were these two names interchangeable? What about *Hindustan*? After all, Hindustan was also a name that was used for India for a very long time. Was India the nation in English, and Bharat the desh, the native land, in Indian languages? Or was it going to be Bharat in Hindi? Did it also signal a contestation between languages, a hierarchy of languages—'India, that is Bharat' rather than 'Bharat, that is India'?

The answer to some questions is simple—the members of the constituent assembly thought of themselves belonging to both Bharat and India. Suggestions were made during the debate on this (17 September 1949) that instead of saying 'India, that is Bharat', the constitution should read, 'Bharat, or, in the English language, India', or 'Bharat, that is known as India also in foreign countries' or simply as 'Bharat, that is India'. One of the members went so far as to say that it should only be called *Bharatvarsha*. But interestingly, none of them suggested Hindustan, a name they used frequently in their own speeches in the Constituent Assembly. So why Bharat and not Hindustan? There could be conflicting reasons for this choice, one that Hindustan had been appropriated by the Hindu right-wing as the name of the land of Hindus and the other is that Hindustan was the name by which the Mughal North India was known and that Hindustan never really indicated the entire subcontinent. So, on the one hand, Hindustan was associated with the Muslim rule while on the other, Hindustan had been appropriated by the North Indian Hindu right-wing in the slogan, 'Hindi, Hindu, Hindustan'.

Thus, to move from Hindustan to Bharat was to move to pre-Muslim rule times, to the previous millennium. As put by one of the members of the assembly, Kamalapati Tripathi,

> When a country is in bondage, it loses its soul. During its slavery for one thousand years, our country too lost its everything. We lost our culture, we lost our history, we lost our prestige, we lost our humanity, we lost our self-respect, we lost our soul and indeed we lost our form and name. Today after remaining in bondage for a thousand years, this free country will regain its name and we do hope that after regaining its lost name it will regain its inner consciousness and external form and will begin to act under the inspiration of its soul which had been so far in a sort of sleep. It will indeed regain its prestige in the world.

So, India had to shift back through time, from India, from Hindustan, to Bharat, a conceptual space which has existed in scriptures and in the Hindu imagination for a long time and was part of the cultural consciousness of the majority. Hence, India, that is Bharat. Ironically, the constitution never refers to the country as Bharat anywhere else!

Interestingly, on 11 March 2016, the Supreme Court of India dismissed a petition to rename India as Bharata. 'If you want to call this country "Bharat", go right ahead and call it Bharat. If somebody else wants to call this country India, let him call it India. We will not interfere', said the Chief Justice of India T.S. Thakur (*The Hindu*, 2016). Why would he? However, the third option was no longer available—the members of the Constituent Assembly had given up the name Hindustan.

While the debates on naming the country are fascinating in themselves, we are referring to them here to demonstrate the central role that languages and translation have had to play in the making of India. India has always been in translation, and translation has always been important in India. Many of our modern Indian languages were not only born in translation, mostly from Sanskrit and some from Tamil; they were also standardised and influenced by Europeans and translations from European languages. Having mentioned modern Indian languages, it is even more obvious that India lives many languages. The country does not work in only the two languages which are the official languages of the Union—Hindi and English (as declared in Part XVII, Chapter 1 of the Constitution), it has 22 languages recognised by the Constitution as languages of India in its Eighth Schedule (though it must be pointed out that the Constitution is not available in languages other than English and Hindi). English, which is not in this list of Indian languages is the official language or additional official language of twelve states and three Union Territories! In contrast, Hindi is the official language of or additional official language of 10 states and three Union Territories. About 33 other languages are official or additional official languages of Indian states and union territories. About 35 languages are the official languages of India, though the Constitution lists 22 while leaving out English and including six languages—Bodo, Dogri, Kashmiri, Maithili, Sanskrit and Sindhi—which aren't the official languages of any state. The only way that we were one civilisation, and can be a union now is through translation.

In a multilingual country like India, it is obvious that governance would depend on translation. For the colonial powers it was even more important. They translated with great zeal. It wouldn't be an exaggeration to say that our ideas of the majority faith and about our nation, including current assertions of its history, have roots in the motivated or simply uninformed translational activity of the colonisers. They needed the translations to understand, to frame, to fix, and to govern the subcontinent, they mapped our minds and culture just like they mapped our terrain. Many of their motivations are still current with those who want power, who want to impose their ideas of nationalism and India. Translation serves very many purposes.

This book seeks to explore the contours of translation of and in India—how Indian texts travel around the world in translation and how Indian texts travel across languages in the subcontinent, and how texts from various languages of the world travel to India. What influences the choice of texts and the translations both within and outside India? Are there different ideas of India produced through these translations? Or do different ideas of India result in such translations? What changes have there been over the last two hundred odd years, from the time of colonialism and anti-colonial struggle to that of globalisation?

The chapters included in the book look at translations from Indian languages as well as from foreign tongues. We look at the politics and practice of translation and at their impact. How does one rate the success or otherwise of a translation? Have these translations had a cultural impact? What is the role of these translations in their host languages, in their cultural and literary polysystems? The book highlights the work of translators even as we examine the role of politico-cultural structures and the motivations of other agencies that commission and publish translations. The book should kindle and partly satisfy the interest in the creation of borders, both national and sub-national and their crossings, and the reinforcement and crossings of generic borders; the role of translations in political, social and cultural movements; and the theory, methodology and language of translation. We look at both pre-colonial and post-colonial translations in this endeavour. The eighteen chapters in this volume examine various facets of the rich and varied translation activity.

• • •

In his chapter, 'Dnyaneshwar's "*Duji Shrushti*": Poetics and Cultural Politics of Pre-colonial Translation in the *Dnyaneshwari*', Sachin C. Ketkar reads the earliest Marathi commentary on the Bhagwad Gita known as the Dnyaneshwari, the Dnyanadevi or the Bhavarth Deepika (1290) by Dnyaneshwar (1275–1296 CE), which is one of the essential religious and spiritual texts of Maharashtra. Ketkar argues that in the writing of this commentary, in taking Sanskrit into Marathi, what seems to happen is not a simple adoption of cosmopolitan models in the local languages but the creation of new models, genres and literary languages, which are created through translation. He further argues that translation needs to be looked at in a nuanced manner, seeing the text in the context of the complex overlapping and conflictual social and cultural formations of sects, patronage of multiple kinds, innovative talents and systems of caste-class-gender intersectionalities of the period within which the literary polysystem is situated.

Gargi Bhattacharya examines the role of Ishwarchandra Vidyasagar in the making of Hindu laws by the colonisers in her chapter on 'Formation of Hindu Laws through Translation in the Rule of British East India Company: Vidyasagar's Contribution in Society and Legislation'. The officials of the British East India Company believed that it was necessary to understand and implement Hindu laws to govern India. Hence, Hindu legal texts had to be translated into English from Sanskrit. However, the chief Hindu Law books, especially the ones traditionally known as significant for the modern age (Kali Yuga) like Parāśara Smṛti, remained unattended for translation till the beginning of the second half of nineteenth century CE. Her chapter explores and examines the translations by Ishwarchandra Vidyasagar whose aim was to garner support from the English rulers for the remarriage of Hindu widows. His translation of two of his own Bengali works into English under the single title *Marriage of Hindu Widows* in 1855 resulted in the Hindu Widows' Remarriage Act in 1856. Bhattacharya explores the various strategies employed by Vidyasagar to achieve his purpose.

In his chapter on 'Translation and the Formation of Gujarati Literary Public Sphere in the early 1850s: A Critical Study of

Dalpatram's *Lakshmi Natak* (1851)', Hiren J. Patel examines the role of translation in negotiating emergent structures of power in the context of colonial modernity in nineteenth-century Gujarat. Translation was used to reinforce and legitimise power relations. However, this led to new contestations and new equations. Patel argues that translation was integral to the nascent Gujarati literary field of the 1850s. He examines Kavi Dalpatram's *Lakshmi Natak* (1851), a prose translation into Gujarati of Aristophanes' *Wealth*, in order to understand the role played by translation in the formation of Gujarati literary public sphere in the early 1850s. Patel argues that the translation partook of the critique of colonial rule and addressed questions of reform and social emancipation.

Tara Menon, in 'Forging Bhakti: Translation, Conversion and Fraud in the Ezourvedam', writes about the famous case of a fraudulent translation—one that supposedly translates Indian mystical devotion, bhakti, but where the original is imagined! This forgery is an eighteenth-century French work, the Ezourvedam, composed by Jesuit Missionaries. It was intended for translation into Sanskrit, Tamil, and Bengali, as an authentic 'fifth Veda'. The aim was to use the text for conversion, bringing in Christian doctrine as a supposedly Hindu text. However, the text served other purposes, such as, being used as a stick with which to beat Catholicism, most famously by Voltaire who believed it to be an authentic translation!

In 'Twice Removed: A Study of the Form and Style of Dina Natha Deva's English Translation of Kashiramadasa's Medieval Bengali *Mahabharata*', Soham Pain looks at an attempt to translate Kashirama's medieval Bengali Mahabharata into English. He reads the translation closely to explore questions of form, and locates it in the zone between the two different theoretical traditions around translation. Soham Pain argues that while the Western theory of translation insists on literalness and complete loyalty to the source text, the Indian practice allows for much more flexibility on the part of the translator. Seen from this perspective, he concludes that Deva's translation is a hybrid text trying to serve both masters, trying to ensure loyalty and authenticity with respect to the theme and content of the original but on the other hand, breaking away in terms of form and style. There is an implicit hierarchy of languages, the translation aimed at the colonial master in their own tongue.

Lav Kanoi explores two acts of translation, which actually becomes three, in his chapter on 'Colonisation, College and Chai: Virgil's *Aeneid* and Okakura's *The Book of Tea*'. He looks at the translation in both the colonial and the postcolonial contexts. He is as much interested in the stories of translation as in the translation themselves. *Aeneid* became one of the earliest non-Biblical works to be translated directly from a classical European language into a modern Indian language when it was translated into Bengali in 1810 by Henry Sargent, who was then a student at Kolkata's Fort William College. This lost translation was discovered only in this century and republished in 2013 along with an English translation co-authored by Lav Kanoi. Kanoi examines the politics of translation and the aims and implications of the re-publication. He then espouses how he translated Okakura's *The Book of Tea* into Hindi, highlighting the anti-colonial politics of the book.

In 'Migrating Stories: The Panchatantra and the Grimm Tales', Priyada Shridhar Padhye examines how children's stories travel the world. While children's stories are unique to each culture, they seem to lend themselves to translation into other languages and cultures, respecting no boundaries. As she observes, the Grimm's fairy tales with their very European style, content and tradition, as well as the 'frame stories' of the *Panchatantra*, so uniquely Indian, have travelled well and are available and at home in many other languages and cultures. She explores the translational traffic between India and Germany to raise and answer questions about the reason for such translations and whether and how they change the received stories to make them translation, adaptation, appropriation and migration of Indian tales/stories.

In a related chapter, 'India in Translation, Translation in India: Translation, Adaptation, Appropriation and Migration of Indian Tales/Stories', Subhendu Mund argues that translation in India has too often been seen as a story of colonialism. He shows how Indian tales have travelled over millennia, both inside the subcontinent itself as well as outside. He posits that in the history of translation of Indian texts, the colonial enterprise is only a blip and that too is needlessly self-important one and calls for new readings of this history.

Amitendu Bhattacharya's 'The Man of His Heart: Tagore's Kabir' explores Tagore's role as a translator of a major Bhakti poet to medieval Indian saint-poet Kabir positing that the translation was an extension of Tagore's own creative, polemical and political writings. Kabir's message, his iconoclasm, his crusade against ritualism, obscurantism, discrimination, authoritarianism and exploitation seemed to serve Tagore's contemporary purpose. Bhattacharya argues that while Tagore has been read as a mystic poet, one who seemed to be a godsend to Orientalist constructions, and his translation of Kabir has been seen as one mystic poet's obeisance to another, it is the political and the social in Kabir that appeals to him. These translations also decentred both English and Sanskrit, which were central to the Orientalist enterprise.

In her chapter on Faiz, 'Transcending Borders, Bridging Cultures: Reading Faiz Ahmed Faiz', Fatima Rizvi gives us a nuanced reading of Faiz's poetry as well as a comparative study of their translations into English. She reads his humanism as a product of his own cultural translation, of his modification of received aesthetics. She then reads English translations of Faiz's poetry, by Victor Kiernan, Estelle Dryland, Carlo Coppola, Agha Shahid Ali and Keki Daruwalla, to show how the translators engage with his aesthetics and philosophy. She finds that each translator has a different approach, as Faiz poses great formal challenges to them, and that 'the translated Faiz is Faiz transcreated, Faiz adapted, Faiz transformed, or Faiz under erasure'.

In the first of the two chapters on translational traffic between India and France, Nipun Nutan examines the Hindi translations of French fiction in his chapter 'Resisting Voices or the Allure of the Centre: French Fiction in Hindi Translation'. He examines the fiction translated between 1910 and 1949 to understand the reason for the selection of various French texts for translation into Hindi. He argues that it was not a simple case of power relations, of centre and periphery, and that the French meant something else to India which was majorly under British colonial rule. He examines both the economic and political reasons for such translations.

In an exploration of the connections between the visions of two writers from different cultures and different times, Huzaifa Omair Siddiqi writes 'The Kafkaesque in Urdu: Naiyer Masud and the Essence of Translation'. Naiyer Masud, one of the earliest translators of Franz Kafka's stories into Urdu, in his collection *Kafka ke Afsaney* (1978), was Kafkaesque in his own Urdu writings. However, Siddiqi argues that it is not that because of his own style that Masud desired to translate Kafka but that it arose from his obsession with the essence of translation. He posits that both the writers were involved with the fundamental issue of translation, that of turning sound into meaning. He argues that, thus, Masud's choice of translating Kafka was motivated by their common obsession with the origin of the Voice.

In 'Translating Gramsci in Bengali: Redefining the *Buddhijibi* in Post-Liberalisation Bengal', Shinjini Basu looks at an important aspect of the activity of translation, that of political and theoretical texts. It is theoretical texts in translation that most readers treat as originals, treating the translator as invisible, and the act as one that conveys everything as intended by the theorist. Basu pays attention to the politics of translation, which is, reading the translations in terms of cultural, historical and political specificities of both the translators and the texts. Antonio Gramsci's writings have been influential around the world, and Basu reads them against the backdrop of developments in the 1990s—the breakup of the Soviet Union, the collapse of the communist rule, the rise of the right, and the economic liberalization in India. She argues that Bengal needed new theoretical models and to redefine the public intellectual and she reads the translations as an attempt to fulfil this agenda.

In the second of the chapters on the traffic between India and France, 'India through a Translation Anthology: An Evolving Perspective', Runjhun Verma examines the India constructed in a specific anthology of Indian literature translated into French. She argues that representing a complex multilingual country like India is a special challenge to anthologists. There is a politics of hierarchisation of languages in India by Indians. Some languages remain on the fringes and are often unseen by other Indians. She accepts that while multilingual translation anthologies shape a more comprehensive and inclusive image of the country by including a diverse range of literary texts, authors/poets, themes as well as genres, the choices made in these anthologies demonstrate presumptions of what constitutes national culture and of course a bias towards writers with literary reputations. She examines the special volume of *Europe* that anthologized Indian literature in French translation in 2000.

In 'Translating Beckett into Indian language/s: Toward World-building', Samudranil Gupta looks at a fascinating writer who translated his own works and constantly questioned how much language can actually communicate. Gupta explores how translating Beckett into Indian languages can lead to understanding translation as an ethical exercise, one that facilitates world-making. Gupta argues that the unfamiliarity between Indian languages can be exploited in a multilingual translation to bring about the kind of linguistic destabilisation that was Beckett's aim. To this end, he examines Ashish Avikunthak's adaptation of Beckett's *Come and Go* into a Hindi-Bengali film titled *Antaral* or 'Endnote'.

In a chapter on the political and social importance of translation titled, 'Making Trans Experiences Visible through Translations', Regiane Corrêa de Oliveira Ramos argues that translation plays a crucial role in espousing the cause of minorities, in both building solidarity and in intervention with the majority. She writes that this is even more important in a multilingual country like India, where only through translation can minority communities come together in solidarity. She examines the translation of texts by people belonging to the transgender hijra community and argues that the translations help to generate both intra- and international solidarities, constituting an alliance of people fighting against heteronormative patriarchy.

In another chapter titled, 'Enabling Translation: Carrying Disability across Cultures', that explores and emphasizes the activist role of translation, Someshwar Sati argues that translation could and should play a destabilising role—one that challenges various norms including those of ability, of normalcy. He asks how translations can challenge the norms inherent in language, in the binary opposition between ability and disability. He explores the emancipatory role of translating a disability text and how it can create a more egalitarian India.

In the last chapter in this volume, 'Money, Work and Family in *Ghachar Ghochar*: A Translational Economy of India', Amrapali Saha explores the idea of India in this Kannada novel that is made available in English translation. She argues that the Kannada novel is in itself an insightful translation of different Indias. She focuses on the networks of money, work and family in contemporary middle-class India. She posits that hybridity is essential to translation, that what we have at the end is two texts, each authentic, each impure. Her reading argues against any kind of hierarchisation and also asserts that to read India in English, one must read India in English translation.

Thus, we begin and end with the felt necessity for translation, that is, translation of and in India.

— G.J.V. Prasad

1

Dnyaneshwar's 'Duji Shrushti': Poetics and Cultural Politics of Pre-colonial Translation in the Dnyaneshwari

Sachin C. Ketkar

The earliest Marathi commentary on the *Bhagwad Gita* known as the *Dnyaneshwari*, the *Dnyanadevi*, or the *Bhavarth Deepika* (AD 1290) by Dnyaneshwar or Dnyanadev (AD 1275–1293) is one of the essential religious and spiritual texts in Maharashtra whose influence on the later development of Marathi literature and culture is enormous. While the *Bhagwad Gita* comprises 700 Sanskrit verses or *shlokas* in the classical '*Anushthuba*' meter, the *Dnyaneshwari* runs into around 9,000 *ovis* or Marathi form of folk verse. In a striking metaphor towards the end of his book, Dnyaneshwar tells his guru Nivrutti Nath, 'O my Master, you have made me create this second universe in the form of this work, and that makes me mock at sage Vishwamitra, who created a transient world for Trishanku, simply to demean god Brahma. But this literary creation of mine will live forever' (Chapter 18, Verse 1886–87). His act is like that of creating '*duji shrusti*', an alternative universe like Vishwamitra creating an alternative world for Trishanku. However, Vishwamitra's world was flawed so he mocks at it, while his own creation is not. This is possible because of the Guru's grace and the grace of saints who he addresses in the '*dharma kirtan*', that is a form of religious performance. This chapter explores the implications of reading this act of creating '*duji shrushti*' as an act of translation from the point of view of contemporary translation studies.

The expanded notion of translation used in order to approach pre-colonial texts like the *Dnyaneshwari* reveals a rich body of metaphors like that of Trishanku's '*duji shrushti*' that can be seen as models of cross-linguistic and cross-cultural communication in pre-colonial multilingual society. An attempt then is made to historically situate these notions in their wider literary, social and cultural contexts.

Vernacularisation and Modern Ambivalent Constructions of Bhakti

The period in which it was composed is significant for South Asia as well as Europe as these places witnessed, in Sheldon Pollock's words, 'transformation in cultural practice, social-identity formation, and political order with far-reaching and enduring consequences'. He understands the creation of such a text as part of the process of 'vernacularisation', or 'the historical process of choosing to create a written literature, along with its complement, a political discourse, in local languages according to models supplied by a superordinate, usually cosmopolitan, literary culture' (Pollock 2006, 23).

Understanding of the cultural politics of texts like *Dnyaneshwari* and bhakti literature in modern times has been ambivalent and controversial. Its legacy has been variously contested. Christian Lee Novetzke extends the notion of vernacularisation into a larger social and cultural context by describing it as 'the strategic use of the topos of everyday life within a social, political, artistic, linguistic, and cultural process in which the quotidian expands at the center of a given region's public culture'. Novetzke reads the *Dnyaneshwari* as an emblem of the process of vernacularisation investing public culture with idioms of the everyday and the quotidian was valorised in public and political expression. It was compelled by a critique of social inequity as a result of this emphasis on ordinary life and the literary sphere engendered by vernacularisation inaugurated the first trace of 'a nascent' or 'rudimentary' public sphere in Maharashtra (Novetzke 2016, ix). Even the phenomenon of 'bhakti' as he notes can be understood not so much as a 'movement' or 'personal devotion' but as an 'ongoing effort to construct publics of belief, maintained through intricate systems of memory' (Novetzke 2016, xi). He points out the parallels in other fields like visual arts or political democracy in the twentieth century (for example, the Shiv Sena) and argues that vernacularisation as a force is 'evident in the thirteenth century Maharashtra as in the twenty-first century India' (Novetzke 2016, 11), but does not claim that vernacularisation (or religion or bhakti for that matter) in thirteenth-century India engenders modern Indian democracy—it does not (Novetzke 2016, 12). He shows that Dnyanadev, 'rejected a world of elite Sanskrit learning such as the Vedas—surely a religious sphere—in order to transpose elite salvational possibilities to a quotidian religious field'. Vernacularisation, according to Novetzke is 'fundamentally about expanding the sphere of everyday life and representing that expansion in expressive forms (literature, art, language, politics, etc.) it is also about noticing difference and distinction in many areas of life experience' (Novetzke 2016, 19). He goes on to say, 'it would be as wrong to say that bhakti is unequivocally and always a form of social protest as it would be to ignore the many examples of social protest enunciated in the language of bhakti' (Novetzke 2016, 21).

The earliest scholars like R.D. Ranade (1933/1982) called bhakti 'democratic mysticism' and Dnyaneshwar an 'intellectual mystic' (p. 16). On the one hand, it is commonplace for critics like Gangadhar Gadgil (1994) to typically hold that Dnyaneshwar, 'laid the foundation of a social revolution. Dharma or spiritual experience in its highest form was brought within the reach of the ordinary people. Potters, cobblers, tailors, maidservants, all shared this spiritual experience' (Ranade 1982, 9). Devy (1993) would also argue that the whole bhakti movements of poetry in India had the desire of 'translating' the language of spirituality from Sanskrit to the languages of the people

(Devy 1993, 136) and the medieval translations from Sanskrit aimed at 'liberating the society', unlike the colonial ones that were merely 'reactionary' (Devy 1993, 150). Devy also calls the author 'a young revolutionary writer' who raised 'several radical questions for Indian society' (Devy 2009, 49–59). B.R. Sunthankar (1947/2017) writing from a Marxist perspective and drawing parallel from the Western renaissance would argue that the saints coming from various sections of society, namely various castes from the traditional agricultural occupations like 'aluteydaar-balutedars' provided a social and cultural leadership to a *class* uprising or some sort of peasant uprising against the feudal Brahmin—and royal establishment.

On the other hand, while historians like V.K. Rajwade would say that these saints ruined Maharashtra with their other worldliness (cited by Sunthankar 2017, 3), the intellectual critics from the Dalit-Bahujan sections would have problems with the very selection of the *Gita* as source language text, described by Dr Ambedkar as 'counter-revolutionary'. Ambedkar's own critical assessment of the Bhakti is sharp and accurate. Commenting on the *bhakti* uprising, he says,

> It was a battle to prove whether the human Brahmin is great or the bhakta. The *bhaktas* did not bother to resolve or even ask the question whether human Brahmin is great or the human Shudra is great. The santas (the saints) won the battle as even the Brahmins accepted the greatness of the santa. However, this victory was of no use in annihilation of the *chaturvarnya* system. You can say that while the *santas* could boast that you can keep your *chaturvarnya* to yourself, we will be bhaktas and put the greatest of Brahmins to shame, they did not even touch the *chaturvarnya* system. Bhakti does not ensure that humaneness is valued. The value of humanism is self-evident and the bhaktas never fought to establish this fact. (translated by the author, cited in Moray 2014, 341)

He also asked what did our people achieve by going to Pandharpur? To Dalits who approached him for supporting their move to build a temple for Chokha Mela, Ambedkar suggested them to build a

Buddhist monastery instead. Ambedkar also threatened that those who go to Pandharpur would be banned from joining his movement (Moray 2014).

In spite of this dismissal, Ambedkar's own position was ambivalent at times. Ashok Kamat draws attention to an interview conducted with him in 1940, where Ambedkar says that while he did not accept the philosophy of Dnyaneshwar, he liked their literature due to the opulence of language and not its philosophy. Kamat also points out that the heading for Ambedkar's own revolutionary periodical *Bahishkrut Bharat* (Oppressed India) carried a quotation from the *Dnyaneshwari* on karma yoga (2003, 179–80).

Ambedkar is actually echoing aggressive critique launched by Jyotiba Phule in the late nineteenth century. Phule believes that after the destruction of Buddhism at the hands of Shankaracharya,

> When the brave followers of the Prophet Hajrat Mohammed destroyed not merely the religious contrivances of the Aryan Brahmins but also destroyed the idols of the Somnath temple with their swords, started to liberate the Shudra farmers from the swindle of the brahmins, the brahmins like Mukundraj and Dnyaneshwar selected some portions of the Bhagwat texts and brought them into Prakrit in the form of the texts like the *Vivek Sindhu* and the *Dnyaneshwari* as part of their conspiracy and deceived the farmers so much that they started considering the Koran as well as Muslims as inferior and started hating them. (cited in Padhye 2017, 12, translation mine)

In a way, Phule's polemic draws our attention to the hegemonic and oppressive dimensions of Brahminism within bhakti and it is indeed valid up to a point. However, transferring the literary language of spirituality to a non-elite audience did undeniably create possibilities of cultural articulation and canonisation among not just women and *shudras* like Namdev, Chokha Mela, Sena Nhavi, Gora Kumbhar, Janabai, or, later on, Tukaram, but also non-'Hindu' writers like Father Stephens who wrote *Khristapurana* or Hussain Ambar who wrote a commentary on the *Gita*.

Patton Burchett (2009) in his analysis of hagiographies of the Dalit saints maintains,

> While the notion of bhakti as an egalitarian, democratizing and revolutionary force uniting an Indian nation is a rather recent one, the idea that devotion is the true path to salvation is far more time-tested.... In presuming (and exalting) the presence of a democratizing and revolutionary spirit in bhakti across history, many scholars have unintentionally presented a notion of bhakti that is far more coherent, consistent, and anachronistically modern than what a close reading of bhakti texts actually demonstrates. (Burchett 2009, 116–17)

He demonstrates that the lack of impact of the perceived egalitarian ideals of bhakti on the social structure is not merely a failure to put bhakti theory into practice but rather that the messages in these hagiographies are themselves far less democratising and socially progressive than they might at first appear that, in subtle ways, these stories also reinforce the social hierarchy and confirm Brahmins as possessing a social identity of higher purity and value than any other. In other words, what appears to be egalitarian bhakti theory is itself, on one level, subtly working against the actual practice of egalitarian social relations and for the maintenance of the purity-based caste hierarchy. He cautions us that we should not approach the theory/ideology of bhakti as some unitary presence inherent in bhakti songs, poetry, and hagiographical stories, but rather as a range constructed variously by different readers and listeners in their encounters with bhakti art forms (Burchett 2009, 117–19). While the current chapter extends this approach, it argues in favour of situating the poetics of the bhakti literature in the historical context of political negotiations of sectarian ideologies and the questions of patronage.

The *Dnyaneshwari* as Translation

However, I seek to demonstrate in my reading of the *Dnyaneshwari* using theoretical advances in translation studies and comparative literary studies, what seems to happen in this process is not a simple adoption of cosmopolitan models (*teeka*/bhashya) in the local languages but the *creation* of *new* models, genres, and literary languages towards different functional ends that are neither 'Sanskrit' nor 'Marathi', but *interliterary* in the sense of the term used by Durisin (1984) and are created through translation, understood as a process of semiotic transformation. In the social and cultural domain, bhakti literature is neither a single or simple political project of social liberation nor simple continuation of Puranic Brahminical hegemony and instead of seeing it simplistically as 'vernacularisation', 'revolution', or 'counter-revolution', the processes of emergence of new literatures have to be understood in context of the complex overlapping and conflictual social and cultural formations of sects, patronage of multiple kinds, innovative intellects, and caste-class-gender intersectionalities of literary polysystem of the period.

Durisin uses the terms interliterary process to overcome 'the vulgarization and one-sidedness implicit in the idea of "influence" or "causality"' as this approach does not take into account 'the factors of autonomous individuality' on one hand as well as

> the factors which integrate in the work the moments of native progressive development, tradition and continuity, activised by factors of natural causation, as well as of creative negation and overcoming... it is for this reason that in comparative research we stress the necessity of taking into account the determining principle of selectivity existing in the recipient element. (Durisin 1984, 50–1)

The notion of interliterariness does away with the assumptions of hierarchy or linear one-directional transmission between Sanskrit and *bhashas* implicit in the term 'vernacularisation'.

I would further argue that instead of using terms like 'vernacularisation' or the binary of 'marga' versus 'desi' to conceptualise the emergence of new literary languages in the subcontinent, the idea of 'translation' in semiotic sense as discussed by Jakobson (2000), William

Frawley (2000), and Yuri Lotman (1994) cannot only help us uncover the cultural mechanisms underlying the creation of new poetics, literary languages, models and the languages of self-description and identity, but also allow us to overcome the Sanskrit-centric (neo-Orientalist) or an Anglocentric view of the cultures in the subcontinent as these semiotic mechanisms are not culture/language specific but are the mechanisms underlying all cultural meaning making.

It is obvious that the idea of translation has to go beyond the Catfordian definition of translation as 'replacement of textual material in one language (SL) equivalent textual material in another language (TL)' (Catford 1965, 20) to be of any use in the study of pre-colonial Marathi literature. Common assumptions underlying the notions of 'culture', 'literature' and 'translation' used widely in literary studies today are extremely restrictive. 'The literary text' is often understood to be 'a printed object', 'translation' is assumed be 'transmission of invariant information across languages' and 'culture' is often thought of in monolingual terms. This becomes even more limiting in the context of pre-colonial South Asian civilisations, where the texts were very often dynamic, largely oral and performative, involving retellings, commentaries and rewritings from multiple linguistic and cultural sources.

As André Lefevere (2000) has argued, reading translation as an instance of 'refraction', that is, 'the adaptation of a work of literature to a different audience, with the intention of influencing the way in which that audience reads the work' (Lefevere 2000, 235), can help make a significant contribution to literary theory as refractions play a very important role in evolution of literatures. He points out that,

> A writer's work gains exposure and achieves influence mainly through 'misunderstandings and misconceptions', or, to use a more neutral term, refractions. Writers and their work are always understood and conceived against a certain background or, if you will, are refracted through a certain spectrum, just as their work itself can refract previous works through a certain spectrum. (Lefevere 2000, 234)

Moving away from the Romanticism based approach to literary studies that relies on assumptions like the authors creating the texts from nothing (ex nihilo), or that the texts have a sacred character which should not be tampered with or the possibility of recovering the author's 'true intentions', Lefevere argues that the approach based on system thinking to literature does not suffer from such assumptions. He proposes a framework for analysis of refractions by describing the spectrum or literary system that refracts the texts. The literary system consists of a set of constraints like the regulatory body of various kinds of patronage, a system of poetics consisting of both an inventory component (genre, certain symbols, characters, prototypical situations) and a 'functional' component, an idea of how literature has to, or may be allowed to, function in society, and the constraint of natural language (Lefevere 2000, 236). Dnyaneshwar's '*teeka*' or '*bhashya*' of the Sanskrit text (source language text) in another language (Marathi) is clearly an instance of refraction involving 'manipulation' of the *Gita* in Marathi. Using the notion of translation in this way, we cannot only understand the cultural mechanisms underlying refractions, but also explain their contribution to the recipient literary systems, especially in the formation of new literary languages, poetics and politics of identity and cultural politics.

Lefevere's theorisation of translation is analogous to Even-Zohar's conceptualisation of translated literature as not only occupying a central position in the literary polysystem but as also being the most active part within it, shaping the centre of the polysystem by becoming the means of elaborating the new repertoire (an aggregate of laws and elements that govern the production of texts) especially in younger literatures (Even-Zohar 1990, 46–47). Translation and transfer according to Even-Zohar are very important modes of literary 'interference'.

William Frawley (2000) defines translation as 'recodification' and 'hence, a theory of translation is a set of propositions about how, why, when, where ... coded elements are rendered into other codes. As such, translation is nothing short of an essential problem of semiosis: it is the problem of transfer of codes (251)'. According to Frawley, this conception of translation subsumes the question of interlingual transfer (as language is not the only code) and it is not solely the question of identity and synonymy as cross-coding and recodification occurs whether or not synonymy or identity exists. Besides, as Frawley demonstrates, translation is always an innovation as a third code is produced. The question is not whether the new code (text) actually individuates itself in the translation. In a sense, the new text gets away from the translator by dictating its own necessities and logic. Instead of asking whether the translation is literal or free we should be asking whether the innovation is moderate or radical. If the new code is a moderate innovation, it adheres closely to either the matrix code or the target code. On the other hand, radical innovations occur when the third code begins to 'break away' from both the matrix and target codes. As the new code establishes its own rules (its own redundancy), the dependency of that code decreases and the possibility of new knowledge from that code increases (Frawley 2000, 262).

Yuri Lotman (1994) has elaborated upon the semiotic dimension of translation extensively. He distinguishes between two major functions of texts. The first function is the adequate transmission of information and the second is the generation of new meanings. The most desirable condition for the first function is the complete overlap of codes between senders and receivers of messages. Since this situation is virtually impossible, an intermediary is developed, which Lotman terms the 'text-code'. The text-code, of which the Bible is the most obvious example, serves an interpretive and prescriptive role in the transmission of texts. The essay shows how the *Dnyaneshwari* became an instance of the text-code. In fact, Lotman develops a full-fledged theory of culture as a polyglot phenomenon, where translation plays a key role in generation of meaning.

The question whether there was 'a theory' of translation in pre-colonial India needs to be addressed here. Just as the terms 'literature', 'culture', 'translation' and even 'history' have to be reconfigured in the pre-colonial South Asian context, the term 'theory' too has to be rethought. Though the term 'theory' has a problematic and historical trajectory, and as a 'working definition', we can use it to imply the conceptual models or frameworks we use to explain and understand social or cultural phenomena. In this sense 'metaphors', understood as cognitive models in Lakoff and Johnson's sense (1981), can also be seen as an instance of 'theory'. Dnyaneshwar has used multiple metaphors to describe his activity of interlingual interpretation and we will look at some striking instances here.

Dnyaneshwar's Poetics of Translation

The term '*anuwaad*' (literally 'saying after' or repeating) which is translated as 'translation' these days, was a common term in the pre-colonial intellectual discourse and Dnyaneshwar uses it often in his commentary to describe his activity. In the tenth *adhyaya* (chapter), he goes on to say that though it is impossible for a common person to comment (*anirvachya*) on the *Gita* composed by the great Ved Vyasa (Chapter 10, Verse 35), it is because of his guru's power (*samarthya*) that he could do it and do it with courage (*anuwaadlo dheet pane*) (Chapter 10, Verse 22). Translation or commentary of the text of great spiritual (and worldly) power like the *Bhagwad Gita* though impossible in theory, is possible due to the grace of his guru (his elder brother Nivrutti Nath) and '*santas*', because with the grace of these people nothing is impossible. In fact, he goes on to say, translation as grace of the Guru by which you can get the Gita '*aaiti*', 'on a platter' and no one should be surprised that I can tell the Gita in Marathi (Chapter 18, Verse 1729). Dnyaneshwar's '*anuwaad*' is actually '*anuwaad*' of Nivrutti Nath's *anuwaad*.

Avadhesh Kumar Singh (2014) cautions that translating '*anuwaad*' as 'translation' is a 'wrong translation', as it implies a pedagogical strategy for knowledge transmission and that Jaimini Nyaymala would define it as '*gnyatasya kathanam anuwada*' or '*anuwaad* is stating something that is already known'. However, *anuwaad* in another language involves interpretation and this is where Jakobson's famous theorisation of translation as the meaning of any linguistic sign is its translation into some further, alternative sign, especially a sign 'in which it is more fully developed', becomes pertinent. He then goes on to lay out his famous tripartite division of translation: 'We distinguish three ways of interpreting a verbal sign: it may be translated into other signs of the same language, into another language, or into another, nonverbal system of symbols' (Singh 2014, 114). Jakobson's theorisation alerts us to the fact that no transmission of knowledge and pedagogical strategy is free from interpretation of one set of signs into other signs. Hence, *anuwaad* across linguistic codes, in a semiotic sense, definitely involves translation.

Interestingly, the *Dnyaneshwari* has a very unusual type of dialogism compared to the *Bhagwad Gita*. While the *Gita* is framed around the discussion of Sanjaya and Dhritrashtra within which we have a dialogue of Krishna and Arjuna, the *Dnyaneshwari* is framed as '*dharma kirtan*' (Chapter 18, Verse 1792) around the addressor Dnyaneshwar himself, the addressees 'Maharashtra Mandali' (Chapter 18, Verse 1802) consisting of the *santas* or saints and his guru Nivrutti Nath who even interrupts Dnyaneshwar when he is digressing saying, 'Enough, you don't have to tell us all this. Be quick and give your thought to the work in hand' (Chapter 1, Verse 83). Thus, the Sanskrit '*teeka*' or '*bhashya*' genre, typically involving commentary and gloss of philosophically ambivalent terms and meant primarily for the literate upper-caste elite reader, is transformed into performative 'dharma kirtan' using folk metres like '*ovi*' meant for different 'publics'. It is that this process is not a simple adoption of cosmopolitan models (*teeka*/*bhashya*) in the local languages in 'top-to-bottom' transmission but the creation of new models, genres, literary languages, that are *functionally* and *contextually* different. While traditionally the *ovi* was a free-flowing folk genre (*janapada ovi*) used by women for singing while working at a grinding stone (*jata*) or a water wheel (*rahat*), Dnyaneshwar developed a more 'literary' form of rhythmic prose or '*granthika ovi*' (literally, the *ovi* of the book). Such models are neither entirely 'Sanskrit' nor 'Marathi', but interliterary in the sense of the term used by Durisin and are created through translation, understood as a cross-linguistic process of semiotic transformation.

A 1,000-odd *ovi* commentary on the 700-odd *anushtubha* shlokas of the *Bhagwad Gita* as recodification is neither adhering to the genre-code of Sanskrit commentary nor the code of traditional folk form of *ovi* literature, but what Frawley terms as 'radical innovation' that establishes itself as what Lotman has called 'the text-code'. This text-code becomes an important component of what Even-Zohar has called 'repertoire' of the emergent literary polysystem. Dnyaneshwar is forging a new language for literary composition in Marathi which becomes a model for later 'bhashya-teeka' of the *Gita*. It set a model for the long and seminal tradition of *bhashyakaars* or commentators on the *Gita* like Dasopanta in the sixteenth century, Waman Pandit in the seventeenth century and Amber Hussein among others.

Dasopanta (1551–1615) is reported to have composed around five commentaries on the *Gita*, out of which *Geetarnava* and *Geetarthachandrika* are available. His *Geetarnava* is a long commentary on the *Gita* in about 1 lakh and quarter *ovis*. Waman Pandit's (1608–1695) *Samashloki* translation of *Bhagwad Gita* is known as *Yathartha Deepika*. He claims to be more precise than Dnyaneshwar, Dasopanta and others. The *Yathartha Deepika* is three times the length of *the Dnynaneshwari* and emphasises knowledge instead of bhakti. Father Stephens (1549–1619) who composed the *Christa Purana* in Marathi is also deeply influenced by the *Dnyaneshwari*.

In Lotman's terminology, *Dnyaneshwari* can be seen as introducing 'explosive' changes, that is, unanticipated and abrupt changes in the language of Marathi poetry. Creativity and innovation in the cultural semiotics model elaborated by Lotman are products of a translational mechanism. All other commentators on the *Gita* after the *Dnyaneshwari* worked with the repertoire expanded by Dnyaneshwar and went on to develop it further.

While Dnyaneshwar and other Marathi composers would use the terminology of Sanskrit poetics extensively they would also come up with distinctively reconfigured poetics that would be distinctively Marathi. In the 10th chapter Dnyaneshwar says,

> I shall tell you that tale, which is full of savour and beauty. With the beauty of this language, the serene sentiment will surpass the amorous sentiment and because of that, these verses will adorn the Marathi Literature. If you will read closely, the original Sanskrit text and its Marathi commentary, you will be at a loss to know which the original text is. When ornaments embellish the beautiful body of a maiden, it is difficult to judge which adorns what. Similarly, both the Sanskrit and Marathi languages have come together to explain the purport of the Gita. Listen now, with a serene mind, how they illumine and embellish the truth.... (Yardi [1991]2011, 41–45)

> When one wishes to disclose the purport to a text, the sentiments receive a boost, and the literary art shown in that regard becomes an object of admiration. I have, therefore, borrowed the beauty and youth of the Marathi language to elucidate the truths contained in the Gita. (Yardi [1991]2011, 475)

While Dnyaneshwar definitely uses the terminology of Sanskrit poetics of the *vangmay*, *sahitya*, *rasa*, *alankara*, and *kavya*, it is not a process of simple adoption as Pollock seems to imply. Pollock's own discussion on the meanings of these terms needs to be taken into account at this juncture. He translates the term 'vangmay' as 'the things made of words', and claims that the theory and practice of Sanskrit kavya was 'the single most powerful determinant of the vernacular conception of literature until it was supplemented or displaced by Persian and English counterparts' (Pollock 2003, 42). He draws upon King Bhoja's *Shringarprakasha* (Illumination of Passion) written in eleventh century for his conceptualisation of 'kavya' and 'sahitya'. Bhoja reiterates the famous definition of kavya as sahitya (unity of word and meaning) and provides a classification of various types of discourses and textualities. He says that *vakyam* or the unit of discourse can be classified as per the species, that is, 'languages' in three ways: Sanskrit, Prakrit, and Apabhramsa. The Sanskrit *vakya* can be classified again in three ways: (*a*) those relating to revelation (the Vedic utterances, subdivided into mantras or liturgical formulas and brahmanas or exegetical texts), (*b*) those related to the seers (the texts that are remembered or the *smriti* and the texts based on ancient lore or the *puranas*), and (*c*) utterances related to the world that are subdivided into the sciences or systematic thought—the shashtras and the 'kavya' or literature. Pollock argues that in spite of the fact that this classification was never watertight and there are elements of *kavya* in the Vedic texts and the *itihasa* (the puranic texts) are termed as kavyas, and the elements from the puranas appear in the kavyas, the non-kavya texts were treated with 'an ontology, authority and referentiality radically different from kavya' (Pollock 2003, 60). There was an 'untranscendable line' drawn between kavya and Veda (Pollock 2003, 55) and the epics were supposed to be performed, taught and reproduced and also read, understood and appreciated differently from *kavya* (Pollock 2003, 59). It should also be borne in mind here that King Bhoja elevated Sringara or the erotic sentiment as the most important *rasa* in *kavya*.

Sadanand Moray has drawn attention to the influence of Kashmiri Shaivism in the form of the Nath tradition as well as the poetics of Abhinavagupta and Anandvardhana that considered the epics as 'paradigm' for literary theorisation on Marathi poetics of the period (*Trayodashi* 21–27). Both these theorists, according to Moray, sought to overcome the compartmentalisation between *itihasa shashtra* and kavya and held that the *dhwani* or artistic suggestion or meaning was the soul of poetry rather than a specific rasa or a form of textuality and genre. Hence in theory, their famous commentaries on the *Gita*, which is both *itihasa* (from the Mahabharata) as well as *shashtra*, should have focused on unfolding the '*dhwanyartha*' or the artistically suggested meaning of the text in terms of *rasa*. However, Anandvardhans' commentary on *Gita* is unavailable and Abhinava's own commentary does not use his own theorisation to read the *Gita*. Dnyaneshwar, Moray believes, completes Abhinava's unfinished task. Like Abhinava, Dnyaneshwar is eulogising the *Shanta* rasa or the serene sentiment instead of *sringara* or the erotic sentiment, and by doing so he is implicitly rejecting the courtly *kavya* tradition expounded by King Bhoja in favour of the poetics of Shaiva ascetics developed by Ananda and Abhinava. Moray would also point out that in Marathi bhakti, *sringara rasa* has never found a prominent place, though it exists, as in other Vaishnava bhakti traditions. Pollock's understanding of vernacularisation overlooks this critical 'principle of selectivity', agency and historicity of Sanskrit-bhasha negotiation. This subtle subversion is also found in Dnyaneshwar's attitude towards Sanskrit-bilingualism.

The common metaphor for this activity is that his commentary is that of translation as an ornament in the desi language ('*desikar lene*'). He uses it to diplomatically negotiate the cultural asymmetry implicit in Sanskrit-bhasha binary by explicitly pitching for Marathi without running down Sanskrit—both the Sanskrit text (the beautiful body) and the commentary (the ornament) are beautiful in their own right, independent of each other and yet have come together to bring out the knowledge in the *Gita*. However, when they come together their beauty makes the difference between the original and the translation vanish in some sort of advaita. This ornament also brings out the poetic potential in Marathi and boosts its power as a literary language, and, on the other hand, it confers youth upon an aged language like Sanskrit.

Dnyaneshwar tirelessly champions Marathi, for instance in the sixth chapter he says,

> This sixth chapter will be told in a literary style, to which you should listen with rapt attention. I shall choose such beautiful diction of the local language (Marathi) that it will easily win by its sweetness, a wager with nectar. Its melodious words will outshine musical notes and in their presence even fragrance will lose its sweetness. (11–15)

Dnyaneshwar's project to forge a new powerful literary language and at the same time enrich it with the wealth of spiritual knowledge by refracting the *Gita* in his book is reiterated. *Anuwaad* and refraction remain essential in this process of creating a new literary language. In Chapter 12, for instance, he says:

> Therefore, O magnanimous mother, [his guru Nivrutti Nath]who is the wish-yielding tree to your devotees, gives me leave to unfold this literary work. Oh mother, pray help me to create oceans of the nine sentiments, mines of figures of speech and cliffs of imports of the Gita. Let me open up in the land of the mother-tongue, mines of gold and cultivate rows of creepers, in the form of thoughts. Let there be laid out always, dense orchards of topics of knowledge, laden with the fruits of discussions. (Yardi 2011, 183)

Dnyaneshwar obviously wants to make it a win-win situation for both the languages. This aspect of Dnyaneshwar's theory of translation draws attention to the fact that the Sanskrit-Desibhasha bilingualism is not exactly analogous to either to bhasha-bhasha bilingualism (say Tamil-Kannada) or English-Bhasha bilingualism that emerged after the British colonialism. This is because bhasha-bhasha bilingualism is largely about two societies separated by two languages like Tamil and Kannada while English-Bhasha bilingualism implies the dimension of social mobility and class that Sanskrit-Bhasha did not offer due to the *varna-jati* rigidity.

Cultural Contexts of Pre-colonial Translation: Poetics and Sectarian Ideologies

However, Dnyaneshwar's own position on Sanskrit-bhasha bilingualism can be contrasted with the writers of the Mahanubhava sect, a sect that emerged in thirteenth-century Maharashtra. The sociologist A.M. Shah has argued that at least since the twelfth century, sects have been a crucial component of Hindu religion and society and should be considered an important component of a social structure in their own right and not just another form of some other structure such as caste (Shah 2006, 209–48). Devy notes that the Indian society during the last ten centuries has been characterised by the processes of sect formation in which they start off as critiques of the caste system and the 'establishment' of the minority elites but turn their key texts and symbols into 'totems' whose hypnotic power appeals to the unconscious instead of reason and hence actually diminishes the ability to reason. Sociologically, Devy notes, sect-formation and canon-formation are analogous movements (Devy 2009, 49–59).

Recent attempt to theorise sectarian formation in precolonial India by Elaine M. Fisher (2017) is a fruitful way of understanding the dynamics sects or *sampradyas* in Hinduism. Avoiding the Orientalist and Protestant constructions of sects as a dissent from some unified Brahminical church or monolithic Hinduism (which never existed), she argues that sectarian communities are not to be understood as Venn diagrams of people and doctrines, demarcated by artificial boundaries, but dynamic social systems composed of networks of religious actors, institutions—temples, monasteries, lineages—and the religious meanings they produce. She draws upon Niklas Luhmann's notion of social system to understand sects as meaning-constituting systems, an operationally closed set of social institutions that maintain—and in fact reconstitutes—its own boundaries internally through the structures of meaning it generates, 'an autopoetic system'. That is to say, Hindu sects function autonomously from one another as meaning-constituting systems, each individually reproducing the religious institutions that endow participation in that community with sectarian-inflected religious identity. Macroscopically, she notes, the aggregate of such mutually independent systems facilitates the balance of an entire ecosystem—or, in our case, a religion inflected to its core by pluralism (Fisher 2017, 13–14).

The organic metaphor in Fisher's depiction of sectarian landscape on the subcontinent as a pluralistic ecosystem should not be understood as implying harmony and amity between the sects. In fact, as Richard Burghart (1978) has shown in the context of the Ramanandi sect in eighteenth-century northern India, the sects were often in conflict and intense competition over three important limited resources: devotees and disciples, pilgrimage routes and pilgrimage centres, and political patronage (cited in Okita 2014, 3). Such sectarian formations are critical, if not the only, institutional contexts of pre-colonial Indian literature.

According to V.B. Kolte (1954/2014), there were three significant centres of religious movements, three sects, in Maharashtra between AD 1275–1290. The first one was the Mahanubhava sect situated in the Vidarbha region on the bank of the river Godavari which was led by Nagdevacharya, It rejected the Vedic scriptures as '*pramana* or authoritative' (that would include the notions of *varnashrama*– the dharma of varna and the ideas of the superiority of Brahmins). It would reject rituals and would be based on the ontological dualism (*dwaita*) and propagate devotion (bhakti) for Krishna. The other was based in Paithan and Nevase which was based on '*puranmatvadi sanatani*' that is the Vedic orthodoxy that upheld 'the *varnashrama* dharma' and was led by Dnyaneshwar, and the third was centred at the southern boundaries of Maharashtra in Pandharpur and was led by Namdev (d. 1350) called the Varkaris who propagated devotion to Vitthala, and though it rejected ritualism and caste-division, it would accept the authority of the Vedas indirectly. They argued that '*nama* bhakti' remembering the name of the God and bhakti *marga* or the path of devotion was the true message of the Vedas. Though the Mahanubhavas rejected the *varnashrama* and Vedic authority, the Varkaris were the people who suffered the most due to the caste system. Kolte accuses Dnyaneshwar of imposing this 'slavish' mentality on the Varkaris who came from a wide range of social backgrounds. He says the Varkaris accepted Dnyaneshwar as he was an outcaste by birth, but he actually co-opted the movement and established himself as the leader thus erasing the possibility of the Mahanubhavas and Varkaris coming together as Marathi Krishna *bhaktas* (Kolte 2014, 37–38). The position comes close to Phule's position mentioned previously.

The Mahanubhava were the earliest writers to use Marathi as a literary language and were equally great champions of the Marathi language. They were the first to ascribe religious meaning to a whole region that they called 'Maharashtra' and assert that it is better in significant respects than other places. They are theologically extremely exclusivist, dualists (*dvaita waadins*), and recognise only one supreme God who has had multiple incarnations. It places an extremely high value on asceticism and for most of history remained withdrawn from the world. Their literature, both prose and poetry which forms a significant portion of the earliest Marathi literature, is preserved in secret code script called 'sakala'. Their key texts include Mhaimbhatta's hagiographies of the founders of the Mahanubhava sect like the *Leela Charitra* a biography of Shri Chakradhar (AD 1194) composed in AD 1278 and considered the first important text in Marathi.

However, their agenda was to create an alternative scriptural universe in Marathi as their primary sacred universe instead of accepting the Vedic scriptural universe as the primary domain, which the poets of the Varkari sampradaya to which Dnyaneshwar belongs, did. This means that the Mahanubhavas used Marathi as 'the language of the gods' and created textual discourse of their own, paralleling the traditions based on the distinctions between shruti-smriti commentary and *kavya*. What is important here is to examine the context of sects (*panthas* and *sampradayas*) and the interaction as well as the conflict between them as being critical to the pre-colonial literary polysystem.

Commenting on why the prose literature that forms a significant component in the Mahanubhava literature does not occupy any space among the Varkaris, R.B. Mancharkar draws attention to the fact that while Marathi was a 'bodh bhasha', the language of literary and spiritual communication, the primary scriptural world of the Varkaris consisted of Sanskrit scriptures like the *Bhagwad Gita*, the *Vedas*, and the *Puranas* like the *Bhagwat Puranas*, it was 'dharma bhasha' for the Mahanubhavas and hence they could not limit themselves to commentaries of the Sanskrit texts (which they did) and insisted on creating their own primary discursive universe in Marathi (Mancharkar 2000, 91–92). The ideological constraint—to use Lefevere's terminology—of sectarian patronage is decisive in not only understanding pre-colonial Marathi literature but also looking at the refractions and pre-colonial bilingualism. Mancharkar has discussed how the sectarian ideology has influenced literary poetics of the period. The poetics of the Shaiva thinkers like Abhinavagupta that emphasise the primacy of the '*shanta rasa*' or the rasa of serenity in his analysis of '*itihasa*' or texts considered as historical like the Mahabharata can be contrasted with the Vaishnava poetics that prioritise 'bhakti' as the prime *rasa*. Dnyaneshwar's own *Natha sampradaya* was a *Shaiva* one and it is not surprising that his commentary on the *itihasa* text eulogises 'shanta rasa' by saying: 'The eight sentiments pale into insignificance before the excellence of that speech, which confers rest and relief to the intellect of good men. Listen to these words, which are meaningful and deeper than the sea, and which will exhibit the serene sentiment' (Chapter 4, Verse 213–14).

Mancharkar points out how the sect ideology inflected the literary retellings in the Mahanubhavas and the Varkari. He says that when the Mahanubhava writer Damodar Pandit retells 'Vachhaharan' from the Srimad Bhagwat it takes on a 'dwaita Vedantic' colour and when the Varkaris like Waman Pandit or Shridhar retell the same story it takes on an 'adwaita Vedantic' colour. As the Varkaris believe in advaita, they perceive the relation not just between god and man but also between the guru and disciple as well as between the composer and the audience as that of intimate oneness of the mother and the child (Mancharkar 2000, 31).

Mancharkar also notes how the intellectuality, the need for objectivity and reclusiveness of the Mahanubhavas is reflected in their tendency to write primarily in prose and how emotive and subjective expressionism of the Varkaris made them write primarily in poetic forms.

The conflict seems to arise from the politics of royal patronage. Though there is no direct evidence of Dnyaneshwar benefiting from royal patronage, the *Dnyaneshwari* refers to Krishna as 'Yadaweshwaru' (Chapter 10, Verse 48) and refers to its place time of composition in the end as the time when King Ramchandra of Yaduvansha ruled justly and who is '*sakal kalaa nivasu*', that is, 'an abode of all arts' (Chapter 18, Verse 1814). It should be kept in mind that *Dnyaneshwari* upholds the Advaita Vedanta, unlike the Mahanubhavas who uphold the dwaita (dualistic) philosophy and are almost anti-Vedic.

Tulpule (1984, 216) draws attention to the view of scholars like Kolte who hold that in some versions of the *Leela Charitra*, there is a mention of the assassination of Sri Chakradhar by Hemadripandit and his subsequent resurrection, though none of the contemporary Mahanubhava texts mention this incident. The conflict between the Mahanubhavas and the Vaidika purohits can be made out by multiple attempts on Sri Chakradhara's life by the royal purohits named Brahmasaanu and Mahadashram. King Ramdevrai's wife, Kamaisey, thanks to the mediation by Aneyraja, took 'shravana' or initiation from Sri Nagdev and Hemadripandit's wife Demati used to visit Sri Chakradhar (Tulpule 1984, 235).

Valerie Stoker in her analysis of patronage to various Hindu religious institutions by the Vijayanagara court notes that it was not always religious and was 'opportunistically flexible' which galvanised Hindu sectarian leaders to pursue certain kinds of intellectual projects as well as to form different inter-sectarian alliances and rivalries which demarcated areas of overlap and distinction in doctrinal and practical matters; they simultaneously articulated a shared religious sensibility and significant sectarian divisions. The conflict between the Mahanubhavas and the Varkaris could be understood on similar lines. Stoker analyses the conflict between the advaita vedanatins and the dwaita vedantins like Vyasatirtha influenced by Madhvacharya and points out how Madhva Vedanta was characterised by its realistic ontological pluralism and realistic epistemology, in contrast to the idealistic monism of Advaita Vedanta in which any experience of difference or plurality was deemed illusionary (Stoker 2016, 3–4). This line of thinking would shed light on the conflictual relation between the Mahanubhavas and the Varkaris.

However, the claim that these translational shifts of discourse from the upper-caste elite spaces to more demotic 'publics' actually resulted in the democratisation of societal structure is a questionable one. Translation as a decision-making process involves agency and ideology. Translation as a mode of refraction is always brought about by the system of constraints of various kinds as discussed previously. These ideological constraints create a series of ambivalences and contradictions in the target language text with reference to caste and gender that undermine the emancipatory ideals associated with bhakti. Though Dnyaneshwar holds that unlike the '*krupan*' or miserly nature of the Vedas which avoid touching the ears of the shudras and women, the Gita is the 'distinctive generosity personified' to overcome the debt by being accessible to the masses (Chapter 18: 1456–60). *Dnyaneshwari* glorifies the superiority of the Brahmins (Chapter 8: 475–89) and instructs the Brahmins not to eat the food cooked at the shudras' home even if it is delicious (Chapter 3: 221). Dnyanadeva's use of the folk *ovi* metre for his bhashya of the Sanskrit text can be simultaneously read as Brahmanisation or sanskritisation of the folk or as democratisation of the spiritual canon, though the use of *ovi* dates back to the Mahanubhava compositions. This has given rise to contradictory readings of not only this text but bhakti literature in general as discussed at the beginning of the chapter.

Conclusion

Expanding the notion of translation in order to approach pre-colonial texts like the *Dnyaneshwari* reveals a rich body of metaphors for cross-linguistic and cross-cultural communication in pre-colonial India. Reading the *Dnyaneshwari* using theoretical advances in translation studies and comparative literary studies, we can conceptualise the process of the emergence of a new literary culture not as a simple adoption of cosmopolitan models (*teeka/bhashya*) in the local languages (vernacularisation) but by the creation of new models, genres and literary languages towards different functional ends, that are neither 'Sanskrit' nor 'Marathi', but interliterary. The notion of interliterariness does away with the assumptions of hierarchy or linear one-directional transmission between Sanskrit and *bhashas* implicit in the term 'vernacularisation'. Thus, we cannot only understand the cultural mechanisms underlying translations as refractions, but also explain their contribution to the recipient literary system and its repertoire, especially in the formation of new literary languages, poetics and politics of identity and cultural politics. We can understand this emergence of the new polysystem in the context of the institutional social structures of the sects and their epistemological grids.

The ideological constraints of sectarian ideologies and competition for patronage are critical in not only understanding pre-colonial Marathi literature but also refractions, retellings, and pre-colonial bilingualism. In the larger social and cultural domain, we discover that bhakti literature is neither a single or simple political project of social liberation nor of simple continuation of Puranic Brahminical hegemony. It is heterogeneous and having many contradictory strands, some of which are radical and many deeply conservative. Instead of reading it simplistically as 'vernacularisation', 'revolution', or 'counter-revolution', the translational processes have to be approached in a more nuanced manner and in the context of the cultural and politics of sects, patronage of multiple kinds, innovative talents, and systems of caste-class-gender intersectionalities of the period.

We can say that though Dnyaneshwar's '*Duji Shrushti*' is not lacking in literary greatness or grandeur, like Vishawamitra's alternative universe, it does happen to be human when we situate it in the context of its cultural history. Then, we also remember that Vishwamitra's world was created out of mythological rivalry with Vashishta which underpinned the politics of Varna.

References

Burchett, Patton, 'Bhakti Rhetoric in the Hagiography of "Untouchable" Saints: Discerning Bhakti's Ambivalence on Caste and Brahminhood', *International Journal of Hindu Studies*, Vol. 13. No. 2, 2 August 2009, pp. 115–41.

Catford, J.C., *A Linguistic Theory of Translation: An Essay in Applied Linguistics*, Oxford, Oxford University Press, 1965.

Devy, G.N., *In Another Tongue: Essays on Indian English Literature*, Chennai, Macmillan India, 1993.

———. *The G.N. Devy Reader with a foreword by Rajeshwari Sundar Rajan*, Hyderabad, Orient Blackswan Pvt. Ltd, 2009.

Dionyz, Durisin, *Theory of Literary Comparatistics*, translated by Jessie Jocmanova, Bratislavia, Veda, House of the Slovak Academy of Sciences, 1984.

Dnyaneshwar, *Sarth Sri Dnyaneshwari.* Edited by D.A. Ghaisas. Sakhre Maharaj Sampradayik Shudhapath. Pune: Manorama Prakashan, 1999.

Even-Zohar, Itamar, 'Polysystem Studies', *Poetics Today: International Journal for Theory and Analysis of Literature and Communication*, Vol. 11, No. 1, 1990 (NA).

Fisher, Elaine M., *Hindu Pluralism Religion and the Public Sphere in Early Modern South India*, California, University of California Press, 2017.

Frawley, William, 'Prolegomenon to a Theory of Translation', in *The Translation Studies Reader*, edited by Lawrence Venuti, London and New York, Routledge, 2000, pp. 250–63.

Jakobson, Roman, 'On Linguistic Aspects of Translation', in *The Translation Studies Reader*, edited by Lawrence Venuti, London and New York, Routledge, 2000, pp. 113–18.

Kamat, Ashok, *Santa Sahitya: Kahi Anubandha*, Pune, Padmagandha Prakashan, 2003.

Kolte, V.B., *Marathi Santache Samajik Karya*, Translated from Hindi by Sumati Kolte. Mumbai: Lokvangmaya Gruha, 2014.

Lakoff, George and Mark Johnson, *Metaphors We Live By*, University of Chicago Press, 1981.

Lefevere, Andre, 'Mother Courage's Cucumbers Text, System and Refraction in a Theory of Literature', in *The Translation Studies Reader*, edited by Lawrence Venuti, London and New York, Routledge, 2000, pp. 233–49.

Lotman, Yuri, 'The Text within the Text', *PMLA*, Vol. 109, No. 3, May 1994, pp. 377–84.

Mancharkar, R.B., *Dharmasampradaya ani Madhyayugeen Marathi Vangmai*, Pune, Pratima Prakashan, 2000.

———, *Tukaram Darshan*, Pune, Sakal Publishers, [1996]2014.

———, *The Quotidian Revolution—Vernacularization, Religion, and the Premodern Public Sphere in India,* Ranikhet, Permanent Black in association with Ashoka University, 2016.

Moray, Sadanand. *Tukaram Darshan* (1996). Pune: Sakal Prakashan,3rd edition, 2014.

Novetzke, Christian Lee. *The Quotidian Revolution—Vernacularization, Religion, and the Premodern Public Sphere in India*, Columbia University Press, 2016.

Okita, Kiyokazu, *Hindu Theology in Early Modern South Asia: The Rise of Devotionalism and the Politics of Genealogy*, Oxford, University of Oxford Press, 2014.

Padhye, Digambar, 'Prastavna', *Maharashtriya Santa Mandalache Aitihasik Karya* by B.R. Sunthankar, Mumbai: Lokavangmay Gruha, [1948]2017, p. 12.

Pollock, Sheldon, ed., *Literary Cultures in History: Reconstructions from South Asia*. Berkeley: University of California Press, 2003.

———, *The Language of the Gods in the World of Men: Sanskrit,Culture and Power in Premodern India*, Berkeley, University of California Press, 2006.

Ranade, R.D., *Mysticism in Maharashtra*, Delhi, Motilal Banarasidas, 1982.

Shah, A.M., 'Sects and Hindu Social Structure', *Contributions to Indian Sociology*, Vol. 40, No. 2, 2006, pp. 209–48.

Singh, Avadesh Kumar, 'Translation in 21st Century', *Translation Today*, Vol. 8, No. 1, 2014, eds Awadesh Kumar Mishra, V. Saratchandran Nair, Central Institute of Indian Languages, Mysore, 2014, pp. 5–44.

Stoker, Valerie, *Polemics and Patronage in the City of Victory: Vyastirtha, Hindu Sectarianism and the Sixteenth-Century Vijayanagara Court*, Oakland, University of California Press, 2016.

Sunthankar, B.R., *Maharashtriya Santamandaliche Aitihasik Karya*, Mumbai, Lokvangmay Prakashan Gruh, 4th edition, 2017.

Tulpule, S.G., ed. *Marathi Vangmayacha Itihas: Khand Pahila: Arambhapasun 1350 AD paryantchya Kalakhandatil Marathi Vangmayacha Vivechak Itihas*, Pune, Maharashtra Sahitya Parishad, 1984.

Venuti, Lawrence, ed. *The Translation Studies Reader*, London and New York, Routledge, 2000.

Yardi, M.R., trans. *Shri Jnandeva's Bhavartha Deepika*, popularly known as *Jnaneshwari*, Pune, Bhartiya Vsidya Bhavan, 5th edition, 2011.

2

Formation of Hindu Laws through Translation in the Rule of British East India Company: Vidyasagar's Contribution in Society and Legislation

Gargi Bhattacharya

In the early days of British India, which was ruled by the British East India Company, the formation of laws was one of the most important issues for the foreign ruler, as the customs, values and beliefs of this country appeared different with respect to their own. The general impression of Europe at that time about the law system of the Indian tradition was quite divergent. *The Asiatic Journal and Monthly Register for British India and its Dependencies*, July to December issue of 1828, recorded:

> A notion seems to have long prevailed in Europe, that the Hindus had no written laws, although the law of the Smritis was in full operation throughout a great portion of India, long after De Gama's invasion, and in many of the provinces neighbouring on Madras, long after Madras became a British possession. (Ellis 1828, 158)

The British East India Company started understanding the huge law system of the Indian tradition, particularly the Hindu customary laws, when, after the concurrence of the Battle of Plassey and Boxer, they achieved the right to deal with the civil cases of the province of Bangla–Bihar–Orissa. The situation demanded that they pay attention to legislation for the stability of the colony. N.B. Halhed (1776), who was deeply associated with the formation of Hindu law in Company-ruled India, clarified:

> The Importance of the Commerce of India, and the Advantages of a Territorial Establishment in Bengal, have at length awakened the Attention of the British Legislature to every Circumstance that may conciliate the Affection of the Natives, or ensure Stability to the Acquisition. (p. ix)

The British rulers were of the opinion that they should treat the Indian law system with enough care and tolerance. Since the conventional customs or laws of the 'Natives' are interwoven with their religious practices, the Company was induced to formulate the laws ensuring that the private laws of the inhabitants of this land would not be suppressed by the new system of the British ruler. As a result, the primary duty for those foreign rulers was to determine the tradition of private laws of the Hindus, which is originally very old as well as complicated, and at times, self-contradictory. The texts that possess the legacy of Hindu code and conduct are many in number and different in category; in addition, the texts, mostly composed in Sanskrit, were available only in manuscript form, which made the job of the British ruler tougher. Therefore, the only possible way for them was to make translations of traditional Hindu law texts. The letter by Sir William Jones to the Supreme Court of Bengal is the evidence here:

> If we had a complete Digest of *Hindu* and *Muhammedan* laws, after the model of JUSTINIAN'S inestimable Pandects, compiled by the most learned of the native lawyers, with an accurate verbal translation of it into English; and if copies of the work were reposited in the proper offices of the *Sedr Diwáni Adálat*, and of the Supreme Court, that they might occasionally be consulted as standard of justice, we should rarely be at a loss for principles at least, and rules of law, applicable to the cases before us, and should never perhaps be led astray by the *Pandits* and *Maulavis*, who would hardly venture to impose on us, when their imposition might so easily be detected. (Colebrooke 1864, viii–ix)

As a result, some translations of the Hindu Law texts were done. Initially, the Persian language acted as an intermediate but later on the Sanskrit texts were translated directly to the language of the foreign ruler.

Obviously, to execute this task the British took the help of some renowned Sanskrit pundits like Ram Gopal Nyayalankar. In the tenure of the British East India Company, we find five major translations.

1. At the request of Warren Hastings, Esq. Governor General of Fort William in Bengal, a digest entitled *Vivādārṇvasetu* was composed by the Bengali pundits with the lead of Bāṇeśvara Vidyālaṃkāra. At first, this Sanskrit composition was translated to Persian; further from the Persian translation the English translation was brought out by Nathaniel Brassey Halhed in 1776 with the title *A Code of Gentoo Laws, or, Ordinations of the Pandits, from A Persian Translation, Made from The Original, Written in The Shanscrit Language*. But the huge effort did not succeed, as the intermediate Persian translation, which omitted many essential passages, was only a 'loose injudicious epitome' (Colebrooke 1864, xi) of the original Sanskrit work.
2. The second project was the translation of the *Manusaṃhitā*, the oldest text of the *Dhramaśāstra* tradition by Sir William Jones. It was published with the title *Institute of Hindu Law or, The Ordinance of Menu, According to the Gloss of Culluca; Comprising The System of Duties, Religious and Civil.* Again, the translation, though being a very brilliant literary piece, did not serve a practical purpose since the direct use of Manu's laws in modern times (*Kaliyuga*) is very little.[1]
3. The British people categorically divided the tradition of ancient Hindu law books under three different heads, that is, (i) the *Smṛti* or the text books, (ii) the commentaries and glosses on those texts, and (iii) the digests. Therefore, after the failure of the translation of Manu's original *Smṛti*-text to attain a practical

1 According to the Hindu tradition, an epoch (a unit of time between the creation and destruction of the Universe) contains four *Yugas*, viz. *Satya*, *Tretā*, *Dvāpara* and *Kali*. It is said in *Parāśara-saṃhitā* that the rules prescribed by Manu are for the *Satya-yuga* and those by Parāśara are for the *Kali-yuga*.

target, the next endeavour was to compile another digest, extracted from already available digests and the gloss or the commentaries of the original source texts and translate it into English. So, next came the translation of *Vivādavańgārṇava*, a *Smṛti*-digest by Jagannātha Tarkapañcānana. In 1796, Mr Henry Thomas Colebrooke, Judge of Mirzapur, translated only some of the portions of Jagannātha's digest, where particularly the laws of succession and contract were discussed, under the title *A Digest of Hindu Law, on Contracts and Successions: With a Commentary by Jagannátha Tercapanchánana.*

4. We find another combined translation of two different *Smṛti*-works on the laws of inheritance, originally composed in Sanskrit, which was not a product of the compilation by the scholars of the eighteenth century. Under the title *Two Treatises on the Hindu Law of Inheritance* in the year 1810 Colebrooke translated Jimūtavāhana's (eleventh or thirteenth century CE) *Dāyabhāga*, a paramount authority in Bengal regarding the law of succession. It also includes a specific portion of the inheritance of Vinjñāneśvara's (eleventh-twelfth century CE) *Mitākṣarā*, a commentary on *Yājñabalkya-saṃhitā*.
5. Reading a reference to *Dāyakarmasaṃgraha* by Krishna Tarkālaṃkāra in Colebrooke's Preface to *Two Treatises on the Hindu Law of Inheritance*, P.M. Wynch translated it as *The Dāya-crama-sangraha, an original treatise on the Hindoo law of inheritance* (1818).

Towards the end of the first part of the nineteenth century, the major focus of the Company's jurisprudence was on the disputes of inheritance and succession. Among the mentioned five translations at least three of them deal with the laws of inheritance, but none of those was the translation of any major *Smṛti*-texts; all were either translations of the digests or of the commentaries. In the process to collect, compile and translate Hindu rules, the British people had to depend on the traditional Pundits and Moulavis, but the traditions of ancient Hindu law patterns were still not clear to them. As a result, no translation came out on some famous and significant law texts. Notable among the translations was *Parāśara-saṃhitā*, the text which according to Hindu tradition is prescribed for the customs of *Kaliyuga*. Again, no translation was made of *Yājñavalkya-saṃhitā*, one of the major texts that deals with the system of court cases of ancient India, though some portion of its commentary, *Mitākṣarā*, had been already published. The first English translations of these two major *Smṛti*-texts, namely *Parāśara-saṃhitā* and *Yājñavalkya-saṃhitā*, were brought out in 1887 by Krishnakamal Bhattacharya and in 1880 by Mr Mandlik respectively.

In this circumstance, a social reform movement and a unique translation regarding the Hindu law pointed out why the understanding of the British ruler towards the Hindu law system should have a new dimension. Previously, the Company used to deal with civil cases by using the strategy of not disturbing the established customs of the 'natives' for the sake of the permanency of their new colony, but a translation, done by an Indian, gave them the strength to make changes in the laws, especially, in the customary laws, if required. The social reform was the remarriage of Hindu widows led by Ishwarchandra Vidyasagar; the translation, entitled *Marriage of Hindu Widows*, was also done by Vidyasagar from his own Bengali writings, just before the introduction of Hindu Widows' Remarriage Act of 1856.

In Hindu custom, before the mid-nineteenth century, second marriage of a woman, after the death of her husband, was not permissible. However, according to W.H. Macnaghten, the second marriage of a girl was very common among the 'inferior castes' (Macnaghten 1862, 60). Here, by the term 'inferior castes' he may indicate the people who were marginalised as śūdras, outcastes and untouchables in the then society. But the rest of the society did not even think of remarriage for widows. After the prohibition of Sati *pratha* (the custom where the wife immolates herself on her husband's pyre or takes her own life soon after her husband's death) by the Law of 1829, the only remaining path for the Hindu widows was to practice penance and celibacy which was no less painful. To bring the misfortune of those Hindu widows to an end, what Vidyasagar needed was public support, but here the main obstacles were the norms set by the traditional Hindu law. It is clearly stated in the *Dharmaśāstras* (law texts of Hindu tradition) that only a virgin girl would be allowed to marry. Hence, it was very difficult to convince the orthodox society for remarriage of Hindu widows without any approval from the *śāstras*. To track the Hindu scriptural permission, Vidyasagar published two writings or 'pamphlets' (Vidyasagar II) in 1855, with thorough logical justifications and evidences taken from some valuable ancient texts, of course in the vernacular language of society, that is Bengali—*Vidhavāvivāha pracalita haoyā ucit kinā* (Whether widow remarriage should be introduced, parts 1 and 2). Very soon, Vidyasagar translated those two Bengali works in English under the title *Marriage of Hindu Widows*. Now, the significant question is: Among so many translations of Hindu laws in the colonial period, why is Vidyasagar's translation singularly important?

It was Vidyasagar's understanding of Indian tradition and society that gave his translated work a distinct honour and clarity. The objective of Vidyasagar's English translation was not to serve the purpose of the British ruler, but rather to accumulate support from the 'English public' (Vidyasagar I) and prepare a new law for the welfare of Indian society. The unlimited authority of the *śāstras* in the Indian tradition made Vidyasagar realise that the only way forward was to refute the opinions and views of the traditional pundits, whom he found exactly at his opposite pole, through the appropriate explanation of the same ancient Hindu *śāstras*. This resulted in his pamphlets and successful translation.

In the case of widow remarriage, along with public support, what Vidyasagar required more was the support of the British rulers for legal sanction. Though the issue may appear purely a matter of social consideration, in fact, it is deeply associated with legal consent. It was probable that if Vidyasagar's venture were to succeed it would lead to a new problem in the legal pattern. An important question for Vidyasagar was whether the son (or sons) from a widow's second marriage would get a valid status of succession. This was the very issue, where, unquestionably, the British rulers would have to interfere. As a result, the target and objective of the translations, until then related to the formation of Hindu laws, attained a new dimension. In the preface of his translation, Vidyasagar unambiguously pronounced:

> ... since the publication of my pamphlets, several parties attempted to misrepresented things to the English public in Reviews and Journals... but as it appeared to me that my pamphlets met all the objections that might be urged against the legality of the marriage of Hindu widows, I thought it best to publish an English version of them, which I now lay respectfully before the English public. (Preface I)

To some extent, Vidyasagar found acceptance among the common people, although the orthodox views in the society also had a strong appeal. A part of the society was eagerly waiting for a new law. Many songs and poems were composed praising Vidyasagar. Among them the poems authored by Dasarathi Ray, the famous bard of Bengal, and the verses woven on the saris of Santipur are noteworthy.

Among Vidyasagar's opponents there were some very influential orthodox pundits, like Gangadhar Kabiraj, Braja Nath Vidyaratna, Bhabashankar Vidyaratna, Ramtanu Tarkasiddhanta and so forth, and some associations like 'Jessore Hindu Dhrama Rakhini Sabha', and 'Calcutta Dharma Shabha' and so on, who tried their best to restrain Vidyasagar's endeavour. The result was a number of conventions, lectures, pamphlets and articles, some of which used vile and scurrilous language. Even after the passing of the Hindu Remarriage Act in 1856, Bankim Chandra Chatterjee, the renowned Bengali writer, who was the first graduate from the University of Calcutta and also the first Bengali judge in the colonial period of India, wrote against it in an article in the Bengali monthly *Bangadarsan* (in June 1880). Declaring the attempt of Vidyasagar as an 'emotional bias' Bankim Chandra stated:

> … we do not think that the hardships of the widows are intolerable. Supposing they are really intolerable, but, at the same time, highly beneficial to the society, what necessity is there for removing them? Those hearts that weep for an infinitesimal number of persons, ought to break down for the thousands of persons in the society.… If it is a cruelty not to relieve the miseries of a handful of widows, then it must be a barbarous inhumanity to cause mischief to thousands of individuals of the society by inaugurating widow-remarriage; … If there are apprehensions of widows turning immoral, those apprehensions cannot be wholly eradicated by giving them away in marriage, for many married women are as well seen to lose their character. (Mitra 1902, 281)

After the publication of the second pamphlet, Vidyasagar hardly entered in those debates, probably because he found them inappropriate to achieve his goal. To gather support from the ruling authority he started translating the pamphlets. Vidyasagar distinctly clarified that his translation was 'neither entire nor literal', as it is not for the 'native population', but rather for a 'different class of readers', that is, the 'English public' (Preface II). From his two ur-texts in Bengali he translated the first one without any change, while he omitted and altered some portions in the second to avoid repetition. Ananda Krishna and Srinath assisted him in his work; Prasanna Kumar Sarvadhikari corrected the proof. Vidyasagar gave a copy of this English translation to the British Indian Association for forwarding it to the Government with its recommendation to pass a new law. On 4 October 1855, Vidyasagar filed a petition praying to declare 'the lawfulness of the marriage of Hindoo Widows'. The bill had its third hearing on 19 July 1856 and was passed into 'Act XV of 1856', which was further received by the Governor-General on the 26th day of the same month.

Before Vidyasagar's success, some other attempts had been made but these failed. Raja Raj Ballabh of Vikrampur, Dhacca, Babu Matilal Sil and Shyama Charan Das, both from Calcutta, were some names who tried to bring this change in Hindu customs. In spite of being very rich and influential, they could not produce any successful result, whereas Ishwarchandra, a poor man, made the mission possible only through his intellectual strategy as well as practical understanding. Some other attempts outside Bengal, specifically in Nagpur and Madras had been made but similarly did not succeed. Therefore, it can be said that Vidyasagar used translation as a vital instrument to combat his powerful opponent, the orthodox thinking of Hindu society. Here is a statistical data to point out how difficult this task was for Vidyasagar. Mr Grant, the committee member to move the Bill, informed that about 40 petitions were against the Bill signed by 50,000/60,000 people, whereas only 25 petitions were filed in favour of the Bill, signed by approximately 5,000 people only (Mitra 1902, 296–97).

It was not that simple for the Company to decide because according to the statistics the opponents were more in number. Why then did the British rulers go ahead with the Bill? We may get the answer in the early history of the East India Company and colonial India. The most dangerous effect of widowhood was child murder and foeticide to conceal the unwilling pregnancy, which was very unhealthy for the social structure. Mr Grant, then Secretary to the Law Commission, mentioned in his letter dated 4 July 1837:

> The Law Commissioners observed with deep regret that Western Sadar Court believe child murder to be a prevalent crime in the provinces under their Jurisdiction. The Law Commissioners think that much of this crime may be owing to the cruel law which prevents Hindu widows from contracting a second legal marriage. (Mitra 1902, 289–90)

With the goal to make a mere alteration in the customs of Hindu widowhood and introduce second marriage, the Commissioners addressed a circular calling for information on the topic and for the views of all four Presidencies; but they found nothing favourable. The Sadar Courts, marking the attempt as 'entirely a dead letter' (Mitra 1902, 290), highly disagreed to disturb the customs of Hindu society. Therefore, in spite of the plan, the foreign ruler could not show their courage unless and until an insider of the Hindu society came forward with the support of the traditional Hindu *śāstras*. In his translation, Vidyasagar carried the same view as the Commissioner:

> If the marriage of widow be allowed, it will remove the insupportable torments of life-long widowhood, diminish the crime of prostitution and foeticide and secure all families from disgrace and infamy. (p. 21)

To convince the society that Hindu sastric tradition permits widow marriage Vidyasagar quoted *Paraśara-saṃhitā*, the *smṛti* text, particularly prescribed for modern age, that is, *Kali-yuga*:

> *naṣṭe mṛte pravrajite klīve ca patite patau/*
> *pañcasvāpatsu nārīṇāṃ patiranyo vidhīyate/*

Vidyasagar translated this as:

> On the receiving no tiding of a husband, on his demise, on his turning an ascetic, on his being found impotent or on his degradation—under any of these five calamities, it is canonical for women to take another husband. (p. 9)

He further announced in unclear terms:

> … that as Parasara plainly prescribes marriage as one of the duties of women in the Kali Yuga under any one of the five above enumerated calamities, the marriage of widow in the Kali Yuga is consonant to the Sastras. (p. 10)

The other significant objection that the Sadar Court had resolved was: 'it [widow marriage] would entirely dislocate the frame of Hindu Law of Inheritance' (Mitra 1902, 290). Vidyasagar was prepared to bring out the solution of that also from the *Smṛti*-texts. The older texts mentioned twelve kinds of sons, but Parāśara admitted only three among them. They are: *Aurasa* (son of body), *Dattaka* (adopted son) and *Kṛtrima* (son made). The opponents argued that no mention of *Paunarbhava putra* (a son born of a woman married the second time) implies the non-sanction of second marriage of women. But Vidyasagar counter-argued that: '... as he [Parāśara] has prescribed the marriage of widows, he has, in effect, legalized the son born of a widow in lawful wedlock' (p. 11). To decide the nature of the son, consequence of a widow marriage, he proclaimed:

> The definition of Dattaka (son adopted) and Kritrima (son made) as given in the Sastras, cannot be applied to the son begotten by a man himself on the widow married to him, but he falls under the description of the Aurasa (son by birth). (p. 11)

While composing the Bengali pamphlets and translating them into English, Vidyasagar quoted a number of ancient Sanskrit texts, especially *Smṛtis* and other related texts with their translations in both Bengali (for the Bengali pamphlets) and English. As a result, we find the translation of a huge portion of *Parāśara-saṃhitā* and *Yājñavalkya-saṃhitā*, *Āditya-purāṇa*, *Udvāhatattva*, *Vṛhannāradīya Puraṇa*, and so forth, which were often used and obeyed in the then Bengali society with deep respect. These translations were the first ever translations of these texts in English, as well as in any European language.

Therefore, in a nutshell, it can be said that the translation *Marriage of Hindu Widows* bridged two ends, both the British rulers and the liberal Hindus found the customs for Hindu widowhood inhuman. Subal Chandra Mitra, in his *Isvar Chandra Vidyasagar: A Story of His Life and Work*, commented: 'There were many obstacles in its way, and the English pamphlet helped to remove those obstacles and clear the way' (p. 282).

Translation from one language to another has several goals to achieve; one of them is to remove the difficulty of communication. The British East India Company used this medium as a tool primarily for the stability of their newly established colony in the Indian subcontinent. The impact of this was multi-dimensional. Before the translations made by the British rulers, we hardly find any translation of Hindu laws in any European language; the only exception was the French translation in the seventeenth century done by Abraham Rogers, a Dutch missionary of Pulicat, who in his translation 'correctly noticed many observations of the Smritis, but without reference to any original authority' (Ellis 1828, 158). Although it was a tough job to understand the entire system of Hindu law, as the tradition was colossal as well as complicated, the endeavour that began in the British colonial period through translating the Sanskrit law texts became the starting point to systematise the Hindu laws. Earlier the laws, specifically the customary laws, were found preserved in the oral tradition or in handwritten manuscripts, both kept under the custody of the traditional Sanskrit pundits; hence, the masses or the non-Brahmin people had no way to reach the original textual sources. According to Carroll, 'By the mid-nineteenth century the texts had replaced the pandits as the repositories of Hindu Law' (2014, 114). Therefore, the translations not only acted as a medium between two languages but the printing of those translations, with or without Sanskrit texts, brought a kind of transparency in the customs and laws; the Brahmanical hegemony of the upper caste faced heavy contestation. It was the juncture of two cultural milieus, where the Sanskrit texts, particularly the *Dharmaśāstra*s, had achieved a wider perspective; as a result, the idea prevalent in Europe that there had been no written law in ancient India was proven wrong. Vidyasagar's translation, *Marriage of Hindu Widows*, played a significant role in that scenario. When the British rulers decided not to disturb the customs of the 'natives', Vidyasagar's translation made them realise that there might be divergent interpretations of Hindu laws and customs, and they had a long path to travel—more significant texts were left to be translated and understood, without which their legislative job would not be easy to handle. Initially, the efforts of Vidyasagar and other progressive Bengalis to introduce a new law of widow remarriage in the then societal structure was limited within the speech community of the Bengali language; but as soon as Vidyasagar translated his two pamphlets into English, the wave of that social reform reached educated people throughout India beyond any provincial language barrier. Again, the knowledge of Hindu law tradition came into the range of that English educated people, as a result, the orthodox pundits gradually lost their supremacy over the Hindu customs. A neo-Brahmanical culture was introduced to the social pattern, where the traditional Sanskrit texts were being translated, as well as interpreted in the English language. The new culture, though upheld by a tiny portion of the then society, envisioned a modern India, through harmonising tradition to contemporary needs.

References

Carroll, Lucy, 'Law, Custom and Statutory Social Reform: The Hindus Widow Remarriage Act of 1859', *Women and Social Reform in Modern India: A Reader*, Vol. 1, Ranikhet, Permanent Black, 2014, pp. 113–44.

Colebrooke, H.T., *A Digest of Hindu Law on Contracts and Successions: With a Commentary by Jagannát'ha Tercapanchánana*, Madras, J. Higginbotham, 1864.

Ellis, Francis Whyte, 'On the Law Books of the Hindus', *The Asiatic Journal and Monthly Register for British India and its Dependencies*, Vol. 25, July to December, 1828, pp. 155–65.

Halhed, N.B., *A Code of Gentoo Laws, or Ordinations of the Pundits, from a Persian Translation, made from the Original, written in the Shanscrit Language*, London, 1776.

Macnaghten, William Hay, *Principals of Hindu and Mohammadan Law*, London, William & Norgate, 1862.

Mitra, Subal Chandra, *Isvar Chandra Vidyasagar: A Story of his Life and Work*, Calcutta, New Bengal Press, 1902.

Vidyasagar, Ishwarchandra, *Marriage of Hindu Widows*, Calcutta, The Sanskrit Press, 1864.

3

Translation and the Formation of Gujarati Literary Public Sphere in the Early 1850s: A Critical Study of Dalpatram's Lakshmi Natak (1851)

Hiren J. Patel

When Dalpatram translated Aristophanes' *Wealth* into Gujarati as *Lakshmi Natak* in the early 1850s, the Gujarati literary field was still in the process of being demarcated and defined. Moreover, the Gujarati language was still in the process of getting standardised and prose forms were yet to become central or canonical. Thus, the examination of early translations made during the period when the Gujarati literary field was in a state of flux, can reveal the role played by translation in the formation and development of the Gujarati literary public sphere of the period. This chapter, in this context, examines Kavi Dalpatram's *Lakshmi Natak* (1851; 1853), a prose translation into Gujarati of Aristophanes' *Wealth.*

Dalpatram Dahyabhai Travadi (1820–1898), generally known as Kavi Dalpatram, was a well-known Gujarati poet and a social reformer of the second half of the nineteenth century. Hailing basically from Wadhwan in Kathiawar, Dalpatram came to Ahmedabad on an invitation to help the then newly appointed assistant judge Alexander Kinloch Forbes (1821–1865) in his endeavour to learn Gujarati and collect manuscripts of old Gujarati poetry (Parekh 1932, 52–53). Much interested in chronicles of the history of Gujarat, local traditions and the Gujarati language, Forbes also established a literary society named Gujarat Vernacular Society in 1848 in Ahmedabad to promote the study of Gujarati language and literature and to preserve collected manuscripts (pp. 8–9, 54). Dalpatram officially joined the Society as an assistant secretary in 1855 and also edited the Society's celebrated journal *Buddhiprakash* for the next twenty-four years. Dalpatram translated Aristophanes' *Wealth* as *Lakshmi Natak* in Gujarati in 1850–1851 with the help of Alexander Kinloch Forbes. *Lakshmi Natak* is considered as the first modern play to be written in Gujarati (Dave 2000, 4). The play was so popular that almost 1,000 copies were sold and it went into four editions just within a decade of its publication (Vasunia 2007, 117). However, no information is available regarding the play's performance on stage.

It would be instructive to review in brief the similarities and differences between the original play and its Gujarati translation. In Aristophanes' *Wealth*, most of the action takes place on the street near Chremylos' house. Chremylos is an elderly, poor farmer facing hard times in life, worried about the future of his only son. Karion is his slave. Chremylos goes to the shrine of god Apollo for consultation regarding his apprehension and receives advice to take the first passer-by he encounters after leaving the shrine to his home. The first person he meets is none other than god Wealth himself, blind and old. Chremylos thinks that if it is possible to restore the eyesight of Wealth, he would distribute money with discretion, only to the good and just people and not to the bad ones. Both Chremylos and Karion take Wealth to the shrine of Asklepios and manage to restore his eyesight. With the restoration of Wealth's eyesight, the good and just people see themselves getting rich while the wicked one faces hard times. At the end of the play, Chremylos and others carry Wealth in a procession to the Acropolis to install him as the new 'guardian of Athena's treasury vault' (Aristophanes 1998, 253). Chremylos and Karion meet several other people in the course of the play. They are: Blepsidemos (Chremylos's friend from a similar background), Poverty (a horrible old woman), Just Man, Informer ('sycophant' or a blackmailer), an old woman and her young lover, Hermes (the messenger from god) and the priest of Zeus.

In Dalpatram's *Lakshmi*, Dhirsinh is an old and poor Rajput landlord facing misfortune and Bhimado is his lower-caste servant. Worried about the future of his son, Dhirsinh goes to the temple of Lord Mahadev and receives advice to take home the first passer-by he encounters after leaving the temple. Dhirsinh encounters goddess Lakshmi as the first person after leaving the temple. She is blind and old. Dhirsinh thinks that if it is somehow possible to restore the eyesight of Lakshmi, she would distribute money with discretion, only to the good and just people and not to the bad ones. Both Dhirsinh and Bhimado take Lakshmi to the temple of Dhanvantari (the physician of gods) and manage to restore her eyesight. With the restoration of Lakshmi's eyesight, the good and just people see themselves getting rich while the wicked one faces hard times. At the end of the play, Dhirsinh and others carry Lakshmi in a procession to install her in a temple. Dhirsinh and Bhimado meet several other people in the course of the play. They are: Daji (the head of the village), Vakil Bhaichand (a lawyer), Zanpado/ Daridra (a decrepit scavenger representing poverty), Lavinga (a female servant), Dhirsinh's wife, Dhanpal and Dolatkhan (Dhirsinh's friends), Shastri (a priest), Chadiyo/Desai (an informer), the old woman Bibi Fatma, her young lover Juvan Madarkhan, the god Hanuman, and Gonsai (a member of the priestly community). The literal reading of both these plays shows that the plot of the Gujarati play follows the plot of the original play very closely. However, the culture specific references and the social status of different characters completely differ from the original. A detailed look at the context and the nature of translation will provide further insights to understand *Lakshmi Natak*.

I

It is quite interesting to look at the context and the time period in which this adaptation was made and how it influences the process of translation. In 1849 Gujarat Vernacular Society (1848) launched a Gujarati newspaper named *Vartaman* (Dalpatram 1878, 11). Bajibhai Amichand, from whose printing press this newspaper used to be printed and published before the Society purchased its own litho press and took it under its purview, used to remain worried and cautious regarding the content of the paper as the writers of the news and the publisher were different people (Dalpatram 1878, 31–32). However, the situation changed when it started to be edited by a native, salaried editor under the aegis of the secretary of the Society (Dalpatram 1878, 32). The newspaper and its content were now the responsibility of the Society. Moreover, the English secretary of the society had no knowledge of the Gujarati language. Hence, the newspaper came virtually under the control of the native editor. The new and relative freedom that the editor experienced led to the publication of news that criticised not only the head of the city (*nagarseth*) but also brought out malfunctioning in the colonial administration. The native editor used this opportunity to exercise the freedom of the press and published materials which were critical of the functioning of the colonial government. It carried news that complained against the administration of the prison in Ahmedabad. This became a controversial issue and its echo was also heard as far away as in Bombay in the newspapers such as *Telegraph and Courier* (Dalpatram 1878, 32–33; Parekh 1932, 17–19). The news was about the jailor of the prison who was functioning under Mr Charles M. Harrison, Judge of Ahmedabad, and who was also one of the members of the managing committee of the Society (Parekh 1932, 17–19). Mr Harrison denied the charge and requested other members of the committee to help remove the content from the newspaper but in vain.[1] Consequently, Mr Harrison resigned from the managing committee. From the notice published in *The Bombay Quarterly*

1 The correspondence between Mr Harrison and the managing committee was also published later in the form of a small booklet by the Gujarat Vernacular Society. See Dalpatram (1878, 34).

Magazine and Review, June 1852, it can clearly be observed that the stand taken by the managing committee against Mr Harrison was not appreciated by the Government.[2] The same newspaper also used to publish news about the malpractices in the functioning of the then Government (Dalpatram 1878, 34). Finally, the Bombay Government brought out a circular ordering the government servants not to write in any newspaper. As the members of the managing committee of the Society were government servants, the Bombay Government also ordered the Society to end its association with the newspaper (Dalpatram 1878, 34).

The same period also witnessed the appearance of two more Gujarati newspapers named *Khabar Darpan* (1851–1855?) and *Shamsher Bahadur* (1854–1855). These newspapers were started especially to combat different types of news and accusations that used to be published in *Vartaman* (Dalpatram 1878, 32; Parekh 1932, 21). However, the decline in this type of journalism can clearly be observed after 1854 as the Company government became aware of the dangers of independent and critical journalism and also began to put a check on it. For example, when the Gujarat Vernacular Society took the publication of *Buddhiprakash* journal in its hands from Vidyabhyasak Mandali in the early 1850s, it decided not to publish any political writings (*rajdwari babato*) in the magazine (Dalpatram 1878, 15). Moreover, the Society's approval was also made mandatory before the publication of any article in the magazine (p. 15). In 1856, the government also introduced an act banning the publication of 'obscene' books, pictures, songs and speech (*Buddhiprakash* 1856, 73).

---

2 The *Bombay Quarterly Magazine and Review* observed: 'This version of the story appears to have excited the indignation of the Judge who sought redress for the attempt to injure the character of his subordinate, and hence arose the correspondence which has been published and to which we must refer all who desire further information. *The course followed by the Committee has been disapproved by Government*' (emphasis mine), see 'Notices of Books, Pamphlets & c.', *The Bombay Quarterly Magazine and Review*, June 1852, p. 235.

While discussing the political views expressed in Dalpatram's poems such as 'Angrji Rajya Prakaran' (A chapter on English rule[3]), 'Vethe kam na karava vishe' (On not forcing people for unpaid labour), 'Prajanu Dukh Varnan' (The description of the misery of people), and 'Angrji Kayda Vishe' (On English Laws) published during this period, J. E. Sanjana, a remarkable Parsi scholar of Gujarati literature, observes that Dalpatram not only praised the good points but also criticised the evil acts of the then Government (Sanjana 1950, 139). Sanjana observes that 'just as he frankly says that no previous regime can come-up to it (the present regime), he condemns with equal frankness the evils he sees in it' (Sanjana 1950, 139). These poems basically took a critical look at the corruption prevalent in the administration of the Company government, the failure of the petty officials in redressing the grievances of the poor, and the multiplicity of laws and acts and their unintelligible language. It was in this context, particularly this nascent phase of *critical* journalism that flourished for a very short period of time in the city that *Lakshmi Natak* was translated into Gujarati by Dalpatram. This critical attitude, ephemeral though, does influence the translation process of the play into Gujarati.

Let us first look at two dialogues from the first scene where both Dhirsinh and Bhimado attempt to explain to Lakshmi her own importance in the material world. While in this particular passage in the original text (line no. 170–85) Chremylous and Karion attempt to explain to Wealth his importance with reference to local political affairs and Athens' relationship with other cities, the translation of this passage in Gujarati takes a jibe at the malpractices prevalent in the system of the present government, especially the judicial system. For example,

> ભીમ૦: આ કારભારી લોકો સરકારને ડંડ ભરવાની કાંઈ ફિકર રાખતા નથી, એ પણ તારૂં જ કામછે.

---

3 Further, all translations from Gujarati are mine, if not mentioned otherwise.

Bhimado: It is because of you that these officials do not worry about paying fine to Government.

ભીમ૦: આ સરકાર માં પૈસાવાળા કજીઓ જીતેછે, અને ગરીબ લોકો માર્યા જાય છે; તે પણ તારૂં જ કામ છે.
Bhimado: In this government rich people win the trial and poor people are killed; this is also because of you. (Dalpatram 1863, Scene 1)

Dalpatram transforms Chemylous' friend Blepsidemos into a Baniya lawyer named Bhaichand in the Gujarati translation. The character of the lawyer seems to have been employed deliberately to facilitate criticism of the legal system. This, in fact, provides Dalpatram a mouth piece, an opportunity to satirise certain malpractices and loopholes in the judiciary. A comparison of the original passages (line no. 373–79) where Blepsidemos suspects the source of Chremylous' sudden wealth with a similar passage from the translation will clarify the above arguments.

Blepsidemos: You claim you haven't been taking anyone's goods?

Chremylos: I certainly haven't.

Blepsidemos: I can't believe his nerve! What can one do? He won't admit the truth.

Chremylos: You've brought a charge before you've learnt the facts.

Blepsidemos [*changing tone*]: I'd like to help, old thing, for a modest sum.
Before the information's public knowledge,

I'll gag the politicians' mouths with—cash.

Chremylos [ironically]: Oh yes, I'm sure you'd prove your friendship then.

You'd spend a sum, then charge four times as much! (Aristophanes 1998, 225)

ભાઈ૦: ત્યારે મને કહો તો ખરા, તમે કેની મિલ્કત લાવ્યા છો?
Bhaichand: Then tell me whose property have you brought (in a sense robbed)?

રાજા: મેર મૂરખા મિલ્કત કોની લાવે.
Dhirsinh: You moron, whose property we can bring.

ભાઈ૦: હે ગણપતી, આ રજપુત વકીલ નું કામ પોતે જ લેશે કે શું? ને સાચું તો બોલતા જન થી, પંડે રાજા એવાં કામ કરશે ત્યારે વાણિયાનાં છોકરાં શું હજામત કરશે?
Bhaichand: O Lord Ganesha! Whether this Rajput will take the job of a lawyer or what? And he does not speak the truth. If Rajput will do such work (of lying), will the children of a Baniya go for a barber's job?

રાજા: ભાઈ અમે હજી કોઈ દહાડો અદાલતમાં આવ્યા નથી જે જુઠું બોલતાં આવડે.
Dhirsinh: Brother, we have not gone to the court yet that we know how to lie.

ભાઈ૦: અરે એમાં શીદ બીહો છો, છોને શેહેરમાં બુમ ચાલી પણ કરભીરી લોકોને થોડીક ભુરશી દક્ષણા આપીશું એટલે કાંઈ ફીકર નથી.
Bhaichand: Why are you afraid? No problem if the city cries about it. We will give some bribe to the officials so there is nothing to worry about. (Dalpatram 1863, Scene 2)

When Dhirsinh refuses to speak clearly about the source of his sudden wealth, Bhaichand thinks that he might have robbed someone's property; he is lying about it and is also not ready to disclose the truth. When Dhirsinh continuously rejects Bhaichand's baseless accusations, Bhaichand comically taunts that Dhirsinh seems to speak like a lawyer, which means he is lying. When Dhirsinh realises that he has been taunted, he sarcastically replies that he does not know how to lie as he has never been to the court yet. Bhaichand at the end also asks Dhirsinh not to worry much about this matter as it can easily be sorted out by giving a 'gift' (*dakshina*) to the officials. The translation of this particular passage in this comic vein shows that Dalpatram very cleverly and subtly satirises the functioning of the court, government officials and their inclination to accept bribery.

Another most telling and explicit example of Dalpatram's comment on the functioning of the government can be seen in the fourth scene of *Lakshmi Natak*. When Bhimado returns from the temple of Dhanvantari to Dhirsinh's house and gives a report to his wife about the restoration of Lakshmi's eyesight at length, Dhirsinh's wife in the end asks:

> રાણી: ત્યારે આપણા દેશંના રાજાની આંખ્યોનું ઓષડ એ ધનવંતરી પાસે કરાવે તો ઘણું સારૂં.
>
> Wife: It would really be very good if the king of our country gets Dhanvantari for treatment of his eyes.
>
> ભીમ૦: એ ક્યાં આંધળો છે? એ તો આંખ્યે દેખે છે.
>
> Bhimado: But he is not blind? He can see through his eyes.
>
> રાણી૦: દેખતો હોય તો આ કારભારી લોકો રૈયત ને ધોળે દહાડે લુટી શકે?
>
> Wife: (If he really does see) then can these officials loot common people in the bright light of the day? (Dalpatram 1863, Scene 4)

Importantly, these lines or many such similar references are not there in *Wealth*. It clearly means that Dalpatram has added these extra lines on his own. Now, it has to be noted here that Dalpatram translated this play in collaboration with his patron friend A.K. Forbes who had invited Dalpatram to teach him Gujarati. Like Dalpatram, the editor of *Vartaman* was also aware of his master's ignorance of the Gujarati language!

It can be observed here that the spirit of the above discussed *critical* journalism controls the translation process. There is an underlying episteme visible here which links the translation process and the editing of the newspapers. It can be argued that the thread of an assertion of the critical spirit that emerges in the period also finds its expression in the process of translation. Thus, this critical attitude becomes the defining feature of the emerging Gujarati literary public sphere and is sustained through translation and other literary forms. 'Dissent' is central to the idea of the public sphere and the use of translation to embody dissent contributes to the production of a new discourse of public criticism. The object of criticism is the exploitation of common people by the colonial government. The context of reforms enables the critical voice to address the common people.

Svati Joshi in her article 'Dalpatram and the Nature of Literary Shifts in Nineteenth-century Ahmedabad' (2004) observes that the urban and traditional social system of Ahmedabad comprising the Jain and Hindu business elites, the *sahukar* (the banker or the small mercantile capitalist), an efficient system of banking and finance, and unique social institutions such as *mahajans* (professional guilds of merchants and artisans developed to safeguard business interest and to maintain checks and balance in the system) were more responsible than the British intervention for the ideological, social and literary changes that occurred in the city during the nineteenth century (Joshi 2004, 328–29). She argues that the mercantile elites of Ahmedabad, on whom the political economy of the city was largely dependent, welcomed and cherished the British rule as it was conducive to and in favour of their business interests (Joshi 2004, 329). As an 'intellectual of the ruling class', Joshi observes, it was Dalpatram who articulated interests and aspirations of the business elites of the city through his literary and journalistic output (Joshi 2004, 332–38). He not only justified 'industrial capitalism', especially in the pages of the journal *Buddhiprakash*, but also couched the same in the new, respectable terms such as 'knowledge' (*vidya*) and 'reform' (*sudharo*). For Dalpatram, 'reform' meant 'material improvement' of the society and development of institutions that support the improvement such as roads, hospitals, schools, colleges, libraries and so forth (Dalpatram uses the word *sudhara na kaarkhana* [factories of reform] for libraries, schools and colleges). Similarly, for him 'knowledge' (*vidya*) meant knowledge of Western modern technology and industrial skills (Joshi 2004, 332–36). The overall argument of the essay is that Dalpatram's discourse of reform (both material and social) is closely linked with the ideological aspirations and interests of the mercantile elites of the city. Svati Joshi observes, 'The decisive shift that occurs in Dalpatram's poetry is that Gujarati literature is almost entirely identified with the interests of the ruling class, as perhaps never before, or after, in the history of the literature' (Joshi 2004, 346). Svati Joshi puts forward these arguments on the basis of her analysis of various articles published in *Buddhiprakash* and Dalpatram's long and important poems, especially *Hunnerkhanni Chadhai—Hindustan Upar* (An Invasion of the Emperor of Industry on India) and *Ven Charitra* (an *aakhyan*—a long narrative poetry, a tale—that discusses widow remarriage and related issues).

However, Svati Joshi does not take into consideration the first important literary work by Dalpatram (this translation of *Lakshmi Natak*) and the unique context in which it was produced in her discussion. And, perhaps, that is why she also misses to comment upon Dalpatram's ambivalent attitude towards the colonial rule that is evident in the translation process of the play. It has to be kept in mind that Dalpatram took the editorship of *Buddhiprakash* in his hands in 1855. It also has to be kept in mind that by 1855 the government had already been alarmed at the expression of critical attitude by newspapers and had started making policies and acts that curtailed the freedom of the press. It can be argued that this non-consideration of the emergence of critical journalism by Svati can also be observed in the reading of the Gujarati play by another scholar named Phiroze Vasunia.

Phiroze Vasunia in his article 'Aristophanes' *Wealth* and Dalpatram's *Lakshmi*' does not take into consideration the context and the time period in which the play was adapted and Dalpatram's ambivalent attitude towards the contemporary regime evident in the play. It would be instructive to turn to a passage from *Lakshmi Natak* and its translation into English by Phiroze Vasunia and the consequent analysis that he provides.

> ભીમ૦: તમે ફાયદો અને કલ્યાણ કીધાં?
> દે૦: હા, હા, અમારા જેવાં બીજા કોઈયે પણ નથી કીધાં.
> ભીમ૦: ત્યારે હું પુછું તેનો જવાબ આપ્ય.
> દે૦: શું કેહે છે?
> ભીમ૦: તમે ખેડુત છો ઘણું અનાજ પકવીને જગતને ફાયદો કીધો?
> દે૦: અમને તું હળખેડુ જેવા જાણે છે?
> ભીમ૦: ત્યારે તમે દેશાવરની મુલકગીરી કરીને લોકોનો ઉપકાર કીધો છે?
> દે૦: ના એ તો કાંઈ નથી કર્યું, પણ અમે કોઈ વખત કાંધાંખત ભરયાં છે ખરાં.
> ભીમ૦: ત્યારે તો એમાં લોકોને ફાયદો ખરો દીવાની તુરંગમાં છે, એટલો પણ તમે કાંઈ નવો કીસબ બજાવ્યો છે? (Dalpatram 1863, Scene 5)

> Bhima: You've worked for benefit and welfare?
> Desai: Yes, yes. No one has done the work that I have done.
> Bhima: Then answer my question.
> Desai: What's your question?
> Bhima: Are you a farmer and has the world benefited from your growing enough grain?
> Desai: Do you think I'm like a farmer?
> Bhima: *Have you ruled over foreign countries for the benefit of people?*
> Desai: No, nothing like that, but sometimes I have composed documents for the repayment of debts. (emphasis mine, quoted in Vasunia 2007, 121–22)

In this passage, Bhimado asks Desai about the ways in which the latter's job/work has benefited the country and its people. Vasunia here, has given importance to the sentence in which Bhimado asks Desai whether he has been benevolent to people by 'ruling over them'. The original Gujarati phrase of that sentence is '*deshavarni mulakgiri*' that has been translated as 'rule over a foreign country' by Vasunia. So far as the context of the conversation is concerned, it is clear that Dalpatram is satirising the petty official's mediating role between the government and people where he exploits the common people because of his position. Moreover, Vasunia does not translate the last sentence in the above quoted Gujarati passage where Bhimado taunts Desai that if he has helped people in composing the documents of repayments, then they surely will go to prison (because of Desai's viciousness in composing documents). Vasunia's translation of the Gujarati phrase '*deshavarni mulakgiri*' as 'rule over a foreign country' seems slightly misleading as a single petty official like Desai cannot be expected to be capable of that. Rather, in my opinion, the phrase seems to connote something related to the collection of taxes. Interestingly, his analysis of *Lakshmi Natak* does not highlight the nuanced comment of Dalpatram where Dalpatram quite explicitly satirises and comments upon the functioning of the present government and administration. Here it has to be kept in mind that Phiroze Vasunia's understanding of the nature of the literary output of Dalpatram and the socio-political contexts of the period are concerned, he has mostly relied upon the arguments put forward by Svati Joshi in her essay discussed earlier.

Both Joshi and Vasunia seem to miss the central issue related to the complex mode of translation and negotiation adopted by Dalpatram in *Lakshmi Natak* and the unique context in which the play itself has been translated. The argument put forward here does not claim to prove that Dalpatram openly or radically criticises the colonial government and its institutions. It also does not claim to repudiate Joshi's apt observation that Dalpatram as an 'intellectual of the ruling class' approved of British rule as it was in favour of the business interests of the elite. The point emphasised here is that the translation itself is the product of that particular socio-political phase which witnessed the rise of critical journalism and production of literature that took a critical and ambivalent look at the colonial rule and its administration. And the same critical and ambivalent attitude also informs the process of translating Aristophanes' *Wealth* as *Lakshmi Natak* in Gujarati.

II

The contemporary discourse of social and moral reform and Gujarat Vernacular Society's aims to enlarge Gujarati literature and to enlighten the general mind of people are important factors behind the selection and translation of the play into Gujarati. Dalpatram in his preface to *Lakshmi Natak* says:

> The original thought of writing this play was to make fun of people of our country who accumulate wealth through injustice, lying and evil means.... By reading this play, good people (*sajjan*) will take a lesson that one should not earn wealth through injustice, immorality and calumny. (Dalpatram 1863, 3)

Dalpatram emphasises in the Preface his fascination for knowledge (*vidya*) and his wish to improve the moral behaviour of Gujarati people by imparting a message through the play. Dalpatram's understanding of the play from the moral perspective can be traced back to the play's reception in English during the eighteenth and the nineteenth century. Phiroze Vasunia observes that the reading of Aristophanes' *Wealth* as 'a moral allegory' is a 'leitmotif that recurs through the play's reception' in English (Vasunia 2007, 118). He argues that when the play was received in English, it was also considered that Aristophanes meant to impart 'a moral lesson' to the contemporary Athenians through this play (Vasunia 2007, 118). He further observes that A.K. Forbes, who recommended this play to

Dalpatram for translation into Gujarati and also collaborated in the translation process, could have studied the play in many versions and especially the school edition of 1834 by H.P. Cookesley which was based on Wilhelm Dindorf's text 'that carefully omitted every verse or expression which would shock the delicacy of the most fastidious reader' (Vasunia 2007, 118). It can be said that Dalpatram perceived Aristophanes as a moralist through 'refractions' made available to him via Forbes' understanding of the writer.

The influence of social reformist context on the process of translation of the play into Gujarati can be observed in several passages of the play where Dalpatram satirises certain social practices and traditions of the contemporary Gujarati communities. The culture-specific references of the original text have been removed and in place of them Dalpatram has inserted satirical comments on prevalent evil customs. For example,

> Chremylos: I've heard Korinthian courtesans don't notice
> If someone poor should make a pass at them.
> But once a wealthy man comes on the scene,
> Without delay they thrust their arse at him.
> Karion: And *boys*, I've heard, behave in just that way.
> The lovers themselves don't matter, it's just the money!
> Chremylos: But not the *good* ones, only the prostitutes.
> The good ones never ask for money.
> Karion: Then what?
> Chremylos [*ironically*]: Perhaps a pedigree horse, or hunting dogs!
> Karion: No doubt they feel ashamed to ask for money,
> And dress their vices up with pretty words. (Aristophanes 1998, 217)

રાજા: વળી અમે સાંભળ્યું છે કે, ગુણકાને ઘેર કોઈ ગરીબ માણસ જાય છે, તેને તુરત કહાડી મેલે છે, અને કોઈ પૈસાવાળો જાય છે, તેનું સનમાન કરે છે.

Dhirsinh: And we have heard that if a poor man goes to a prostitute, she turns him away. But if a rich man goes, she respects him.

ભીમ૦: વળી જુઓ કે, પૈસા વિના કેટલા એક વડનગરા નાગર વાંઢા મરી જાય છે, તેનું એક ભજન બોલું છું.
(પ્રભાતી) શીદને સરજાડ્યાં પ્રભુ નાગર ની નાતે; સામી વળગણિયે સાલ્લો ન ભાળ્યો રાતી રે ભાતે.
Bhimado: And see, without money many *Vadnagara Nagars* die unmarried. I will sing a *bhajan* of it:

Oh God, why was I born in the Nagar caste?
I cannot even see a sari with red pattern hanging on a wooden pole opposite.

રાજા: આપણા જાડેજા રજપુત દીકરિયોને જન્મતાં જ કશુંબો પાઇ દે છે. તે લક્ષ્મીની જ કસર થી કે નહીં?
Dhirsinh: And our Jadeja Rajputs make infant daughters drink *kasumbo* (opium mixed in water), is it not because of lack of money?

ભીમ૦: હા, ઠાકોર આપણાં ઠકરાળાં ને કેવળ પીતળનાં ઘરેણાં કરાવીને ઉપર સોના નો ગલેફ લગાવવો પડે છે તે પણ એટલા જ સારૂ
Bhimado: Yes, and for the same reason Thakors have to have ornaments of brass and get them plated with gold for their wives. (Dalpatram 1863, Scene 1)

It can be observed here that Dalpatram does not translate the passage where Chremylous and Karion attempt to help Wealth realise his own importance with examples that refer to Korinthian courtesans and male lovers. Instead, Dalpatram shows Dhirsinh and Bhimado explaining to Lakshmi her own importance by arguing that in the absence of money many male Vadnagara Brahmins die without getting married. Dalpatram inserts two lines from a *bhajan* which states that the man of this particular Nagar caste is so low down on the social scale that he requires money to have a wife, and there is no possibility for him to see a red sari in his home in the absence of money. He also satirises the practice of female infanticide prevalent in the upper castes of Gujarat by making Bhimado argue that many Rajput families kill their newborn daughters in the absence of money. Another example of the same type can be found in the seventh and the last *swang* (scene) of *Lakshmi Natak*. Here, Dalpatram adds several lines on his own that make fun of the character of the priest named Gonsai, a Vaishnavite priest. When the surprised Dhirsinh asks why he needs money, Gonsai abuses him and angrily replies that he has got three daughters and seven uneducated sons to be married off. He also laments that none of his sons help him in worshipping the Lord Mahadev. The sentence where Gonsai even hurls an abusive word at Dhirsinh acquires importance in the play as the rest of the translation does not use such language or abusive words though the original play abounds in it. This particular mockery of the Vaishnavite priest can also be understood with reference to Dalpatram's belief in the Swaminarayan sect which gained currency during this period and was against certain licentious and immoral practices prevalent in Vaishnavism at that time. The reception of the play caused some commotion in the 1850s among Hindus of Ahmedabad and they even communicated to Forbes about it (Vasunia 2007, 129). It seems that they might have got perturbed by Dalpatram's satire on the socio-religious practices of Hindu high-castes and native officials. A.K. Forbes' discussion about this communication with a British member of Gujarat Vernacular Society also proves the above-mentioned point. Commenting on the communication received from the Hindu community of Ahmedabad, Forbes observed:

> We come now to *Lakshmi* which you tell me is considered to be too keen in its satire and too severe upon all sects of Hinduism

> except that of Swami Narayan to which the author belongs. I am not surprised at this nor do I see any great cause for regret in it. (quoted in Vasunia 2007, 129)

III

The context of social and moral reform seems to influence the translation process in yet another way too. Though *Lakshmi Natak* has been translated following the Bhavai tradition, the play does away with coarse wit and humour, and the 'gross vulgarity and open indecency' that are considered to characterise the Bhavai play (Jhaveri 1924, 182–83). Interestingly, Aristophanes' *Wealth* in the original is full of sexual humour, taunts and physical and verbal ribaldry. In fact, *aischrologia*, the Greek term for 'speaking what is shameful' is an important feature of the comedies of Aristophanes (Aristophanes 1998, xix). However, when Dalpatram rendered *Wealth* into Gujarati, he not only removed sexual explicitness and banter of the original play but also tampered the form in which the play was cast.

Stephen Halliwell in his Preface to *Wealth* observes that the character of Karion—the slave in *Wealth*—is much 'livelier' and more prominent than the slave characters of his previous comedies (Aristophanes 1998, 204–05). He has been presented as a 'more thrusting comic persona' who even seems to usurp the place of the protagonist Chremylos. Halliwell observes that he has been 'allowed a free rein in usurping the position which might be expected to belong, by both social and comic logic, to his master' (Halliwell 1998, 205). Now the character of Karion has been replaced with a lower-caste servant named Bhimado in *Lakshmi Natak*. The character of Bhimado has been employed here in the manner of *rangalo* (the clown or jester) of Bhavai (Vyas 2009, 16). Rangalo is an important character in Bhavai who remains ubiquitous in the play and makes the audience laugh 'by coarse allusions, shameless jests, and obscene gestures' (Jhaveri 1924, 183). He lampoons and denigrates almost all the characters of a Bhavai play. However, Bhimado in *Lakshmi Natak* becomes a diluted version of *rangalo*. He has been rendered submissive so far as his language and his relationship with his master are concerned. For example, the very first passage of *Wealth* where Karion calls his master 'quite insane' and goes on to explain his master's stupidity to the audience has completely been removed from the translation. As has been shown in the analysis of the passage where Aristophanes refers to Korinthian courtesans and male lovers, Dalpatram has either removed or naturalised such expressions with sexual connotations. Similarly, Karion's bawdy conversation with Chorus (lines 290–315) has also been removed from the translation. Vasunia rightly observes that the version of the 'popular' that Dalpatram offers is 'stylized, carefully demarcated, and often moralizing in its intent' (Vasunia 2007, 122).

Dalpatram, like his contemporary social reformers and writers such as Mahipatram Rupram Nilkanth[4] and Ranchhodbhai Udayram Dave,[5] harboured an 'elitist' bias towards the Bhavai. They were of the opinion that this 'obscene' form of performance either should be purged of its 'obscenity' and 'vulgarity' or should be completely removed from the scene (Patel 2017, 46–48). As an alternative of the Bhavai, they favoured and encouraged 'natak', a more respectable form of performance. Dalpatram's use of the word *natak* in the title of the play and *swang* for a scene (rather than the popular word '*vesh*') can be seen as an attempt to move away from the popular tradition of the Bhavai.

---

4 Mahipatram Rupram Nilkanth (1829–1891) was a social reformer, an educationist, a novelist and a biographer. He edited 19 Bhavai plays and published as the book *Bhavai Sangrah* in 1874. See Madhusudan Parekh (1981).

5 Ranchhodbhai Udayram Dave (1837–1923) was the most important, prolific and popular Hindu Gujarati playwright of the second half of the nineteenth century. The author of the first Gujarati tragedy *Lalitadukhdarshak Natak* (1866), Ranchhodbhai was also a good translator and scholar of Sanskrit prosody. See *Ranchhodbhai Udayram Shatabdismarakgranth* (1938).

Another interesting aspect of this translation is that Dalpatram presents the Old Woman and her adulterous male lover of Aristophanes' play as Muslims; they are Fatma Bibi and Juvan Madarkhan. This is quite striking considering the fact that the rest of the characters are Hindus and the play itself teems with references to Hindu religion and culture, evoking the conception of Hindu village and community. Moreover, unlike other characters of the play who speak in Gujarati, these two characters speak in Hindustani. It seems that Dalpatram was hesitant in giving these particular roles of the Old Woman and her adulterous lover to Hindus. However, this can also be explained with the fact that the high-caste Hindu intellectuals of this period harboured a strong bias against Muslims and the Gujarati spoken by them. J.E. Sanjana, in his remarkable critical evaluation of the literary oeuvre of Narmad and Dalpatram, observes that there is no room for non-Hindus in their purview (Sanjana 1950, 143). He further observes:

> This purely Hindu outlook has been and is a constant and important, though often not consciously realized factor in the mental outfit of all Gujarati writers, from Dalpat and Narmad down to Govardhanram and Gandhi, Mashruwala and Munshi. (Sanjana 1950, 144)

It has been observed that Gujarati spoken by Muslims and Parsis was considered 'impure' and 'sub-standard' by the high-caste Hindu intellectuals during the second half of the nineteenth century (Patel 2017, 32–42). And they also attempted to remove Persian and Arabic words from Gujarati considering them 'impurities'. The ideological impetus behind it was high-caste Gujarati intellectuals' desire to carve out their own exclusive regional identity and to establish its hegemonic dominance over the vernacular sphere during the period (Patel 2017). In this peculiar context, this ascription of Hindustani language and sexual immorality to a Muslim couple acquires significance. It can be argued that the contemporary Hindu bias against Muslims and Gujarati spoken by them also informs the process of translating *Wealth* into Gujarati. Phiroze Vasunia aptly observes:

> In that sense, it is perhaps true to say that the socio-moralistic perspective precedes and shapes the literary exploration rather than the other way around.... With Dalpatram, the ethical or moral point is made emphatically, from the beginning, and the play trails in its wake. (Vasunia 2007, 125)

Conclusion

Lakshmi Natak is a product of the socio-political milieu of its times. And the critical attitude, manifests in the journalism of the period, informs the translation process. The discourse of reform that radiates through this play addresses not only prevalent irrational and evil socio-religious practices but also the malfunctioning of the new regime. Dalpatram's affiliation with the particular form of Hinduism, its belief system and his own ideological perspectives also dictate his translational strategies. Though *Lakshmi Natak* seems to move away from the popular tradition of Bhavai, its impact at the subliminal level cannot be denied. The contemporary disdain, especially that of the Hindu intelligentsia, towards Gujarati spoken by Muslims also plays an important role in the translation process. In the light of the previous discussion, it can be strongly stated that translation was integral to the Gujarati literary field of the 1850s as it was still in the process of being demarcated and defined. The Gujarati language was in the process of getting standardised and prose forms were yet to become central or canonical. In such a context, translation addressed problems of reform as well as social and political emancipation. There is an underlying thread of critical attitude running through the periodical literature, the new forms of literary expression such as drama and the novel and the public criticism of the colonial government in various forums. Translation shares this underlying critical attitude and embodies its spirit in the translation of a text like Aristophanes' *Wealth.*

References

Aristophanes, *Birds and Other Plays*, translated and edited by Stephen Halliwell, New York, Oxford University Press Inc., 1998.

Buddhiprakash, 'Sane 1856 no Act 1. Bhunda Pustako, Cheetaro, tatha Bhunda Geeto, thatha Bhundu Bhashan band kare chhe' (Act 1 of AD 1856 Banes Obscene Books, Paintings, Songs and Speech), Vol. 3, No. 3, 1856, pp. 73–76.

Dalpatram, 'Gujarati Vernacular Society no Itihas', *Buddhiprakash*, Vol. 25, Nos 1, 2, 1878, pp. 3–13, 27–34.

———. *Lakshmi Natak*, 3rd edition, Ahmedabad, Gujarat Vernacular Society, 1863.

Dave, Jagdish J., *Gujarati ane Marathi Samajik Natako, 1850–1900*, Ahmedabad, Vasant Prakashan, 2000.

Jhaveri, Krishnalal M., *Further Milestones in Gujarati Literature*, Bombay, 1924.

Joshi, Svati, 'Dalpatram and the Nature of Literary Shifts in Nineteenth-century Ahmedabad', in *India's Literary History: Essays on the Nineteenth Century*, edited by Stuart Blackburn and Vasudha Dalmia, Delhi, Permanent Black, 2004, pp. 327–57.

Parekh, Hiralal Tribhuvandas, *Gujarat Vernacular Society no Itihas. Vol. 1 (1849–1878)*, Ahmedabad, Gujarat Vernacular Society, 1932.

Parekh, Madhusudan, *Arvacheen Gujarati Sahitya no Aaswad*, Ahmedabad, Chandramauli Prakashan, 1981.

Patel, Hiren J., 'Translation and the Making of Literary Public Sphere in Nineteenth Century Gujarat, 1850–1880: A Critical Study', PhD Thesis, Central University of Gujarat, 2017.

Ranchhodbhai Udayram Shatabdismarakgranth, ed., Shree Ranchhodbhai Udayram Shatabdi Samiti, Mumbai, 1938.

Sanjana, J.E., *Studies in Gujarati Literature*, Bombay, The University of Bombay, 1950.

The Bombay Quarterly Magazine and Review, 'Notices of Books, Pamphlets & c', Vol. 2, 1851–1852, pp. 232–35, *Hathi Trust Digital Library.* Available at: https://babel.hathitrust.org/cgi/pt?id=uc1.b3042597;view=1up;seq=245 (accessed on 4 March 2016).

Vasunia, Phiroze, 'Aristophanes' *Wealth* and Dalpatram's *Lakshmi*', *Aristophanes in Performance, 421 BC–AD 2007: Peace, Birds and Frogs*, edited by Edith Hall and Amanda Wrigley, London, Modern Humanities Research Association and Maney Publishing, 2007, pp. 117–34.

Vyas, Sateesh, *Gujarati Natak*, Ahmedabad, Gujarati Sahitya Parishad, 2009.

4

Forging Bhakti: Translation, Conversion and Fraud in the Ezourvedam

Tara Menon

The project of which the following is an exploratory excerpt began with an interest in what Subrahmanyam calls the 'career of "religion" as a master concept' and in his attempt to 'understand how it was deployed within Christian discourses of similarity and difference' (2017, 62). I wondered how the project of conversion ended up distilling an idea of 'pure religion': on the one hand, something like the ideal substrate underlying the empirically given historical religions, and, on the other, something like the movement of conversion itself, removed from the liturgical and doctrinal particularities of its given historical context. Conversion always involves, among other things, the work of literal translation and I believe there is something similar to this 'pure religion' to be glimpsed in Walter Benjamin's 'pure language' (74): something whose definition Benjamin does not explicitly provide, but which might be said to consist in the *force* of translation as endowed with the *form* of a language.

I hoped, in tracing the genealogy of the contemporary pseudo-creed 'I'm spiritual but not religious', to uncover by what mechanisms of literal, metaphorical and conceptual translations it came into being. A large part of the history of this discourse of unaffiliated spirituality involves the Romantic inheritance of Jesuit Indology—if Romanticism is, to borrow T.E. Hulme's spiteful but compact phrase, spilt religion, Jesuits did a lot of the spilling. The present chapter builds on research by Ludo Rocher, Urs App, Ines Zupanov and many others, and moves in the direction of theoretical problems in the history of religions. The Ezourvedam provides an exemplary optic for certain problems that I here attempt to explore in a preliminary form.

I would like to begin by narrating to you the rather picaresque history of a text. Many of you may know some or all of this story. I will begin my account of its mottled career in 1760, when it worked mischief upon that most mischievous of French philosophers, that trenchant critic of religion in general and Catholicism in particular, Voltaire. Voltaire received with delight a copy of a supposed translation from Sanskrit of one of the most ancient books in the world—perhaps, he would contend at points, the most ancient book in the world. The original to beat all originals. It was presented to him by Louis-Laurent de Féderbe, Chevalier de Maudave, on the recommendation of the famous mathematician and philosopher Jean le Rond d'Alembert.. Maudave was ostensibly a 'close friend of one of the principal brahmins' of the Coromandel coast—this proximity to a privileged native informant rendered Maudave reliable in Voltaire's eyes, while the Brahmin himself (an invented Brahmin, it turns out) seemed trustworthy in his assurance that the translation was 'very, very faithful' because he was supposedly a regular correspondent of the French East India Company, who rendered the Company invaluable services. Voltaire made sure to deposit this translation at the Bibliothèque Royale in Paris, now the Bibliotheque Nationale (you can find it today as number 452 of the nouvelles acquisitions françaises). He was thrilled at this revelation, at long last, of the secrets of the Hindu Vedas. I quote his exultation from a letter he wrote to his friend Jacob Vernes on 1 October 1761:

> this manuscript is destined to become the sole treasure that will remain of our East India Company... It is definitely very authentic

> [you can sense some anxiety here] and must have been composed long before Alexander's expedition, for not a single name of rivers, mountains or cities resembles the Greek names which Alexander's companions introduced into the land.... The manuscript is called Ezour Vedam, which means: commentary on the Veda. Another reason why it must be very old is that in it the author combats the beginnings of idolatry. I am convinced that it antedates Pythagoras by several centuries. I have sent the manuscript to the King's Library, where it is preserved as the most precious gem of their collections. (quoted in Rocher 1984, 29)

A curious feature of Voltaire's attachment to this text is his insistence on its value as an object to the French empire. He asks, facetiously, why we should not obtain wisdom too from those who have provided us with pepper across the ages (Voltaire 1877, 140).

The Ezourvedam shot to fame primarily by Voltaire's handiwork. Raymond Schwab, in his magisterial work *The Oriental Renaissance*, attributes to Voltaire the 'launch of India' as the 'cradle of civilization' in the European consciousness (1950, 20). It is an amusing and illuminating irony that this launch was motivated initially by what was very soon exposed as a modern Jesuit concoction. Urs App speculates that the Ezourvedam was initially devised by a Jesuit posted in India as a device for the purposes of conversion, as a kind of *preparatio evangelica*, or even as an aging Jesuit's Sanskrit practice (2010, 61). The translation from French into Sanskrit occurred in order for the text to be presented as a supplementary Veda, the title of which would vaguely recall the Yajurveda, the last of the four real Vedas—in addition to evoking a euphonic transformation of something like 'Yesu Vedam', a Veda of Jesus. The intention was to transpose Christian theology into Vedic form. Voltaire, convinced of its authenticity, found in it a polemical weapon against Catholicism—if a text of apparently more ancient provenance than the Hebraic tradition expressed the same essential wisdom, the legitimacy of the Christian revelation and the Church that assured its transmission through history was in danger of being replaced by the universal religion Voltaire so ardently sought, a worldwide, transcultural consent to original monotheism.

As Ludo Rocher demonstrates, the ostensible French translation was actually the original. The spelling of the words and other such features all attest to this fact. In the Indian context, the text had little effect. App identifies one possible appearance of it in an anecdote he culls from the Jesuit archives in Pondicherry—a Brahmin, addressed by a Jesuit with this spurious document in hand, beat him and chased him out of the village (2010, 380). The Ezourvedam presents itself as a corrective, a return to the truth, of the 'false Vedas'—Hinduism's original four are, from this point of view, subsequent distortions. In App's words:

> This effort to undermine the authority of the Indian Vedas (and thus also of the Brahmins) was sure to enrage Indian clergy, who must have been astonished by this kind of brazen hijack attempt by outcaste Johnny-come-latelies who had no idea of the Vedas. For the missionary author and 'teacher' of this text, on the other hand, the genuine tradition was now coming back to India, the cult of the true God was about to be restored, and the reigning cults of Vishnu and Shiva were on their way to extinction. (2010, 391)

The Ezourvedam consistently presents the contents of the 'false Vedas'—that is, the 'real' Hindu texts, usually Puranic rather than Vedic—and then provides a refutation. In Europe, the text was widely read, even though it was soon exposed and derided as a forgery. Ellis declared that this is an 'imitation of the Vedas', 'an instance of literary forgery or rather of religious imposition without parallel'; Max Müller called it a 'very coarse forgery'; August Wilhelm Schlegel—otherwise fairly sympathetic to what he considers the Ezourvedam's poetic and metrical proficiency in Sanskrit—mocks the venerable Indologist, Anquetil-Duperron, who continued all his life to defend the text's authenticity along with Voltaire in these vivid terms: the one milked a he-goat, and the other held a sieve under it. Schlegel also comes up with one of the most apt terms for the Ezourvedam—he calls it a 'pious fraud' (quoted in Rocher 1984, 21–33). What interests me here is exactly how a fraud can be pious—what the nature of this devotion might be, and how it might be compatible with a serious Christian mission—assuming, for the sake of argument, that the intention was in fact not malignant but sincere and committed to some sense of truth.

Certain great Indologists—Sainte Croix and Anquetil-Duperron most prominent amongst them—held adamantly to the idea of the Ezourvedam's authenticity. What motivated this blind devotion to the trickster text? Most important for readers like Voltaire was that the Ezourvedam was evidence of a natural or universal religion, a kind of primitive monotheism. A sort of tautology governs Voltaire's enthusiastic embrace of this text. It is the oldest text because it is monotheistic; at the same time, it provides evidence that monotheism existed in ancient India and preceded the 'corrupt' polytheism of contemporary Hinduism. For the Jesuits too, the theory of primitive monotheism may have justified the creation of this deception. It is after all not really a falsehood if one is only manufacturing a text out of the materials of Hinduism to convert Hindus to a truth already inherent in the true form of their religion. It was through such texts and practices that the division of religions—including Christianity—into 'esoteric' and 'exoteric' forms came about. The esoteric content—such as a belief in one universal God—were privileged over the exoteric practices; it did no harm to the Christian doctrine to be cloaked in Hindu names. Underlying Jesuit practices such as the concoction of the Ezourvedam was a belief in what Zupanov calls 'fragments of esoteric truth' (1999, 4) in other religions—fragments to be brought back to life, energized, and set to work to take over, to inseminate the entire religion. Zupanov notices that the maverick Jesuit de Nobili cites church precedents for this practice of transferring Christian doctrine into other ritual and mythological structures. He calls on the sixteenth-century cardinal Cesare Baronio to say, 'We indeed find no Gentile customs, which the church did not transform into a practice consonant with faith, that all those who formerly worshipped the devil might, to his greater confusion, render honour to Christ' (1999, 53). In de Nobili's observation, the fervour of devotion displayed by converts before conversion remained intact. What changed was the *object* of devotion—as well as the guru. Something like what A.K. Ramanujan terms the 'white heat' (1973, 27) of bhakti can be simply redirected into a translated form.

Confusions abound in Voltaire's description of the text. Sometimes it appears as the Veda itself, sometimes as a commentary explicating the Veda. A note is in order regarding the structure of the text itself. It consists of a dialogue between Chumontou (Sumantu) and Biach (Vyasa), master and student. Chumontou deploys Indian terminology and Hindu concepts in order to justify what he terms the true Veda and to disprove or disqualify the idolatrous beliefs of contemporary Hinduism—which he claims has deteriorated from its pure origins. The 'true Veda' is startlingly close to Christian doctrine. The text consistently relies on proximities of words and sounds—vague echoes, usually with no etymological basis—a mode that obtains throughout the early history of Indology, in associations such as those that claimed that the 'brahmins' were the descendants of Abraham; a deduction made from the typological similarity of the words in Roman script. A good example of this mode is the Ezourvedam's account of God's creation of man and woman: 'Adam is the name of the first man to come from the hands of God' (Rocher 1984, 113). We readily identify this Adimo as Adam, and the Hindu gods, whom Biach 'falsely' claims as anterior to men, are his children. Eve is replaced by Prokriti—and this use of the term demonstrates that the author of the Ezourvedam had some familiarity with Indian philosophy, despite his systematic garbling, because Prakriti is, in various yogic texts, the feminine force, the energy of nature and life itself. Another example of the way in which, at the verbal level, the Ezourvedam serves as a 'semi-Christian halfway house' (Aravamudan 2006, 33) is Chrixnou—Christ and

Krishna in one. But this Chrixnou is far from Christ-like. It is the homonymity that matters, that performs the syncretism of the text. These words function as subliminal messages, limning Hinduism with Christianity—not dissimilarly to the method by which P.N. Oak, much later, who invented etymologies to support Hindutva, claiming Abraham as a corruption of Brahma. One could, as Rocher does, read 'Ezourvedam' not just as a distortion of Yajurveda, the fourth Veda, but also as a Sanskritised version of Yesuvedam—the Veda of Jesus. Ezourvedam thus becomes code for the gospel of Jesus, promulgated in whatever distorted form. I follow Zupanov in identifying in this slippery 'Jesuitical' mode of 'translation' a Steinerian 'trust in the other', a sense that there is a meaning out there to be translated. Also, a conviction that, once brought into contact with others, human inventions and institutions cannot 'possess or sustain autonomous semantic fields'. The convertibility of things and thoughts is postulated as unlimited—hence this mode's seemingly unstable position on the 'threshold of cultures' (1999, 197).

In terms of genre, it is safe to say that the Ezourvedam is one or several authors' attempt to 'translate' Christianity into a Hindu idiom. The emotional reaction this forgery provoked in both its defenders and its critics has much to do with the monstrosity of translation—but as a Jesuit summary and adaptation of Hindu text, the Ezourvedam fits comfortably into the capacious scope of the Indic commentarial tradition. It was part of the Jesuit enterprise to adapt the caste system to their own purposes—and to position themselves as the new gurus, true Brahmins in a spiritual sense. Chumontou provides Biach with a fairly standard explication of the caste system—directly from the Manusmriti, according to which Brahmins are naturally more endowed with spiritual virtue—and then repeatedly alludes to his status as Brahmin and guru in order to rebuke Biach (Rocher 1984, 117, 135, 195). The Ezourvedam may simply have been a Jesuit's attempt to fulfil his Brahminical duties, engaging with and managing scripture.

Elisa Freschi provides the following rubric to assess what makes a text a commentary: (*a*) several given texts are their main interlocutors, (*b*) they belong to a genre in their own right and are not a minor specialisation for authors at the beginning of their careers, (*c*) they are characterised by a varied but strong degree of textual reuse, (*d*) they use a shared interlanguage that the author assumes is known to the audience, and (*e*) they allow for a significant degree of innovation (2015, 7). By these terms, the Ezourvedam's only fraud seems to be the misrepresentation of its age. In his masterful and mischievous *Guru English*, Srinivas Aravamudan points out how texts like the Ezourvedam (a case of 'Guru French', of course) produce new religious meanings. Zupanov employs the metaphor of a 're-tying' (that is, *re-ligio*—religion as rebinding) to characterise the way in which the Jesuits acted on the strands of Indic religious alterity in order to produce a kind of new 'nomadic knowledge'. One of the by-products of the forged syncretism to be found in the Ezourvedam—and other texts like it—is our set of idées reçues regarding Bhakti (as monistic, as largely anti-caste, or as at least privileging individual expression over ritual and doctrine).

The Ezourvedam performs a fairly consistent inversion of teacher and pupil, primary and secondary, anterior and posterior. Schlegel finds this feature of the Ezourvedam's composition confusing and cites what he sees as a mistake of this sort as evidence that 'A learned Brahmin would not have made Vyasa a pupil of Sumantu, since it should be the opposite' (Rocher 1984, 33). (Sumantu is 'well-known, easily known, friendly sentiment or evocation, of a king, of a son'—but he is also the sage to whom the Atharva Veda, the fourth of the four Vedas, is ascribed). Vyasa—the 'Biache' of the Ezourvedam—is the mythological author of the Mahabharata and one of the most ancient Hindu sages. To position him as a humble student of Chumontou, that modern fiction and reprimanded by the Ezourvedam's sage for his distortions of Hinduism, is to reverse the order of precedence and authority as Hindu texts prescribe. Many such reversals obtain throughout the Ezourvedam—the final one being the positioning of the god Narayena himself as not just Adimo's son but as Chumontou's student. If the student is in (Hindu) fact anterior to the teacher, why should not the later text, the Ezourvedam, become the original in some sort of spiritual sense?

By way of speculative conclusion, I would like to return briefly with which Schlegel characterised Anquetil-Duperron's dogged defence of the Ezourvedam's authenticity: 'the one milked a he-goat, and the other held a sieve under it'. In reaching for this analogy, Schlegel must have had in mind its famous appearance in the *Critique of Pure Reason*. Kant, who ascribes the striking image to 'the ancients', uses it in the introductory part of the Transcendental Logic to give an idea of what ensues when the attempt is made to turn 'general logic'—logic in its classical form, conceived as the 'canon' or standard against which thoughts can be measured to detect faults in their form, but never in their content—into an 'organon', an instrument for the production of fundamentally new truths. This attempt, Kant suggests, involves the asking of dead-end questions of the type 'What is truth?' (this is the milking of the he-goat) and the consequent production of absurd, unintelligible answers (this is the holding of the sieve).

The case of Anquetil-Duperron would appear to be markedly simpler: no more than an inexpert application of the philological canon, the measuring rod of acquired linguistic and literary knowledge, to a text that, regardless of its content, is recognisably defective in its form. But Schlegel's words—he belonged, after all, to a school of thought that indeed hoped to translate philology into an organon, into a culturally generative and regenerative discipline—leave open the possibility that, beyond the easily resolved question of authenticity, there is another vein of questioning better suited to the strange textual object that the Ezourvedam represents.

It was Kant's essential innovation (the Romantic school to which Schlegel belonged would later borrow Kant's name for this innovation—*Kritik*—to characterise, among other things, their new and ostensibly organic approach to textuality) to split the difference between 'general logic' (the procedures by which one can ask, of a given proposition, whether its *form* violates the norms of truth) and 'metaphysics' (questions like 'what is truth?'); it was his achievement to detect, in the invalid metaphysical question, something like the misdirection of an original impulse, the garbling of a hidden question that he—as he would have it—was the first to pose distinctly: 'What *kinds* of thing may be judged to be true? What is the range of judicability? What kinds of content are predisposed to fit into the form of logical truth?'

It seems to me that the Ezourvedam represents exemplary material for the critique of Indological reason—for the attempt to elucidate, to bring out, retrospectively, the valid questions prefigured in garbled form by figures like Anquetil-Duperron and the Ezourvedam author himself. The equivalent, in this case, of the 'metaphysical impulse' would be something like the faith in a single, universal, natural religion that would, of course, manifest itself in every part of the world, if unearthed through the work of devoted philology; words like Ezour (Yajur/Jesus) and Chrixnou (Krishna/Christ) are like impatient anticipations of this pseudo-messianic desideratum.

The Ezourvedam project (and, on Anquetil-Duperron's part, the hope against hope for its legitimisation) is in turn something like an anticipation of a much later turn in the discipline of Indo-European philology. In its first incarnations, of course, Indo-European scholarship consists largely in the identification of genealogical relations and the abstraction of phonetic laws from a vast body of linguistic material. Later the discipline begins a fundamentally new project: the construction of the proto-Indo-European language, the assembly of a lexicon consisting—as Giorgio Agamben puts it in his *Signatura Rerum*—of words 'like **deiwos* or **med*, forms that linguists customarily introduce with an asterisk in order to distinguish them from words attested in historical languages' (2008, 92). If this project is to escape condemnation as 'the *monstrum* of a historical investigation that produces its own documents', one must acknowledge that 'each of these forms, rigorously speaking, is simply an algorithm expressing a system of correspondences between forms existing in historical languages' (2008, 92, my translation). In other words, the twentieth century in Indo-European linguistics tends not so much to abolish the set of 'laws' and correspondences that the nineteenth century established over and above the historical material but rather to organise these correspondences into the form of a virtual and supplementary pseudo-historical language, to fold them back into the material itself, or to render them unnecessary by the adjunction of a new and partly artificial linguistic corpus. Perhaps something of the same tendency can be charted out in the—in some respects murkier—history of religions. In this case, it might not be illegitimate to regard **Ezour* and **Chrixnou* as two early, 'algorithmic' entries in the virtual lexicon of modern religiosity.

References

Agamben, Giorgio, *Signatura rerum. Sul metodo*, Torino, Bollato Boringhieri, 2008.

App, Urs, *The Birth of Orientalism*, Philadelphia, University of Philadelphia Press, 2010.

Aravamudan, Srinivas, *Guru English*, Princeton, Princeton University Press, 2006.

Benjamin, Walter. 'The Task of the Translator', *Illuminations*, trans. Harry Zohn, NY: Harcourt Brace Jovanovich, 1968.

Chakrabarty, Dipesh, *Provincializing Europe*, Princeton, Princeton University Press, 2000.

Freschi, Elisa, 'The Reuse of Texts in Indian Philosophy', *Journal of Indian Philosophy*, Vol. 43, No. 2–3, May 2015, pp. 85–108.

Ramanujan, A.K., trans. and ed., *Speaking of Siva*, Harmondsworth, Penguin, 1973.

Rocher, Ludo, ed., *Ezourvedam, A French Veda of the Eighteenth Century*, Philadelphia, John Benjamins B.V., 1984.

Schwab, Raymond, *La Renaissance Orientale*, Paris, Payot, 1950.

Subrahmanyam, Sanjay, *Europe's India: Words, People, Empires, 1500–1800*, Cambridge, Harvard University Press, 2017.

Voltaire, François Marie Arouet de. *Oeuvres Complètes*, Paris, Garnier, 1877.

Zupanov, Ines G., *Disputed Mission: Jesuit Experiments and Brahmanical Knowledge in 17th Century India*, New Delhi, Oxford University Press, 1999.

5

Twice Removed: A Study of the Form and Style of Dina Natha Deva's English Translation of Kashiramadasa's Medieval Bengali Mahabharata

Soham Pain

Kashiramadasa and His *Mahabharata*

Kashiramadasa's Bengali verse translation of the *Mahabharata*, called the *Kashidashi Mahabharata* after his name, and also called *Bharatapanchali*, is a prized possession in Bengali homes. Historians believe that Kashirama was born towards the end of the sixteenth century in an upper caste family belonging to the *kayastha* subcaste, and his *gotra* (family designation signifying lineage) was *Shandilya*. His *Mahabharata* was composed before 1642. The earliest recorded ancestor of Kashirama was Daityarideva. Six generations after Daityari appeared Kamalakanta, the father of Kashirama. Kashirama had two brothers, Krishnadasa and Gadadhara, both poets of considerable merit. Kashirama's inspiration was his teacher Abhirama Mukhuti, a *brahmana* from the Hariharapura village.

Manuscripts mention the village of 'Singi' in the 'Indraini' *pargana* (subdivision) as the place of Kashirama's birth. Some manuscripts replace 'Singi' with 'Siddhi'. Asit Kumar Bandyopadhyay speaks of two possible identifications of the place, one with the now-extinct Siddhi village near Agradwip and the other with Singi village in the Katwa subdivision, both in the Burdwan district of West Bengal, but finally votes for the latter (1980, 465–67).

The internal evidence of Kashirama's *Mahabharata* attests to the fact that it is not the work of a single author. Different sources testify to the fact that Kashirama himself could finish only the first three *parvas* or sections and at best the fourth. Dineshchandra Sen has argued that many of the portions attributed to Kashirama's followers are actually plagiarised from other works (1993, 979).

By common consent, poetic merit is at its height in the sections attributed to Kashirama himself. As is evident from his surname 'Dasa', which is sometimes substituted by 'Deva', Kashirama was a Vaishnava by faith, and his *Mahabharata* is permeated by a Vaishnava sensibility and the composition is oriented towards a glorification of Krishna. While critics such as Haraprasad Shastri had assumed that Kashirama did not know Sanskrit, Bandyopadhyay disagrees with them and his research proves that Kashirama's diction and style betray formidable knowledge of Sanskrit and first-hand familiarity with the source text (1980, 469). However, much of Kashirama's material has also been drawn from popular oral traditions, Saraladasa's Oriya and Kavindraparamesvara's Bengali translations of the *Mahabharata* and the *Puranas*.

Kashidashi Mahabharata: Rediscovery

The first printed edition of the text was undertaken by the missionary William Carey (1761–1834) and he did succeed in bringing out a volume or two. A revised, one-volume edition was subsequently published in 1836 under the supervision of Jaygopal, Professor at Sanskrit College, Calcutta. Thus, the text was in a sense 'rediscovered' by the British in the late eighteenth and early nineteenth century. Seen from this perspective, then, Kashirama's text can be considered to be in the same line as that of the *Bhugwud Gita* or Kalidasa's *Abhijnanashakuntalam*, both of which were 'unearthed' by colonial Indologists and presented to not just the European reader but to Indians themselves in a new package.

Colonial engagement with Indian texts and especially English translations commissioned by the East India Company involved considerable politics related to the consolidation of administrative and legal power over the native population. Summarising the arguments of scholars who have dealt with the nature and methodology of translation in colonial India, we may note the following trends:

1. There was a certain disregard for India's present. The translation projects generally sought to recreate an Indian past, glorious or otherwise and therefore mostly Sanskrit texts were chosen.
2. Even when literatures in the other Indian languages were considered, the texts chosen were almost invariably pre-modern ones. Thus, in Bengali, the Asiatic Society of Bengal funded the translation of *Chandimangal*, a medieval religious poem.
3. Though translations ranged from legal to religious to literary texts, as Mahasweta Sengupta puts it, 'Texts that appealed to the English were basically those that spoke of the "faiths" of the "Orient"' (1995: 163). Hence, the dominance of religious texts.
4. Whatever the nature of the text, it was translated in a way so as to suit the taste of the Europeans, and always judged according to European standards. For instance, in his preface to the English translation of the *Bhagwad Gita*, Charles Wilkins creates a 'One God-One Book' version of Hinduism that runs as a close parallel to Christianity (Kothari 2006, 12).

Since the beginning of the nineteenth century, however, we find Indians themselves undertaking translations of Indian works into English. This was in many senses a disruptive process as the Indian intervention into the colonial stage of translation challenged the Western constructs about India. As Rita Kothari puts it:

> ...the discussion on British translators serves to demonstrate how translation began as an administrative tool and by the time of Jones' *Shakuntalam*, it had become a tool to "discover" India. In the hands of the Indian translators, translation acquired a different significance, that of a tool for self-definition and the revision of history. (Kothari 2006, 23)

Kothari, however, is also conscious of the fact that 'in many cases the West informed terms of argument'. Thus, the process of self-definition that the Indians sought through these translations was also problematised by a colonial presence. The Indian intelligentsia had nevertheless bought the Western theory of the existence of an ancient Indian Golden Age which was followed by a subsequent decline of Indian culture and civilisation. Nineteenth-century translators, therefore, like historians and religious reformers, were motivated to recreate this past. Such a belief naturally led to a preference for Sanskrit texts and a certain degree of abhorrence for medieval ones. The hierarchy between Sanskrit and other Indian languages, therefore, remains with the Indian translators of the time. Indeed, Raja Rammohun Roy, the first Indian to undertake the translation of Indian texts into English, picked up Vedanta texts for translation, with the sole aim to project a 'pure' form of Hinduism 'uncorrupted' by superstitions and polytheism (Kothari 2006, 17). It is from this perspective that we need to approach Dina Natha Deva's translation of Kashirama's text.

Kashirama and Vyasa: The Question of Fidelity and Colonial Response

As we have already mentioned before, Kashirama's text is a product of Medieval Bengali devotional Vaishnavism. Despite the many literal translations of verses from Vyasa's original epic that are discernible throughout the text, in the final assessment it turns out to be an original work, shorn of the elaborate descriptive passages (including the lengthy battle scenes), philosophical discourses, and epic digressions in the

Sanskrit *Mahabharata*. Elsewhere I have tried to show how Kashirama's symbolism is drawn from Bengal Vaishnava theology as opposed to the Vedic symbolism of the Sanskrit *Mahabharata*, and how he rewrites certain very grave episodes of the epic in a way to tickle the lay reader.[1] The *Bhagwad Gita*, which runs for 700 verses in the original, is concluded in just 121 verses. Especially notable is Kashirama's attempt to narrate the story in rhymed couplets called *payaar*, which often do not do justice to the grandeur and sound effect of the Sanskrit original. It must be noted that while the Sanskrit *Mahabharata* originated as part of an oral genre, it was also canonised early, and given the sanctified and elite status of a *dharmashastra*, a book of *dharma* or moral law and religious merit. Kashirama, though fully aware that he is composing a version of the same text, is interested only in the narrative portions, and presupposes a not-so-learned readership.

However, it must also be noted that for the pre-modern Bengali reader/listener not familiar with Sanskrit, Kashirama's text had been the primary source of his/her knowledge of the *Mahabharata*. For the medieval Bengali reader/listener, Vyasa's text was apparently no more 'original' than Kashirama's. It hardly mattered to him/her that Kashirama had played with Vyasa's text, as s/he never faced the problem of an ancient/pure versus later/corrupt binary. The colonial intervention brought this distinction, and, therefore, in the early nineteenth and twentieth century, we find the Sanskrit *Mahabharata* being prioritised over Kashirama's text. Mahasweta Sengupta mentions some Bengali religious lyrics being translated into English in the 1920s but neither Krittivasa's *Ramayana* nor Kashirama's *Mahabharata* seems to have garnered adequate attention (1995, 163). Romesh Dutt, whose early literary achievements were in Bengali, also chose to render the Sanskrit versions of the epics into English and not the Bengali ones. One

1 'When God Decides to Die: A Study of the Muṣalaparva in Kāśīrāmadāsa's *Mahābhārata*,' paper presented at Conference, University of Delhi, 2017.

of the most glaring specimens of prejudice against Kashirama's *Mahabharata* is to be found in Bankim Chandra Chatterjee's *Krishnacharitra*, where the author clearly sets aside all non-Sanskrit sources for Krishna's character as spurious (and even creates a hierarchy among the Sanskrit sources themselves) (Chatterjee 1886, 11–76). It is, however, interesting to note that despite this prejudice, Kashirama's text made its entry into the Anglophone world via Talboys Wheeler's *The History of India*. In this book, Wheeler gives a summary of what he believes to be the original *Mahabharata*, and in the Preface acknowledges his debt to a certain Bengali gentleman named Obenash Chunder Ghose who, in response to his request, had apparently rendered chunks of the *Mahabharata* into English. Ironically, a reading of Wheeler's summary leaves no doubt that he had been deceived by Ghose who had resorted to Kashirama's version instead of Vyasa's, a point which did not escape Bankim's attention and taunt (Chatterjee 1886, 31). In retrospect, however, Ghose's act of deceit can be considered to be a reassertion of the Bengali sentiment with respect to the Kashidashi *Mahabharata*. A modified text which has enjoyed the status of being the 'original' within a particular cultural and linguistic space seems to have superseded the true 'original' even beyond its immediate cultural contours.

Dina Natha Deva's Translation

Dina Natha Deva's translation of the selected portions of Kashirama's *Mahabharata* was published in 1872 by Day & Co., Calcutta. Not much is known about the translator and this particular book is a rare find. Dina Natha Deva's choice of translating selected portions of the Kashidashi *Mahabharata* is significant as it challenges the hierarchy between Sanskrit and Bengali.

Before getting into the specific question of Deva's translation, I would like to focus on a few formal aspects of the book. First of all,

I would like to focus on the title. It is titled *Specimens of Translation into English Verse from the Bengali Mahabharata of Kasi Rama Dasa*. Thus, the title itself makes it clear that the primary intention of the translator is neither to narrate the story of the *Mahabharata* nor to provide the reader with an idea about the faiths and beliefs of medieval Bengal. Deva is intent on proving the *purely literary* merit of both Vyasa's and Kashirama's works through his translation. This is all the more evident when we see the portions that Deva has selected for translation. The two chunks that have been selected are the ones in which Yudhishthira is leaving for his exile and Vyasa instructs Yudhishthira to take lessons from Bhishma who is lying on his bed of arrows, respectively from the *Vanaparvan* and the *Shantiparvan*. For this chapter, we may focus only on the first one. This chunk can be divided into three parts: First, the residents of the city are not willing to abandon Yudhishthira. They curse Duryodhana and want to accompany the Pandavas to the forest. Yudhishthira, however, convinces them to stay back. The Brahmanas, however, accompany Yudhishthira and this invites a lament from the banished prince who regrets his inability to nourish the Brahmanas with his meagre resources. Sages Shaunaka and Dhaumya, however, comfort him with their soft words and enlightening lessons and boost his morale.

In the Sanskrit version, this entire sequence runs through three large cantos, extending a little over 200 verses (Dutt 2001, 1–6). In Kashirama's work, it has been cut short and is complete in just 96 rhymed couplets. The dominant rasa in this episode, as is evident, is the *karuna* rasa, or the rasa of grief. The Sanskrit text, however, finally subdues the plaintive note of the lament by the citizens and Yudhishthira to a sombre tone of dense philosophical discussion. The sages Shaunaka and Dhaumya are made to impart not just soothing words but lofty discourses on the cycle of destiny and the duties of a king. Kashirama, fully conscious of his readers' expectations and also the musical effect of his rhyming couplets, completely dispenses with these complex discourses. Deva's originality, however, lies in his decision to render Kashirama's work into blank verse. We are going to return to this issue a little later but having taken a note of the title and contents of Deva's book, we need to focus on the preface first.

In the Preface, Deva introduces the *Mahabharata* with the following words:

> This celebrated work contains *the ancient history of India* and *the chief mythological narratives* of the Hindu race. The poem abounds in *moral reflections*. It contains also many *pathetic passages and beautiful descriptions of nature*. Sanskrit being known only to a few of the natives of India, Kasi Rama Dasa composed a *version of the original* for the sake of Bengali readers.... (Deva 1872, I, emphasis mine)

The Preface, therefore, describes the *Mahabharata* as a historical document, a source of myths and legends, a manual of Hindu ethics and a work of poetry. The first two descriptions project the epic as a text of antiquarian interest and the third as a document that encodes the 'faith' of Indians. It is more than evident that Deva is here aspiring to make his own translation relevant to the Orientalist discourse of his times.

The second important point that Deva makes in his Preface is to blur the difference between Vyasa's and Kashirama's texts. He cleverly uses the term 'version' which may equivocally refer to a literal translation and a rather free one. Again, the use of the words 'a version of the *original*' adds to the vagueness. Kashirama's text is certainly a version of the *Mahabharata*, but if the 'original' in Deva's mind refers to Vyasa's work, then the former is a 'version of the original' only in a limited sense.

A passing glance may also be taken at J. Murray Mitchell's declaration and Jibananda Vidyasagara's letter, both prefixed to the book. Mitchell claims to have read through the work and certifies that it 'is carefully composed, and the versification is almost always correct' (Deva 1872, iii). Vidyasagara writes that he has 'compared it with the original, and... found it exact and satisfactory' (Deva 1872, iv). It is apparent from the language that while Vidyasagara is commenting on the merits of the translation, Mitchell's engagement is restricted to the versification of the translated text only. While Vidyasagara's declaration that Deva's translation is 'exact and satisfactory' is problematic, because the latter is certainly not so, Mitchell's declaration adds a different angle to the entire story. Apparently, Mitchell is located at a more privileged position compared to Deva simply by virtue of his being the white coloniser. It is implicitly assumed that however proficient an Indian translator may be in English, the final product must pass through the hands of an Englishman. Apart from this obvious issue, however, we also need to ask the following questions: Did Mitchell actually manipulate and alter Deva's renderings? If yes, to what extent has Mitchell contributed to the printed book? Who is to be held responsible for the omissions of the culture-specific terms and phrases in the translation? Mitchell or Deva himself? Perhaps we can only speculate.

Now we may return to the particular question of Deva's use of blank verse while translating Kashirama. It is more than evident that Deva is here consciously attempting to cloak Kashirama's work into the standards of British epic poetry, especially Milton's *Paradise Lost*. Ironically, the *Mahabharata*, let alone Kashirama's, is a text not only temporally and spatially removed from the Miltonic epic, but also differs widely in character and spirit. Leaving aside the obvious difference between primary and secondary epics, we can say that while Milton has a unidirectional moral and ethical message for his readers, the *Mahabharata* is a work which takes no final stand on the question of ethics and morality. Moreover, while the Miltonic style has been historically used by poets (most memorably by Wordsworth in *The Prelude*) to express a multitude of feelings not restricted to grandeur and heroism, the truth remains that it cannot do justice to a selected chunk where the dominant note is one of sorrow. However, Deva's use of blank verse also opens up a new possibility where the occasional monotony of the rhymed couplets is broken. Thus, Deva's attempt may be considered to run parallel to the experiments of Michael Madhusudan and Rabindranath Tagore with versification in Bengali. The legacy of *payaar* is taken up in both cases and revised and recreated under the influence of Western standards of versification.

We may wind up by scrutinising a few lines from the text. In these lines, the sage Shaunaka is made to advise Yudhishthira. The original reads:

> *Shaunak bolilo raja, chinta dur koro/*
> *Dharma ke shoron loho shunon ripoboro//*
> *Indra Chandra Aadityo aupor dikpaale/*
> *Trailokyo-jonere tara dharma-baule pale//*
> *Tumiho koroho raja topo-aachoron/*
> *Topobole dwijogone koroho paalon//* (Lahiri 2014, 328)

Deva's translation reads:

> O sovereign! Banish all thy mournful thoughts,
> To piety alone have thou recourse;
> The sun, the moon, the regent of the sky,
> And Indra, through devotion's force protect
> The heaven, the earth, and nether world:- thou too
> To him, the Great Eternal Lord, thyself
> Devote, and so uphold the twice born men. (Deva 1872, 8)

Let me first point out that the equivalents that Deva has resorted to for some of the Bengali words and phrases:

Bengali	English
Dharma	Piety
Dikpal	Regent of the sky
Dharma baule pale	Through devotion's force protect
topo-aachoron	To him, the Great Eternal Lord, thyself Devote

Let us first focus on the word '*Dikpal*', the second in the list. '*Dikpal*' most satisfactorily translates as 'guardians of the directions', and refers to a specific mythical group of ten deities in Hinduism. Deva seems to take a rather easy way out by substituting it with 'regent of the sky'. '*Dharma*', again, is a highly technical term with a variety of meanings and has traditionally been translated as 'righteousness', 'moral law', 'religion' and more, depending on the specific context. In the context of the *Mahabharata*, '*Dharma*' is a cosmic law of moral goodness which everybody should abide by. However, if the word is being addressed to Yudhishthira, then in the epic context, it also refers to his divine father, Dharma, the personification of the cosmic law just mentioned. Drawing on this connection, Yudhishthira himself is called 'Dharma-raja'. These are important nuances which are *totally* lost in Deva's translation. While 'piety' *may be* a poor equivalent of 'Dharma', 'devotion' is a completely faulty one. But Deva seems to know enough English to realise his mistake. Why then does he (and Vidyasagara) stick to the term? Is it simply for the sake of versification? It does not seem to be so. The real reason is perhaps properly understood when we focus on the succeeding case. The correct translation for '*topo-achoron*' should be 'performance of austerities'. In fact, though in popular myths, austerities are mostly undertaken to propitiate a deity, the word '*tapas*' etymologically refers to 'heat', and in this original sense, the performance of austerities or penance need not specifically imply the performer's allegiance to a deity. Therefore, 'To him, the Great Eternal Lord, thyself Devote' seems to be a deliberately distorted translation. The present writer is of the opinion that this is a conscious attempt on Deva's part to shear the text off its culture-specific terminology and manipulate it to suit the expectation of the Christian reader. Dharma, a specific term with deep roots in Indic philosophy, is supplanted by universal terms such as 'piety' and 'devotion', and similarly, '*tapas*' is given a Christian, devotional spin, by bringing in the presence of a 'Great Eternal Lord'. At the same time, the English reader not familiar with Hindu mythology is exempted from the labour of knowing the identity of the '*dikpala*s', and is presented a simplified list where only the sun and the moon, along with Indra, the king of the gods, feature as 'regents of the sky'.

Conclusion

Deva's translation is a piece of document that seems to exist in a limbo. At one level, it is *twice removed* from the Sanskrit original, being the *English rendering* of a *Bengali version* of the epic. But unlike Kashirama, Deva has some restrictions that he cannot willingly transgress. Kashirama's text belongs to the Indian tradition of '*anuvada*' (speaking after) which allows much space for originality. Deva's is a text that sets out with the ideal of faithfulness and literalness. However, the unequal power relations between the coloniser and the colonised complicate the process and the aim is never achieved. The final text ends up privileging the coloniser and the target language. While the theme and content of the original has been retained, the structure of a foreign language is superimposed, thereby rendering the final product into a hybrid text stuck in an in-between space.

References

Primary Sources

Deva, Dina Natha, *Specimens of Translation into English Verse from the Bengali Mahabharata of Kashirama Dasa,* Calcutta, Day & Co., 1872.

Dutt, Manmatha Nath, ed. and trans. *A Prose English Translation of the Mahābhārata, Vol. III., Vana Parva,* Delhi, Parimal Publications, 2001, rpt.

Lahiri, Subimal, ed., *Kashiram Das Birachita Mahabharat,* Kolkata, Dey's Publishing, 2014.

Secondary Sources

Bandyopadhyay, Asit Kumar, *Bangla Sahityer Itibritto,* Vol. 3, Part 1, Kolkata, Modern Book Agency, 1980.

Chatterjee, Bankim Chandra, *Krishnacharitra,* Kolkata, Bangiya Sahitya Parishad, 1886.

Kothari, Rita, *Translating India: The Cultural Politics of English,* Delhi, Foundation Books, 2006.

Pain, Soham, 'When God Decides to Die: A Study of the Musalaparva in *Kāśīrāmadāsa's Mahābhārata*', Paper presented at 'The Mahabharata and Inter-Asian Cultures: Transmissions, Adaptations, Performances and Histories' Conference, University of Delhi, 2017.

Sen, Dineshchandra, *BrihatBanga,* Vol. 2, Kolkata, Dey's Publishing, 1993.

Sengupta, Mahasweta, 'Translation as Manipulation: The Power of Images and Images of Power,' in *Between Languages and Cultures: Translation and Cross-Cultural Texts,* edited Anuradha Dingwaney and Carol Maier, Pittsburgh and London, University of Pittsburgh Press, 1995, pp. 159–72.

6

Colonisation, College and Chai: Virgil's Aeneid and Okakura's The Book of Tea

Lav Kanoi

Pre-text

Translation has a long pre-colonial history in our country. अनुवाद (*anuwaad*)—the word often used for 'translation' can mean 'to say again' (as in repetition), as well as 'to repeat by way of explanation' (a commentary). A lot of *anuwaad* was done in/to *apabhramasha* (literally a 'falling down'), or what may be called vernacular, languages that came into their own or into authority by becoming the neo-receptacles of Sanskrit texts or by demonstrating Sanskrit standards (for example, Nagaraju 1995, 12–13).[1] The process of carrying different standards into other Indian languages can also be seen during the colonial period in India. This chapter will set up the politics of translation in colonial contexts and introduce a 'collegiate' perspective on the colonial knowledge project. It will then return to an idea of *anuwaad* as being executed in a different translation (worked by the author of this chapter) of an anti-colonial text. As such, this chapter is concerned with specific acts of translation in colonial and post-colonial contexts. Although it may be trite to say that the act of translation can often be a story in its own right, it should be

1 Vernacular languages also came into their own by first imitating Sanskrit standards (as in the प्रशस्ति) and then by displacing Sanskrit as a literary and *written* language to express the everyday; for this, see particularly Chapters 2, 8 and 9 in Sheldon Pollock (2006).

noted that texts are carried over across languages in a variety of ways and some of these stories-of-translation can be as interesting, if not more interesting, than the story-in-translation. In this chapter, I will consider three acts of translation, two of which relate to the same text and a third that deals with an entirely different time and subject. The first text is Virgil's *Aeneid* and the second is Okakura's *The Book of Tea*.

The Colonial College

Fort William College would be, it is attested to in a Minute by the then Governor-General of India and the College's founder, Lord Wellesley, 'a becoming public monument to commemorate the conquest of Mysore' (Danvers, Monier-Williams, Bayley, Wigrand, Sapte et al. 1894, 238). This is supported by the fact that the law to establish the college was passed on the anniversary of the fall of Srirangapatnam (Danvers et al. 1894, 238).

The colonial purpose of the college is well known. It had a stated objective to provide for 'the instruction of … junior civil servants in such branches of literature, science, and knowledge as may be deemed necessary to qualify them for the discharge of their duties' (Danvers et al. 1894, 237–38). In addition to the apparently noble task of creating a generation of trained civil officers for the administration of what was to the British a complex, alien land, the College sought to execute a well-defined and programmatic operation to appropriate Indian knowledge, essentially through language study and translation (for example, Cohn 1996, 21). In the process, it did play a seminal role in the formation of many modern Indian literatures and languages, particularly Bengali and Hindi. It had a formidable line-up of the then contemporary scholars: foreigners such as William Carey and J.B. Gilchrist and Indians such as Lallu Lal and Mahapandit Ishwar Chandra Vidyasagar. While it is outside of the scope of this chapter to weigh the works of these giants, let it suffice to say that these formidable individuals translated, and they taught. But whom did they teach?

Their students were young 'writers', as they were called, aged usually between sixteen and eighteen, some of whom might have been 'educated with a view to the Indian Civil Service, but on utterly erroneous principles' (Danvers et al. 1894, 237). The aforementioned minute states that, oftentimes, their training prior to Fort William College did 'in no degree extend to liberal studies' and was 'confined to commercial knowledge' (Danvers et al. 1894, 237). As a side note, it must be observed that the East India Company did at least some good in recognising that though commercial knowledge is important, it is inadequate for governance. These 'writers' would often be stationed in the interiors of Company provinces, where it would be required of them to be 'conversant with the language, laws, and customs' of Indians (Danvers et al. 1894, 237). Therefore, equipping students with the languages of India in order that they might acquire knowledge of Indian literature, science and customs was a required pedagogic outcome. To test the achievement of learning standards, many of these writers-in-training were tasked with translating texts that could prove their linguistic mettle. Here, translation becomes a tool to test the language skills of colonial operators. One such distinguished operator was Henry Sargent.

Henry Sargent

We are told by Abhijit Gupta that Sargent's mysterious name would 'occasionally turn up in accounts of Bengali literature of the early 19th century' (Gupta 2013, 56). Sargent was supposed to have masterfully translated the first book of Virgil's *Aeneid* from the original Latin to Bengali as a student or writer-in-training at Fort William, but the translated work had been lost. Although translating European texts was perhaps customary for students at Fort William then,[2] Sargent was apparently an exceptional student. He received degrees in Hindustani and Bengali in the same year and was awarded a medal of merit in both these subjects (Gupta 2013, 58).

The prose translation of the *Aeneid* was necessary to but not sufficient for his degree. Sargent had to prove his linguistic ability in speech. Of the two disputations he gave, one was titled 'An accurate knowledge of the manners and genius of the Hindoos is to be acquired by an attentive examination of their written compositions' (Gupta 2013, 58). If on the one hand, the colonial project required an appropriation of Indian knowledge as evinced by the title of the disputation, it also involved the introduction of European standards into the Indian psyche. The Governor-General stated upon Sargent's successful examination that Sargent's 'classical execution', that is to say, translation of classical European poetry or writing, into 'even ... a prose version' could 'set before the native scholars of the provinces ... that model of epic genius and Augustan taste' (quoted in Gupta 2013, 58). In the words of the Governor-General then, it could set before the poets of Bengal the 'chaste and polished composition of the Western ancients' and present a preferred choice over 'the vicious glare of figurative and hyperbolical exaggeration ... of the East' (quoted in Gupta 2013, 58–59). Translation, then, could become not just a way to carry knowledge of natives into the tongue of the coloniser; it could also be a mode by which the standards of 'culture' would be introduced into native tongues and thus contribute to the 'civilising mission' of the colonial project (for example, Mantena 2010, 'Introduction' and Ch. 1; or Fischer-Tiné 2004, 229–31).

---

2 We are also told that at about the same time another student by the name of Monckton was supposed to have carried out a translation of Shakespeare's *Tempest* into Bengali, but this too could not be located. (Gupta 2013, 56)

We remember that the agents of translation were not just old and venerable figures such as William Carey, they were also young 'writers' in their late teens or early twenties. These young individuals, 'once landed in India … [we]re no longer subject to any regulation, restraint or guidance', and were 'abandoned … with affluent income, to pursue their own inclinations, without the superintendance (sic) or controul (sic) of parent, guardian, or master' (Roebuck 1819, viii; 'Introduction'). Consequently, and perhaps unsurprisingly, they 'often acquire[d] habits destructive to their health and fortunes' (Danvers et al. 1894, 237). Henry Sargent, notwithstanding his brilliance, was also subject to such weaknesses. Thomas Roebuck tells us in his commendation for Sargent's successes at modern Indian languages: 'Mr Sargent holds the first place in Hindoostanee, the first in Bengalee, and is reported proficient in Muhratta'[3] (quoted in Gupta 2013, 57)—and that Sargent 'has not only accomplished the difficult labours which have been recited … but he has achieved the more arduous task of subduing himself, and breaking through the strong control of indolent and enervating habit' (quoted in Gupta 2013, 57). Roebuck also presents Sargent as an exemplar of individual brilliance who could overcome weak habits and could furnish 'a powerful invitation and encouragement to those, who may yet be held in the chains which he has broken' (quoted in Gupta 2013, 57–58), which suggests that such (mal)practices were not uncommon on the premises of Fort William College. The great colonial project of knowledge, built on the foundation of languages and languages in translation is cemented, it seems, by 'indolent and enervating habit'. Translation, by this account, does not just serve to further

3 'Muhratta' means the Marathi language. The British had developed no systematic way to represent the sounds and words of various Indian languages in the Roman script. Their alternative—and I daresay incorrect—ways of spelling haunt us in various forms to this date.

the colonial cause or function conveniently as an examination tool; indeed, it can also perhaps furnish a powerful antidote to addiction.

Anuwaad 2.0

The lost Bengali translation of Henry Sargent was happily rediscovered in St Agnes' College.[4] This finding presented a new challenge for scholars of Bengali prose. If Sargent was to be recognised as a pioneer of Bengali writing there had to be a way to assess his Bengali translation. But many readers of Bengali would not be familiar with Virgil's *Aeneid* in its original Latin. The new publishers of Sargent's rediscovered work (Jadavpur University Press) decided to prepare a trilingual edition: containing Sargent's Bengali, Virgil's Latin and a new literal English translation to facilitate the appreciation of the text by Bengali readers. In this context, the primary text of Virgil's *Aeneid* resurfaced in a translational (and transnational) context not only in Fort William College in Calcutta, but also in Jadavpur University, another collegiate space. The task before the next set of translators (Professor Amlan Das Gupta and the present author) was to provide a basis for the meaningful appreciation of Sargent's own translation. If Sargent had translated Virgil's *Aeneid* into Bengali notwithstanding his 'indolent and enervating habits' as part of his student duties, Professor Das Gupta and I sought to repeat a scholastic translation of the *Aeneid* from the Latin, this time into English. Sargent's translation was lyrical and sought to recreate Virgil's lyricism in Bengali. Our English translation sought to reproduce a Latin-like texture even at the risk of compromising the natural cadence of this language. Ours was a secondary '*anuwaad*' and was designed to serve an ancillary

4 The text had been catalogued with the wrong title and was discovered by Abhijit Gupta.

purpose—to support the reading of Sargent's translation. Let us look at two examples, the first (Sargent, Das Gupta, Gupta and Kanoi 2013, 2–3) lifted from the beginning of the poem:

Bengali

অস্ত্রের এবং যে পুরুষ অদৃষ্ট বশে ত্রয় দেশের সীমার নিকট হইতে পলায়ন করিয়া ইতালীয় দেশের লবীনার তীরের উপরে উপস্থিত হইলেন তাহারই উপাখ্যান গীতদ্বারা কহি। তিনি যাবৎ লবিনিয় নগর নির্ম্মাণ না করিলেন এবং যাহা হইতে লাটিনিয় বংশ ও আলবনীয় কুল এবং রুমনগরবেষ্টনী উচ্চ প্রাচীর প্রকাশিত হইল এমন যে লাতিয় দেশ তাহার মধ্যে যাবৎ আপনার দেবসমূহ না আনিলেন তাবৎ পর্য্যন্ত দেবগণের পরাক্রমে এবং দেবেশ্বরীর কোপ দ্বারা সমুদ্রের উপরে পোত যাত্রায় ও পৃথিবীতে পাল্কারে আন্দোলায়মান হইয়া যুদ্ধেতে অত্যন্ত ব্যাকুল হইলেন।

English

Of arms, I sing, and of the man, who, being propelled by fate, went first from the shores of Troy to Italy and the Lavinian beach. Much was that man tossed on land and sea by the gods above on account of the mindful anger of cruel Juno. And the same man suffered much in war, until he could build a city and carry in his Gods to Latium, from which comes the Latin race and the Alban fathers, and the walls of high Rome.

Latin

Arma virumque cano, Troiae qui primus ab oris
Italiam, fato profugus, Laviniaque venit
litora, multum ille et terris iactatus et alto
vi superum saevae memorem Iunonis ob iram;
multa quoque et bello passus, dum conderet urbem,
inferretque deos Latio, genus unde Latinum,
Albanique patres, atque altae moenia Romae.

Outside of the inverted sentence structure, which becomes evident when we read the English and the Bengali, we notice how Juno is translated as '*debeshwari*' here (and later) as '*sureshwari*', similarly, the 'Gods' are rendered '*debasamooha*'. At other places, Sargent uses '*brihaspati*' for Jove, '*adrishter kartaa*' for the Parcae, and '*pavanadeva*' and '*varunadeva*' for Aeolus, the wind god, and for Neptune, the sea god respectively (Das Gupta and Kanoi 2013, 54).

Towards the end of the first book as the dinner between Dido and Aeneas concludes, we hear of long-haired Iopas (Sargent et al. 2013, 50–51).

Bengali

আত্‌লাস যে রাগ তাহাকে শিক্ষাইয়াছিলেন দীর্ঘলোমশ যোপাস তাহা কনক বীণাতে প্রকাশ করিলেন এবং চন্দ্র বিভ্রম ও আদিত্যের পরিশ্রম ও পুরুষের বংশ এবং পশু সকল ও বৃষ্টি আর জ্বলনবৎ ধুমকেতু এই সকলের উৎপত্তি গান করেন তিনি আর্ক্তুরস এবং বর্ষাজনক হৈয়াদিস ও ত্রিয়োনিস্দ্বয় এবং কিমর্থে হৈমন্ত সূর্য্য আপনাকে এত শীঘ্র সমুদ্র মধ্যে মগ্ন করেন অথবা কি নিমিত্তে বিলম্ব স্বল্পগামি গ্রীষ্ম রাত্রির ব্যাঘাত করেন এই সমুদায় ও গান্ধারা সুস্পষ্ট প্রকাশ করেন।

English

Long-haired Iopas,
whom mighty Atlas had taught, played
[music] on a gilded lute. He sang [of] the
errant moon and of the sufferings of the sun;
whence the race of men and cattle [came];
whence rain and fire; [he sang of] Arcturus
and [of] the rain-causing Hyades, and [of]
the Twin-bears; [of] why the wintry suns
hurry so much to dip themselves in the
ocean, or what obstacle hinders the slow
[moving] nights.'

Latin

Cithara crinitus Iopas
personat aurata, docuit quem maximus Atlas.
Hic canit errantem lunam solisque labores;
unde hominum genus et pecudes; unde imber et ignes;
Arcturum pluviasque Hyadas geminosque Triones;
quid tantum Oceano properent se tinguere soles
hiberni, vel quae tardis mora noctibus obstet.

It is notable that here, long-haired *jopaas* performs a 'raga' and does not just sing; and that the 'cithara aurata' (or 'gilded lute') is the 'konok beenaa' (or golden veena). Sargent is careful to make even as foreign a text as the Latin *Aeneid* sound natural in the Bengali. The quality of Sargent's rendered Bengali, as evinced in the previous examples, is very high. It should be pointed out that in Sargent's *Aeneid*, we find one of the earliest direct translations into Bengali, and possibly into any Indian language, of a non-biblical, classical European work.

Our own fairly literal and modest translation of the Latin into English, which allows us to trace some of Sargent's translational decisions, was done in rather different circumstances from Sargent's: we were still very much within an educational space, but there was no examination and there was no disputation. On the contrary, there was a scholastic desire to present a mirror to the world—all of this interspersed, in true Calcutta tradition, with chai.

Storm in a Teacup

And it is on that heady substance that I wish to bring up the other text-in-translation: that of Okakura's *Book of Tea*, first published in 1905–1906. The book, like tea itself, is almost 'irresistible and capable of idealisation' (Okakura 2016, 11). Okakura's collection of essays is at once a guide to the intricacies and philosophical simplicity of the Japanese tea ceremony, and simultaneously, a strong critique of Eurocentrism and Western imperialism. Both critiques retain political relevance, especially in the Indian context, today. Okakura writes that Western 'information' (as against 'knowledge') of Japan is 'based on the meagre translations of our [Japanese] literature, if not on the unreliable anecdotes of passing travellers' (Okakura 2016, 8). Further, when Okakura writes that '[c]ommerce has forced the European tongues on many an Eastern port. Asiatic youths are flocking to Western colleges for the equipment of modern education' (2016, 7), he could as readily have been describing nineteenth or twenty-first century India, as early twentieth century Japan.

Consider these lines in translation:

> हमारे रहने-सहने पर, रीत-रवैय्यों पर, पोशाक और पक्वानों पर, पोर्सीलेन एवं प्रलाक्ष के वस्तुओं पर, चित्रकारी पर – हमारे अपने साहित्य पर – हर चीज़ पर चायवाद का प्रभाव पड़ा है। जापान की संस्कृति का कोई भी अध्येता इस बात को नज़रअंदाज़ नहीं कर सकता। आलीशान रनिवासों में यह महकती है तो आम निवासस्थानों में भी यह सुशोभित है। हमारे किसानों-हलवाहों को फूलों की सजावट आती है, हमारे सबसे मुफलिस मज़दूरों को भी पहाड़ों और पानी की आराधना करनी आती है। [...]
>
> किसी साधारण पशचिमवासी को अपनी चिकनी खुदपसंदी की आड़ में से चाय समारोह में पूरब की हज़ारों सनक और अजीब-ओ-गरीब खेलों का एक और उदाहरण ही मिलेगा। जब जापान शान्तिपूर्वक ललित कलाओं का अभ्यास करती थी तब उसके लिये यह देश बर्बर ही था। मंचूरिया के युद्धक्षेत्र में जब से जापान हत्याकांड करने लगी तब से उसके लिये यह देश सभ्य हो गया। हाल में हमारी सामुराई संहिता पर बहुत चर्चा होने लगी है – मृत्यु-दर्शन मौत की कला पर जिसके

चलते हमारे सैनिक सोल्लास खुद को कुर्बान कर देते है; लेकिन चायवाद पर उतना ध्यान नहीं गया है, जिसमें हमारे जीवन दर्शन का एवं जीने की कला का कितना कुछ समाहित है। अगर सभ्यता के आधार युद्ध-क्षेत्र की भीषण खूनी महिमा हो तो हम खुशी खुशी बर्बर ही रहना चाहेंगे। हम खुशी खुशी उस समय का इंतज़ार करेंगे जब हमारी कलाओं और हमारे आदर्शों का दुनिया में सही सही आदर हो।

पूरब को पश्चिम कब समझेगा या समझने की कोशिश करेगा? हमारे बारे में पश्चिम द्वारा रचे गये सच और झूठ के अजीबोगरीब जाल से हम एशियाई लोगों को अक्सर हैरानी होती है। हमें ऐसे दरशाया गया है कि हम कमल की गंध पर जीते हो, ना कि चूहों और तिलचट्टों पर। या तो लाचार धर्मांधता में हम डूबे हैं या अति नीच विलासिता में। भारतीय आध्यात्मिकता को मूर्खता कहकर, चीनी शिष्टाचार को बेवकूफी कहकर और जापानी देशभक्ति को नियतिवाद का परिणाम कहकर उपेक्षित किया गया है। [...]

हमारी हंसी ही क्यों नहीं उड़ा लेते? ऐशिया भी यह तारीफें लौटायेंगी। और कितना मज़ा आयेगा अगर तुमको पता चलें कि तुम्हारे बारे में हमने क्या क्या सोचा है और लिखा है।[5]

Okakura wrote his work in English, and indeed, appeared to be writing for a European audience, addressing them directly in several places. In Hindi, however, it has been this translator's attempt to repeat Okakura's Japanese anti-colonial point of view for an Indian audience. The Hindi retains the overt address to Europeans, although the real audience of the translation are Indians. As a result, the Hindi 'we' is at times expanded, sympathetically, to refer to not just the Japanese, but also the Hindustani. It helps, of course, that Japan and India share a history and culture, and so the Buddha Sakyamuni (a very important figure in the development of Japanese Zen) is as much Indian as Japanese. Moreover, Okakura's anti-imperialistic stance resonates in the translator's own post-colonial and nationalistic politics; and being aware of this, there is a conscious attempt to let that resonance increase

---

5 Extracts from the WIP Hindi translation of Okakura's *The Book of Tea*, or चायवाद, by the author of this chapter.

and carry forward into the Hindi reader. As a result, Okakura's own text acquires a new, albeit parallel, politics of post-colonialism in translation. This exercise represents a different category of '*anuwaad*' where the translated text is at once a 'telling again' or a 'telling after' of the original text, as much as it is an elaboration of the original politics in a different idiom.

Post-Script

Consequently, if Sargent's act of translation was non-political (at least as far as he was concerned), and if the secondary act of translation that resulted from the rediscovery of Sargent's text was scholastic, the third act of translation is deliberately and consciously political. It is also, perhaps, no accident that the subject of the third translation is tea—a produce which has both a colonial and a private history, especially, in the context of India. But that, this author hopes, will be 'chai par charcha' on another occasion.

References

Cohn, Bernard S., *Colonialism and its Forms of Knowledge: The British in India*, New Jersey, Princeton University Press, 1996.

Danvers, Frederick Charles, Sir M. Monier-Williams, Sir Steuart Colvin Bayley, Percy Wigram, The Late Brand Sapte, et al., *Memorials of Old Haileybury College*, Westminster, Archibald Constable and Company, 1894. Available at: https://archive.org/details/memorialsoldhai00collgoog (accessed on 28 January 2018).

Das Gupta, Amlan and Lav Kanoi, 'A Trilingual Rendition of the First Book of *Aeneid* with a New English Translation and Notes,' *The First Book of Virgil's* Aeneid *Translated in to the Bengalee Language by Henry Sargent: Being a Facsimile of the First Edition Published in 1810 from the Mission Press, Serampore*, by Henry Sargent, Amlan Das Gupta, Abhijit Gupta and Lav Kanoi, Kolkata, Jadavpur University Press, 2013, pp. 1–51.

———, 'Note on Texts and Translations,' *The First Book of Virgil's* Aeneid *Translated in to the Bengalee Language by Henry Sargent: Being a Facsimile of the First Edition Published in 1810 from the Mission Press, Serampore*, by

Henry Sargent, Amlan Das Gupta, Abhijit Gupta and Lav Kanoi, Kolkata, Jadavpur University Press, 2013, pp. 52–55.

Fischer-Tiné, Harald and Michael Mann, eds. *Colonialism as Civilizing Mission: Cultural Ideology in British India*, London, Anthem Press, 2004.

Gupta, Abhijit, 'Henry Sargent', *The First Book of Virgil's* Aeneid *Translated in to the Bengalee Language by Henry Sargent: Being a Facsimile of the First Edition Published in 1810 from the Mission Press, Serampore*, by Henry Sargent, Amlan Das Gupta, Abhijit Gupta and Lav Kanoi, Kolkata, Jadavpur University Press, 2013, pp. 56–61.

Mantena, Karuna, *Alibis of Empire: Henry Maine and the Ends of Liberal Imperialism*, New Jersey, Princeton University Press, 2010.

Nagaraju, S., 'Emergence of Regional Identity and Beginnings of Vernacular Literature: A Case Study of Telugu', *Social Scientist*, Vol. 23, Nos 10–12, October–December, 1995, pp. 12–13.

Okakura, Kakuzo, *The Book of Tea*, Great Britain, Penguin Classics, 2016.

Pollock, Sheldon, *The Language of the Gods in the World of Men: Sanskrit, Culture, and Power in Premodern India*, USA, University of California Press, 2006.

Roebuck, Thomas, 'Minute in Council at Fort William', *The Annals of Fort William College*, Calcutta, Hindoostanee Press, 1819. Available at: https://archive.org/details/annalscollegefo00roebgoog (accessed on 2 February 2018).

Sargent, Henry, Amlan Das Gupta, Abhijit Gupta, and Lav Kanoi. *The First Book of Virgil's* Aeneid *Translated in to the Bengalee Language by Henry Sargent: Being a Facsimile of the First Edition Published in 1810 from the Mission Press, Serampore*, Kolkata, Jadavpur University Press, 2013.

7

Migrating Stories: The Panchatantra and the Grimm Tales

Priyada Shridhar Padhye

Hertel, a German Indologist and scholar, has translated the word 'Tantra' in the Panchatantra tales as a 'case of good sense' in English and '*Klugheitsfall*' which means a case of cleverness in German (Lanman 1915, ix). Theodor Benfey says that the tales speak about '*Regierungskunst*' (the art of ruling) (1859, xvi) and Hans Wegener, the editor of the German Translation of '*Bidpai: Das Buch der Beispiele alter Weisen*', refers to the Panchatantra tales as '*Standardwerk angewandter Philosophie*'—standard work of applied Philosophy (1925, 149). The Grimm Tales are referred to as 'Kinder-und Hausmaerchen' which means children's and household stories. The titles and the content of the two could not be more different. In spite of this, they are both comparable in terms of their success which can be gauged by the sheer number of cultures, languages and countries they have traversed. Even though the two works have very little in common, they still are fertile territory for studying the forces at play that affect translation and are unleashed by translation.

The focus of this chapter is to find out what these two success stories say about the countries, people and narrative tradition in their home and host cultures. An attempt will also be made to explore whether the study of the translation of these two tales reveals possible norms (as used by Toury) for the translation of this genre. This chapter also envisages to locate, situate and compare the movement of the Panchatantra tales and the Grimm Tales from their homelands to a few specific host countries in order to understand the dynamics of translation as manifested in their appropriation, adaptation and translation into some languages of the world.

The Panchatantra tales are ancient and have had a very long existence as compared to the Grimm Tales. The two works differ from each other with respect to all parameters, be they the text-based parameters like authorship or perhaps the lack of it, as is in the case of the Panchatantra, the style, the content and form. The two works essentially differ also in their non-textual factors like their history, sheer difference in the size and the linguistic make-up of their homes, the time and reasons for their origin, narrative traditions existing at the time of their creation, paths they have traversed in the world and their reception in their host cultures through their translations. They are also ideal prisms through which one can study and also question notions of translation ethics believed to be associated with nations, the very concept of national literatures, the idea of canon, authorship, translational norms (Toury 1995) and the societal hierarchical structures, be they political, social, cultural, traditional, religious or philosophical (Even-Zohar 1990). The date, location, title and sub-title of publications, forewords and introductions, glossaries, the name of the publisher, the agents commissioning the translation and the patronage received for the translations help to historicise and hypothesise the product of the translation of the stories. Some of these aspects form the basis of this chapter. The chapter is concluded with a few questions which need exploration.

The translation of the Panchatantra and the Grimm Tales till the mid-nineteenth century have been taken into consideration for this purpose as a result of which the audio, video, and animated renditions of these stories will not be discussed. The translation of the Panchatantra tales within India with regard to their recensions especially by the Jain monks, their translation in Marathi, and their translations into the two non-Indian languages, English and German, will be crucial to the deliberations in this chapter. As regards the Grimm Tales, their Danish and English translations will be central to the commentary.

This chapter largely draws on the detailed research done by two researchers: For the Panchatantra tales the book by Johannes Hertel titled '*Das Pancatantra. Seine Geschichte und seine Verbreitung*' ('*The Panchatantra: Its History and Spread*'), which was published in 1914, has been mainly referred to. In the case of the Grimm Tales, Cay Dollerup's *Tales and Translation*. The Grimm Tales from Pan-Germanic Narratives to Shared International Fairy Tales was referred to. Both the works are well researched and help in situating and locating the two works as well as their reception in translations adequately.

The Panchatantra has no author though it has been believed to be written by a Brahmin Vishnu Sharman, which, according to Hertel, is a pseudonym (1914, 7). The Panchatantra has been written sometime between 300 BC and AD 570. In the beginning of his previously mentioned book, Hertel writes: '*Orient und Occident sind nicht zu trennen*' ('Orient and occident cannot be separated') (1914, Preface I). He is referring to the fact that the stories have migrated so far and wide and even returned to their homeland as translations of the translations that one cannot tell which of them are the oriental versions and which are the occidental versions unless closely scrutinised and researched. Hertel compares the main recensions of the Panchatantra and plots the trajectory of each recension in their respective translated languages. His book mainly deals with the major translations of the Panchatantra into 70 languages. In the Foreword to the book, he mentions the difference between the stand of the West and the orient to the phenomenon of translation:

> *Was bei uns als niederträchtige Fälschung oder schamloses Plagiat gebrandmarkt werden würde, rechnet sich der indische Philologe der alten Schule als Verdienst an und vergleicht seine Arbeit mit der Wiederherstellung eines verfallenen Tempels* (1914, xii).

> (That which would be denounced by us as disgraceful imitation or shameless plagiarism, is considered by the Indian Philologist of the old school as a service to the author and his work of translation is compared to the reconstruction of a dilapidated temple.)

What Hertel means is that from the point of view of the West, the numerous adaptations and translations of the Panchatantra would be considered as shameless plagiarism and poor imitations of the original. The Indian philologists though consider the work of translation as a service to the author of the original work. He cites a Jain monk, Purnabhadra's, comments mentioned in the '*prasasti*', a sort of an epilogue, in 'Panchakhyanka'. The Jain monk compares his work as a translator to that of a person rebuilding a dilapidated temple.

If we take into consideration Hofrath Professor Buehler's quotation in C.H. Tawney's translation of the *Prabandhachintamani* on the work of the Jain monks, the above-mentioned 'service rendered to the original work' will have to be interpreted in a different light. The Jain monks, according to Buehler, were the ones who had the singular distinction of translating most Hindu literature because they wanted to use it to further their own faith:

> The Objects with which the caritas and Prabandhas were composed were, to edify the Jain community, to convince them of the power and glory of the Jain religion, or in cases where the subject is a purely secular one provide them with an agreeable entertainment. (Tawney 1901, vi)

So, the Jain monks were chroniclers of sorts. They also wrote histories, or maybe I should say rewrote Indian histories, where again to use Tawney's words they had a '*custom of annexing all the heroes of Indian tradition*' (Tawney 1901, vii; emphasis added).

As mentioned previously, the act of translation by the Jain monks does not come across as a selfless act of rebuilding the fallen temple but of using the Hindu texts as readymade literature to be appropriated for the spread of Jainism. Is the dilapidated temple also a reference to the way the Jain monks perceived the Hindu religion, as being one on a decline, and the rebuilding of it as a reference to the rise of Jainism as the new religion? One cannot help wondering.

If we follow the trajectory of the Panchatantra we see that it has been translated into many languages and the translators have been representatives of major religions who converted from one major religion to another and dedicated the translation to the religion they converted to. The Panchatantra tales reached Europe via Persian, Arabic and Hebrew translations. The Latin translation was done by Johannes von Capua between 1263 and 1278 and his translation was titled 'Directorium vitae humanae'. Capua was a Jew who had converted to Christianity. He dedicated the translation to the Cardinal Matthäus Rubens Ursinus (Hertel 1914, 396). Anton von Pforr, a member of the clergy, translated Johannes von Capua's text into German called '*Das Buch der Beispiele alter Weisen*' in 1480. He was the vicar of Jechtingen and had been commissioned by the Count Eberhard of Württemberg (Wegener 1925, 152). It was this book that was used for the translations into Danish, Dutch and Icelandic (Hertel 398). This translation was also used as a text for retranslating them into German by Hans Wegener in 1926. Wegener mentions in the Afterword how the tales from so distant a culture were given a Christian touch by Anton von Pforr: '... *er begnügte sich damit, der Auslegung ein christliches Gewand zu geben*' (He had to be contented with giving the Panchatantra a Christian touch) (1925, 151).

Abdallah-ibn-al-Moquaffa translated the Panchatantra into Arabic based on the Persian version called 'Kalila and Dimna'. He came from Persia and converted from Zoroastrianism to Islam (Hertel 1914, 391). At home it was extensively translated into Marathi, Gujarati, Tamil and so forth, at times not only in the standard language but also dialects. Hertel mentions a translation titled *Panchopakhyana* written in a Marathi dialect spoken near Aurangabad. The translator belonged to the Bhagwat sect and the translation was written in the 'Ovi' metre so that it gains more acceptances among the people (Hertel 1914, 262–67). The Marathi translation sanitised the text of Jain beliefs and appropriated the text so as to suit the tenets of the Bhagwat sect (Hertel 1914, 273).

In short, the tales were brought to distant cultures through representatives of varied religions of the world and appropriated to make them suitable for their religions. The translations of the Panchatantra were hence much influenced by different religions and initiated by members of religious institutions giving them a canonical status within their host cultures.

Hertel is of the opinion that the biggest folk narrators of India were the Jains especially the Svetambaras who had a large reservoir of literature not only in Sanskrit but also in Prakrit and Gujarati. Because the literature was also available in the language of the common people, it travelled with the people, with the wandering gypsies and caravans of travelling businessmen. This is how the stories reached the East Africans directly through travelling businessmen and indirectly through their translations in Semitic literature (*Kalila and Dimna*, *Tutinameh*, and *One Thousand and One Nights*, and so forth). From there they travelled from one tribe to another till they reached West Africa and with the slaves they reached America (Hertel 1914, ix). In fact, in America they appear in the form of an advertisement for the American Telephone and Telegraph Company and Associated Companies in 1912 (1914, 68). It has been proven that the Persians and the Turks were responsible for taking the Panchatantra to the Mediterranean and Armenia from where they reached the Russians. It is from these two routes—the Mediterranean and Russia—that the stories reached the rest of Europe (Hertel 1914, ix).

If religion was one of the major factors and very often the only factor in deciding the fate, content and the form of the Panchatantra tales, it was also one of the many (and not as important as in the case of the Panchatantra tales) factors playing a role in the making of the Grimm Tales. The Grimm Tales were written keeping the tenets of

Christianity in mind. Dollerup says that Wilhelm Grimm 'introduced religious sentiment into the content layer of the tales as part of his editorial filter' (1914, 248). The Grimm Tales owe their success to the then existing vacuum in children's literature at a time when schools were under the clergy and church and what the children read had to have the approval of the church and the elders (Shavit 1986, 61). This also explains the multiple editing the Tales went through right from the time they were first published in 1812 till the last publication in 1857. Hence the Grimm Tales were some kind of readymade, ideally suitable, material for children which had the stamp of approval from all authorities, be they institutions like the church or the adults who had to approve of what their children read. This appears to be one of the main reasons for their success in Europe.

Another crucial factor for their extensive translations in other European languages was the political situation and the power relations between the European nations. The German stories were written on the background of a Germany in the making where a concept of 'Nation' was still taking root amongst the Germans and in a Germany ravaged by the Napoleanic wars (Dollerup 1999, 291). The idea to have something 'German' was of immense importance. Ironically, it has been proven that in style, the German tales are inspired by the Norwegian myths and in content they are partly French in origin (Zipes 1988, 11). In spite of it, they have been introduced to the world as German legacy. One does not find recensions of the Grimm Tales like one finds of the Panchatantra leading to their appropriation and adaptation in their translations. One would then expect the Grimm Tales to have been rendered faithful to the original in other European languages because they have authors whose life and history have been well documented, which is not the case with the Panchatantra tales, for which there is no documentation regarding the exact date of their writing nor the name of the author. In spite of this, both the Panchatantra and the Grimm Tales exhibit faithful and unfaithful translations, at times because of the incompetence of translators and at times because of the political relations and the effect of narrative traditions of the host culture on the translations.

Dollerup draws attention to certain facts about the translation of the Grimm Tales while comparing the British translations with the Danish ones. He is of the opinion that the Danish translations were more faithful to the original as compared to the British (1999, 175). The reason for that lies in the respective traditions of the countries and the power relations that exist between Germany and the two nations Britain and Denmark. He maintains that whichever country has a live and rich tradition of oral narrative, and where the written word is not necessarily the ultimate authority, the notion of authorship and proprietorship affects the activity and quality of translation as well as the visibility of the translator. He goes on to prove that in Denmark the translation of the Grimm Tales was a translator's affair. Translators of high repute and standing with very sound knowledge of the German language were involved in the activity; there were poets like Adam Oehlenschläger, noblemen like Chamberlain Lindencrone, and academics like Professor Christian Molbech. Their translations bore their name and they were rendered faithfully (159). Which stories they chose for translating was a translator's decision alone. So, one sees that the 20 Danish translations published between 1816 and 1858 of the tales always carried the names of the translators (280). Same is true with the translations of the Panchatantra in India. One sees in the translations of the Panchatantra that some stories were added and some were deleted, but it was always a translator's work and the translators were given due visibility because the different versions of the Panchatantra were identified by the presence of the name of their translators like Nirmala Pathak's *Panchopakhyana* or Büd's *Kalilag* and *Damnag*. The liberal tradition of freely choosing from a dilapidated original what one felt was appropriate and rebuilding the temple was not considered as amounting to plagiarism.

On the other hand, in Britain, the translation of the Grimm stories was from the beginning an activity regulated by the publishers.

Britain not only lacked a live tradition of oral narration but also had more stringent copyright laws as compared to Denmark. The publishers decided which stories were translated and the translators were not people of standing or even well versed in German. The British translations, according to Dollerup, abound in 'contrastively identifiable errors'. The British translations also exhibit a lot of recycling of previous translations which is not seen in the Danish translations (Dollerup 1999, 321). Most British translations of the Grimm's Fairy Tales do not bear the name of the translators. There were 16 translations published between 1823 and 1858 (Dollerup 1999, 283), mostly by women translators (1999, 322), but hardly any translations carried the names of the translators.

Another factor that played a role was the power dynamics between Germany and the two countries, Denmark and Britain. At the time the Tales were written, of the two nations Germany and Denmark, Germany was the dominant nation. One third of Denmark was German speaking (Schleswig Holstein) (Dollerup 1999, 321) and German was the 'first foreign language most educated Danish people could speak' (Dollerup 1999, 170). Britain, on the other hand, was a firmly established colonial empire which shared no history and culture with Germany. This explains probably the lack of translators with a sound knowledge of German as well as the poor quality of the translations. For the British translators, the Tales were just a 'publisher's affair' and the activity of translation a derivative of the original (Dollerup 1999, 321).

As it has already been mentioned previously, the English translations of the Grimm Tales exhibited many inconsistencies with the original so did the Panchatantra's translations outside India. The British translations of the Grimm Tales played a crucial role as gateway language for translations in other languages, in spite of their unfaithfulness and also their poor quality. They came to be used as relays for most translations in Europe as well as for the Chinese and Japanese translations. The first Chinese translations beginning from

1903 till the first 'Complete Grimm' by Wei-Yi-Hsin were done from English by using English translations as relays. The Japanese edition was translated from English in 1887 (Dollerup 1999, 278) The same norm seems to be in operation in the case of the Panchatantra. Hertel comments on the Pahlavi translation and says that though it was done with the help of an Indian Pandit, the translator seems to have not understood parts of the text dealing with political content and Indian customs and views. Hence, a lot was left out. The sequence of the stories too was changed (1914, 389). It was the Pahlavi translation of the Panchatantra which played a major role as relay for the Syrian translation from which important later translations in Arabic, Hebrew, and Latin were made. These, in turn, served to be the major sources for the translations into Spanish, Greek, Italian, German, and so forth.

It is also evident in the case of both the tales that instances of the translation being commissioned by political patrons, or, for example, in case of the Grimm Tales, publishing houses, led to a bad translation. Where the act of translation had been triggered by the translators themselves, the translations were good. There may not be a need to mention that this alone does not translate into the success or failure of a translation and that the phenomenon is impacted by other considerations, some of which have already been discussed earlier.

Sanitising of the tales seems to be the case with both the works. The Grimm texts were sanitised by their authors while the translations of the Panchatantra show that entire arguments are missing and texts have been corrected politically and modified to suit the host cultures. A case in point is the reference to characters in the Indian translations of the Panchatantra. Very often a character is referred to by his or her profession. In the Marathi translation of the first story of the first Tantra, 'The Ox in the Forest' by Kashinath Anant Joshi and Pandhurang Ramchandra Dhamdhere, the story begins with the protagonist who is a businessman. In the story he is referred to as '*wani*' in Marathi which is his caste name. This is replaced in the

German story by the businessman's name '*Vardhaman*' every time the word '*wani*' occurs. Referring to people by their caste names is commonplace in Indian languages but not so in Europe, hence the modification was made by the translator.

In the case of both the tales, female translators have no visibility. As already pointed out, the British translations were done by women, but their names are not on the translations.

The spread of the Panchatantra can be attributed to a competition between major and minor religions and religious sects whereas the spread of the Grimm Tales can be attributed to a need for suitable and acceptable children's literature.

The Panchatantra tales show—probably because of the sheer cultural specificity of their contents and the hundreds of years of their existence—more radically naturalised versions than the Grimm Tales. The development of copyright laws could also be another reason for this.

When we observe the dates of publication of most of the translations and the scholarly research work done on the Panchatantra, one sees that it is the end of the nineteenth century and the beginning of the twentieth century till the beginning of the First World War. One wonders why the German Indologists like Hertel and Benfey, epigraphists like Eugen Hultzsch, French linguists like Jules Bloch, patrons in the form of foundations like the Lamey foundation, Saxony and die koenigliche Gesellschaft der Wissenschaft zu Goettingen, Universities of Strassburg, Leipzig, Goettingen, publishers Teubner, Brockhaus, amongst others would want to take such a keen interest in India and also the Panchatantra when by the time of their publications the Grimm Tales had already firmly established themselves on European soil. The British interest in their capacity as the colonial masters is understandable but the German interest can only be attributed to their idea of common Indo-Germanic roots. The *Zeitgeist* in which all these translations happened appears to be some kind of a build-up of an 'India consciousness'.

Hertel's critique with regard to the Panchatantra recensions and translations being referred to as plagiarism in the beginning of the nineteenth century comes across as hypocritical especially in light of the fact that the Grimm's Tales referred to as original German were anything but German.

In conclusion, it can be said that in the case of any migration there is a push and a pull factor. By the time the Grimm Tales were published, the idea of authorship had firmly taken root in the Western world due to the possibility of printing technology. This was again not possible in the case of the Panchatantra which had a fictitious author to satisfy itself with.

The Grimm brothers were very keen on the acceptance of the Tales by the wider public which is proven by the amount of editing work carried out by Wilhelm Grimm. From the original to the translated versions, the tales remained exclusively their work. Editing and adapting also happened with the Panchatantra but it was a free for all. Anybody who wanted to 'contaminate' them, to borrow the word from Hertel, were allowed to do so. It can be seen more in the light of what in modern terms can be called 'brand building'. The Grimm Tales are a brand which does not allow any wilful tampering.

The Grimm stories came at a time when there existed a vacuum in children's literature of Europe. It was a time when the notion of childhood changed in Europe and children suddenly became a social group with their specific needs in clothes and reading material far removed from those of the adults. The stories were further sanitised of their sexual references and violence to mould them in the Christian ideals of the time to make them more and more acceptable as children's literature for the adults and the educators who were controlled by the clergy and the church. This was not the case with the Panchatantra. Instead, the Panchatantra's translations into Indian languages show that the tales unabashedly refer to topics which would be considered taboos for children. The Marathi translation is a good example. There is a reference to adultery (Tantra 1, story no. 4, the story of

Ashadabhuti and Devsharman), insatiable sexual drives, especially of women (Tantra 1, story no. 3, the story of the businessman Dantil) and there is even a mention in verse form about the sexual prowess of women which they use to control men (Joshi/Dhamdhere). In fact, the Panchatantra tales have content unsuitable for children and yet it was most widely translated and came to be known as children's literature.

The flip side of the notion of authorship and subsequent proprietorship that goes with it is the static nature and rigidity of the product, as well as a sense of insecurity of the author who ensures that other claims to the product are effectively erased by simply not mentioning the sources. In the case of the Grimm brothers, the source of their tales, as discussed earlier, were Norwegian and French stories, whose mention one does not find in the two volumes. Every recension of the Panchatantra mentions its source and since most of the recensions are written by Jain monks, the 'prashasti' gives details of what liberties they have taken with the original text.

The Panchatantra tales were highly naturalised in whichever language they were translated. Hertel maintains that such a development is justified in the light of their long existence on foreign cultures (1914, xi). That extent of naturalisation of the Grimm Tales is not seen.

In the case of the Panchatantra, the original form, which is a combination of prose and verse, has been manipulated into only prose or only verse and also in content. This is probably due to the attitude prevalent in its home culture to the very act of translation which has been discussed previously. Comparatively, in the Grimm's stories one sees such appropriation less, probably because of the Western notion of the original and the translation being faithful.

Both the tales show that the number of tales does not remain the same. Tales are added and deleted. In the case of the Panchatantra, this tendency is seen in spite of the fact that they are frame stories.

In the case of the Panchatantra, the translations seem to be inspired by competing religions, at times used even to poke fun at competing religions, whereas in case of the Grimm Tales the translations seem to be inspired by a vacuum created by a lack of children's literature, the demand for which was high (Dollerup 1999, 167).

The Panchatantra tales returned to their home in the form of translations of the translations. One does not find the Grimm's Fairy Tales being translated into German from a Danish or English translation. Nor do we hear of Grimm Tales in a Bavarian or a Swabian dialect. There is only one German version. This probably has to do with the times in which the two were written. Whereas German as a language had been standardised, and the one nation, one language theory as a notion and symbol of nationalism had come to stay in the case of the Grimm Tales, the notion of '*Vasudhaivakutumbakam*' (The entire universe is one family) seemed to be the philosophy behind the Panchatantra tales which is reflected in their openness to plurality—since they have not just one original and one translation but many versions and many translations—for the world which is viewed as one family, hinting at a joint universal proprietorship.

References

Benfey, Theodor, *Panschatantra: Fünf Bücher indischer Fabeln, Märchen und Erzählungen. Erster Theil*, Leipzig, F.M. Brockhaus, 1859.

Dollerup, Cay, *Tales and Translation: The Grimm Tales from Pan-Germanic Narratives to Shared International Fairytales*, Vol. 30, Amsterdam/Philadelphia, John Benjamins Publishing Company, 1999.

Even-Zohar, Itamar, 'The Position of Translated Literature within the Literary Polysystem', *Poetics Today*, Vol. 11, 1990, pp. 45–51.

Grimm, Jacob, and Wilhelm Grimm, *Kinder und Hausmärchen. Gesammelt durch die Brüder Grimm*, München, Winkler, 1977.

———, *Kinder- und Hausmärchen*. Göttingen: In der Realschulbuchhandlung, 1857. Volume 1.

———, *Kinder- und Hausmärchen*, Berlin, In der Realschulbuchhandlung, 1812. Volume 1.

Hertel, Johannes, *Das Pancatantra seine Geschichte und seine Verbreitung*, Leipzig and Berlin, Vlg. Von B.G. Teubner, 1914. Available at: https://archive.org/details/daspancatantrase00hert (accessed 5 January 2018).

Joshi, Kashinath Anant and Pandhurang Ramchandra Dhamdhere, *Panchatantra*, Audio files downloaded from https://archive.org/details/Panchtantra (accessed 10 January 2018).

Lanman, Charles, ed., *The Panchatantra: A collection of Ancient Hindu Tales in its Oldest Recension, the Kashmirian, entitled Tantrakhyayika*, Cambridge, Harvard UP, 1915. Harvard Oriental Series Volume 14. Available at: http://books.google.com/ (accessed 12 January 2018).

Shavit, Zohar, *Poetics of Children's Literature*, Athens and London, The University of Georgia Press, 1986.

Tawney, C.H., *The Prabandhachintamani or Wishing-Stone of Narratives*. Calcutta: The Asiatic Society, 1901. Available at: http://books.google.com/ (accessed 9 January 2018).

Toury, Gideon, *Descriptive Translation Studies and Beyond*, Amsterdam and Philadelphia, John Benjamin, 1995.

Wegener, Hans, ed., *Bidpai: Das Buch der Beispiele alter Weisen*. Berlin: Wegweiser Publisher Ltd., 1925. Available at: http://archive.org/details/bidpaidas00pfor (accessed 12 January 2018).

Zipes, Jack, *The Brothers Grimm: From Enchanted Forests to the Modern World*, USA, Routledge, Chapman and Hall Incorporated, 1988.

8

India in Translation, Translation in India: Translation, Adaptation, Appropriation and Migration of Indian Tales/Stories

Subhendu Mund

The two aspects—*Translation in India* and *India in Translation*—are not only complementary to each other but also throw open a number of speculations related to the role of translation in India. It may not be wrong to say that the entire corpus of Indian literature, the bhashas, have more or less been the consequence of many different avatars of translation: transcreation, adaptation, appropriation and the like. Lakshmi Holmstrom, in her essay called 'Let Poetry Win: The Translator as Writer—An Indian Perspective', refers to India's multilingual milieu and points out that there has been for centuries a 'translation consciousness' and a 'translation culture' in India (2007, 33). Many other communities may also have such culture or consciousness but in the case of India it has far greater significance.

However, this is only one side of 'Translation in India'. There are many other aspects which have either not been noticed or selectively excluded from scholastic discourses. Let me begin with a few theorisations by some of our renowned scholars who are also well-known translators.

The complicity between coloniality and the act of translation has of late been developing as an influential discourse. Tejaswini Niranjana, in her *Siting Translation* (1992) identified this complicity. According to Harish Trivedi, Niranjana uses the term 'translation' by and large 'to denote the colonial power-play between the British rulers and Indian subjects' (2007, 284). Indicating the underlying power structure in the act of translation, K. Satchidanandan, points out that 'Most of the pre-colonial translations were what Gianfranco Folena would call "vertical translations"'[1] where 'the source language has prestige and value which transcends that of the target language'. In this context, in his essay 'Do you understand me?', he alludes to translations undertaken from hegemonic Sanskrit to a bhasha. He cites the example of Jnaneswar who translated the *Bhagavad Gita* into Marathi, and we can add any number of such works, such as Jagannath Dasa's translation of *Srimad Bhagabata Mahapuranam* in Odia in the early sixteenth century. Maybe we can use the same terminology for the translation of English and other Western texts into Indian languages during the colonial era.

But did we have instances of the so-called 'horizontal translation' ('between languages of a similar structure and strong cultural affinity') in our literary history? In her essay called 'Power and the Case of Horizontal Translation', Meenakshi Mukherjee, while talking about 'translation and structure of power', seems to suggest that there is no hierarchy 'between languages of a similar structure and strong cultural affinity' (2008, 207–08). But I beg to differ. When she talks about horizontal translation among the bhashas and gives the examples of Bankim Chandra Chatterjee, Rabindranath Tagore, Sharat Chandra Chatterjee and others being translated in other Indian languages, she does not mention that English was almost always the filter language through which all these renderings were done. In other words, there was some kind of verticality involved in all these apparently innocuous translations which signified yet another kind of hegemony. During the colonial era some Indian languages did experience the burden of this verticality of translation. There was a hierarchy indeed and this

1 Gianfranco Folena's essay '*Volgarizzare e tradurre*' was originally included in the proceedings of a conference on translation held at Trieste (Italy) in 1973 (*La traduzione. Saggi e studi*, Lint, Trieste, 1973, pp. 57–120). It was published as a book with a Preface as '*Volgarizzare e Tradurre*' (1991).

I can say at least about the power relationship between Bangla and Odia and to some extent Hindi and Odia. But that is not within the premise of this chapter.

This brings me to the third premise. In 'Translating Culture Vs. Cultural Translation', Harish Trivedi says, '... perhaps the first instance when readers in English and in other European languages were similarly shocked and exhilarated by the discovery of an alien [*read* Sanskrit] literature', when 'Charles Wilkins, Sir William Jones and other orientalists began translating from Sanskrit and caused in Europe what Raymond Schwab has called *The Oriental Renaissance* and J. J. Clarke *The Oriental Enlightenment*' (2007, 278). Like Sujit Mukherjee, Trivedi also apparently looks upon the act of translation as 'discovery', though he indicates a postcolonial angle by mentioning Edward Said, and 'further and more effective colonization' (2007, 278).

Now I wish to draw your attention to the one aspect where *Translation in India* and *India in Translation* converge. Although India has had a very active history of translation since the earliest known times, in our contemporary discourses this aspect is lost in amnesia, maybe because of our colonial hangover. Although it is difficult to ascertain the times of the Vedas and the Brahmanas, the Upanishads and the epics like the Ramayana, the Mahabharata and the Astadasha Puranas, they can certainly be traced to very ancient times, the oldest being at least 500 BC. Quite a few Indian languages have been active for at least 1,500 years,[2] and arguably, there has been a good deal of creative transaction among them down the ages. It is astonishing as well as heartening to notice how creativity in the Indian literary tradition has been associated with translation. For example, we have hundreds of Ramayanas in Indian languages written during the last 2000 years or so, but only a few of them can be called literal or faithful rendering of Valmiki's original. The same is the case

2 Six languages of India (Sanskrit, Tamil, Malayalam, Telugu, Kannada and Odia) have been officially conferred the status of 'Classical' languages on the basis of their proven literary existence for a considerably long time.

with Vyasa's Mahabharata and *Srimad Bhagabata Mahapuranam*. Many of these versions may be seen as 'transcreations',[3] and have evolved independent lives of their own. The originals have often been refashioned, retold and re-interpreted down the ages changing along with time and place. They are told in various forms and mediums without much harm to the essential in them. The implication is far more intricate: these adaptations have branched forth and have given birth to thousands of new works. This is such a well-known feature of Indian literature(s) that no examples are required to substantiate my arguments. Thus, it may not be wrong to say that a major part of Indian literature(s) has been constituted of translation.

Nonetheless, in the recent times, the discourses on translation have been a little too much intertwined with coloniality and power-play. Whenever we talk about translation, somehow we tend to relate it to coloniality and tend to create a binary of pre-colonial and post-colonial (with hyphens). We also forget the fact even a little before the so-called colonial era—say between the twelfth and the eighteenth centuries AD—bhashas thrived on *adaan-pradan* (give-and-take) amongst each other—texts were translated directly, and sometimes used Pali, Sanskrit, Paisachi, Persian or some other bhasha as the mediator. I can say this at least in the case of Assamese and Bangla texts with Odia literature.[4] This might have also happened with other

3 P. Lal, an Indian English poet, critic and translator and the founder of Writers Workshop (Calcutta/Kolkata) gave currency to the term 'transcreation' through his works like *Great Sanskrit Plays in Modern Translation* (Norfolk, CT: New Directions, 1964) and *Transcreation: Two Essays* (Writers Workshop, 1972).

4 Sanatana Vidyabagisha, who was the first to render the *Srimad Bhagabata Mahapuranam* in Bengali [*Bhasabandha Bhagabata*] acknowledges in his work that he could not have translated the tenth skandha without taking Jagannath Das's *Bhagabata* in Odia as his model (*"Dashamer shes sastha bhakha na paina/Anekata pasi grame grame bedaina/E hetu Utkala bhasha karila likhana/Jagannath Dasa krita apurba varnana/Grantha samapana hetu utkantha haiyan/Bangala bhasaya Utkala misaiyan"* [After reaching up to the Tenth Skandha, I could not get the language for my composition. I went from village to village to look for appropriate material, but in vain. That's why I had to write in Odia language. Being eager to complete the work, I took the help of the exquisite narration of Jagannath Das and mixed up

languages with close geographical or cultural affinities. This is how intertextuality among the bhasha developed and it almost gave us a vague concept of the much-debated Indian Literature.

This brings me to the third part of my chapter: *India in Translation*. I look at this aspect as a wonderful historical phenomenon in Indian literature(s) in which English or coloniality has no role at all. India has been translated since the ancient times. Let me give a few examples to substantiate my argument.[5] In his Introduction to the scholarly re-issue of *Fables of Bidpai: The Morall Philosophie of Doni* (1570) in 1888, Sir Thomas North's (1535–1601?) translation of the Italian writer Antonio Francesco Doni's (1513–1574) *The Moral Philosophia* (1552), Australian folklorist and literary critic Joseph Jacobs (1854–1916) informs:

> It is the English version of an Italian adaptation of a Spanish translation of a Latin version of a Hebrew translation of an Arabic adaptation of the Pehlevi version of the Indian original. And this enumeration only indicates one of many paths which these fables took to reach Europe. (*Fables of Bidpai* xi)

In the 'Prologue' to his work, North shows his awareness of the migration of the tales he was going to present before his readers: 'A worke first compiled in the Indian tongue, and afterwardes transferred

my Bangla composition with Utkalabhasha]. In his *Bhumika* [Introduction] to the 'authentic version' of the sixteenth-century Odia saint-poet Jagannath Das's *Srimad Bhagabata* (1989), Pandit Nilamani Mishra makes a detailed discussion of this scholastic borrowing/appropriating of the original Odia text (p. 33) by the Bengali poet. The sixteenth-century Mahabharata of Kashirama Dasa is believed to have been inspired by Sarala Dasa's Mahabharata (early fifteenth century) in Odia. Similarly, the Assamese saint Sankaradeva (1449–1569) was also inspired and influenced by Jagannath Das's *Bhagabata* to write the *Bhagabata* in Assamese. See, Kanak Chandra Deka, *Sankaradeva: The Great Vaishanva Saint of India*, Chapters I & II (1988).

5 I have made a detailed study of these aspects in my paper called 'Travelling Tales: Migration, Translation, Adaptation and Appropriation of the *Jataka Katha*', presented at the SARI Colloquium at Paris University 13 in June 2016, and later on published online with the same title in an anthology called *Indian Births and Western Rebirths of The Jataka Tales*, Publications numériques de l'ERIAC, 2017; http://publis-shs.univ-rouen.fr/eriac/index.php?id=183.

into divers and sundrie other languages: as the Persian, Arabian, Hebrue, Latine, Spanish, and Italian: and now reduced into our vulgar speeche' (1888, 13).

Similarly, in his very elaborately researched Introduction to *Kalila and Dimna: Or the Fables of Bidpai. Being an Account of Their Literary History, with an English Translation of the Later Syriac Version of the Same, and Notes* (1885), I.G.N. Keith-Falconer affirms: 'All that we know for certain is that it originated in India' (1885, xvi). He provides 'a concise account of the literary history of this collection of tales', as 'Many readers may be interested in the wanderings and transformations of a book which has probably had more readers than any other except the Bible' (1885, viii–ix). He further informs that these tales travelled from India 'not later than 570 A.D. into Persia'. From Pehlevi, the literary dialect of Persia, 'the book was rendered about A.D. 570 into Syriac by an ecclesiastic named Bud (or Bod), and about A.D. 750 into Arabic by "Abdullah Ibn al-Mokaffa"'. According to him, 'The Greek version, made about A.D. 1080 by Symeon son of Seth, gave rise to an old Italian one first published in 1583', and that he has translated from the later Syriac version 'of the tenth or eleventh century' … 'ascribed to a Christian priest' (1885, xiv). Providing a detailed genealogy, he continues,

> A Hebrew translation of the Arabic, of uncertain date and authorship, was the parent of a Latin one, made between A.D. 1263 and 1278 by John of Capua, a converted Jew, and styled by him *Diredoriumhumancevitce*. This Latin version had a numerous progeny, including translations in German, Spanish, Italian, French, English, Danish and Dutch. (1885, xiv)

In fact, Doni has acknowledged that he had used John of Capua's rendering as his source. He also refers to several renderings and appropriations of the tales, the most influential being *Pantschatantra: fünf Bücher indischer Fabeln, Märchen und Erzählungen*, the German translation by Theodor Benfey (1809–1881).

Keith-Falconer furnishes the details of the migration of the Indian tales in the following manner:

> Already at the beginning of the second century A.D. Indian stories had begun to travel East and North. Along with Buddhism they penetrated straight into China, where they found a ready reception. Stan Julien discovered two Chinese encyclopedias containing a number of Indian tales translated into Chinese. The oldest of these encyclopedias was finished in A.D. 668. From one of these collections he has selected a number of such tales and published them in a French translation under the title, *Les Avadanas, Contes et apologues Indiens,* (Paris 1859). Similarly they reached Tibet, and thence Mongolia... Anton Schiefuer has mentioned about German renderings of a number of Buddhist tales.... (1885, xiii)

Jacobs as well as many other scholars concur that nearly all the stories, tales, fables and so forth in the rest of the world owe their origin to the translation/adaptation of the Jatakas and Panchatantra, as well as the mahakavyas and puranas which were eventually appropriated by the various communities in accordance with their own culture and religious predilections.

Besides, the art of storytelling, creating Frame stories was also India's gift to the world. According to Jacobs,

> In making Buddha the centre figure of the popular literature of India, his followers also invented the Frame as a method of literary art. The idea of connecting a number of disconnected stories familiar to us from *The Arabian Nights*, Boccaccio's *Decamerone*, Chaucer's *Canterbury Tales,* or even *Pickwick*, is directly traceable to the plan of making Buddha the central figure of India folk-literature. ('General Notes', 2015)

In his review of *Kalila and Dimna: Or the Fables of Bidpai*, Richard Gottheil makes these significant observations:

> Perhaps no one book in the world's literature has had such a unique history as the collection of stories which goes under the name of '*Kalilag and Damnag.*' Originating above two thousand years ago in the pious circles of the followers of Gautama and destined only for a small band of the faithful, they have, by means of their inherent *humanity*, traveled thousands of miles beyond their original home, had formed a sort of human bond between different peoples divided

> by nationality, religion and history, and have been translated into almost every human tongue. (1889, 67)

The travelling of these tales tells many a tale, because they kept being adapted to various cultures, times and histories. Even in India, the place of origin of these tales, there has been a good deal of intertextuality through the overlapping of the stories in different frames. The Jatakas, *Panchatantra*, *Hitopadesha*, *Kathasaritasagara* and so forth migrated in translation and it happened not only in countries and cultures elsewhere, but also in the subcontinent itself. Interestingly, even in the subcontinent of their origin the tales have been the fountainhead of inspiration to many a literary creation, even scriptural writings. For example, a Jataka story called 'Rama and Sita' (Francis and Thomas 1916, 325–31) in 'DasarathaJataka' may have been the source for Ramayana. In this tale, the locale is Benares, not Ayodhya. Dasaratha, the king had 'sixteen thousand wives', and that 'the eldest and queen-consort bore him two sons and a daughter, the elder son was named Rama-pandita, or Rama the Wise, the second was named Prince Lakkhana, or Lucky, and the daughter's name was the Lady Sita' (Francis and Thomas 1916, 325).

In fact, the story of the migration of tales and fables has been as old as the story of the migration of human beings. The migration of these ancient Indian tales and texts in various languages to many lands and islands also tells tales of adaptation and appropriation. For instance, North 'englishes' the Indian tales by anglicising many terms and habits. In the very first tale, North puts the protagonist as 'a husbandeman of Persia' (1888, 17), and also uses British terms like 'courtier'. He seems to follow the geographical or cultural locations of the text from which he translated. Thus in the tale of 'Three Great Fishes', it is 'upon the borders of Hungarie there was a certayne Lake' (1888, 132).

This is not a stray example. The migration and translation of the ancient Indian tales in a period of about 2,000 years in languages all over the world witnessed marvellous illustrations of acculturation. I would like to present here two examples which would demonstrate the extent of migration, appropriation and adaptation of the Indian stories. The first example is about relating the 'Kachchhapa Jataka' ('The Tortoise and the Geese') in various times and places. In this story, a tortoise lived in a lake that was beginning to dry up. Pitying the future suffering of their friend, the geese suggested they fly off with it. They flew with the tortoise who was made to hold a stick between its teeth while they took hold of the two ends. While passing over a village, children saw this strange sight and exclaimed, 'There are two geese carrying a tortoise by a stick!' (Francis and Thomas 1916, 179). The Tortoise cried out, 'Well, and if my friends do carry me, what is that to you, you caitiffs?' (Francis and Thomas 1916, 179)—and 'he let go the stick from between his teeth, and falling into the open courtyard he split in two' ('The Tortoise and the Geese', Francis and Thomas 1916, 179). The Panchatantra has its earliest Indian version which is slightly different. The story was eventually included in the *Tales of Bidpai* and travelled Westward through translations in Persian, Syriac (Syrian), Arabic, Greek, Hebrew, and Latin, from which it began to be rendered/retold in other European languages at the end of the middle ages. Doni's tale is closer to the original, a version of which is also included in the *Jataka Tales* (1916) by Francis and Thomas. However, the tale has been told differently by North in the English version. Interestingly, in many of the European renderings, crows, eagles, and so forth take the place of the geese of the original.

The French poet and fabulist Jean de la Fontaine (1621–1695) included the tale in the tenth volume of his *Fables Choisies* (12 volumes, 1668–1694) as '*La Tortue et les deux Canards*' (The Tortoise and the Birds). Fontaine treats it as a story of human vanity and imprudence.

'Frog the Traveler', the Russian version of the story by Vsevolod Garshin (1855–1888) has been retold several times by various hands and has also been made into a cartoon strip in 1965 (*Epitome of the Pali Canon* 2012, 206). In the Mongolian version, it is a frog, not a tortoise, jealous of the geese that can migrate to a warmer climate. While being carried thus by the geese, the frog shouts in excitement and tells his clan about his great fortune and falls, back to where it belongs (*Epitome of the Pali Canon* 2012, 206).

Many more similar variants are available in various languages. Interestingly, it also appears in Chapter XI of Chinua Achebe's (1930–2013) *Things Fall Apart* (1958), a little differently. The tortoise is delineated as a West African trickster figure. He hears of a feast being given by the sky-dwellers to the birds and persuades them to take him with them, winged in their feathers. There he tells his hosts that his name is '*All of You*' and when they provide the food, saying, 'This is for all of you', the imposter claims the entire feast. The enraged birds ask for their feathers back and leave. However, a parrot agrees to take a message to the wife of the tortoise asking her to spread the bedding from his house on the ground. Instead, the parrot tells her to spread all the hard things so that when the tortoise jumps down its shell is broken. However, the tortoise survives, and the broken shell is glued together. This provides the explanation of why the tortoise's shell is so uneven. The Swazi people and the Kikuyu [the largest ethnic group in Kenya] also share a similar story.[6]

The second example I wish to cite demonstrates a much more complex level of assimilation and appropriation through translation. The representation of the Buddha that emerged out of the Jatakas made him a Prophet of sorts even in the Christian world. *Barlaam and Josaphat: English Lives of Buddha*, 'edited and induced' by Joseph Jacobs and published in 1896 chiefly dwells on 'the near canonization of Buddha' in the Western Christian world. The legend of Barlaam and

6 For details, see *Epitome of the Pali Canon*, pp. 205–07, and http://goatrevolution.com/blog2/2009/05/31/a-tortoise-story.

Josaphat is about two Christian martyrs and saints, based on the life of the Buddha. In the Preface to *Barlaam and Josaphat* Jacobs says, 'The fact that by its means Buddha had been, if only informally, canonized a Saint of the Church, would be enough to attract attention to it' (1896, viii). After their story was included in a famous thirteenth-century hagiography called *The Golden Legend* it became more popular and it was translated into most of the major vernacular languages of Europe. Annabella Pitkin informs that the legend was more widely printed even than the Bible prior to 1500. The following excerpt from her review of *In Search of the Christian Buddha: How an Asian Sage Became a Medieval Saint* by Donald S. Lopez, Jr. and Peggy McCracken (2014) succinctly establishes the point I have been trying to make:

> What on earth, we might ask, is the Buddha's life story doing disguised in the tale of a Christian saint? A preliminary answer is that stories travel, even more widely than the individual human beings who tell them. Across language barriers and between civilizations, people translate stories that grip their imaginations, exchanging them along trade routes or after conquests. Tales are carried on voyages together with fashion, science, or medicine; they are included in histories of foreign lands. Stories even seep through the fierce perimeters of (supposedly) alien religious belief and practice and the mutual distrust, or worse, that may separate religious communities. (Pitkin 2014)[7]

---

7 The legend of Barlaam and Josaphat tells how an Indian king named Abenner (aka Avenier) persecuted the Christian Church in his realm, founded by the Apostle Thomas. When astrologers predicted that his own son Josaphat would one day become a Christian, the king kept the young prince in isolation. However, Josaphat met the hermit Saint Barlaam and converted to Christianity. Eventually, Abenner also embraced Christianity, and retired to the desert to become a hermit after abdicating his throne to Josaphat. Josaphat himself later renounced his throne and went into seclusion with his teacher Barlaam. The two were entered in the Eastern Orthodox calendar with a feast-day on 26 August, and in the Roman Martyrology in the Western Church as 'Barlaam and Josaphat' on the date of 27 November.

For more details on the historiography of the legend, see, https://www.britannica.com/topic/Barlaam-and-Josaphat; Maria Stanciu Istrate, 2013; Lang, 1957; Stefan Andrews, 2017; Donald S. Lopez, Jr. and Peggy McCracken, 2014; and the reviews ofthe last mentioned book, Kristin BeiseKiblinger, 2017, pp. 277–81, 10.1353/bcs.2017.0023. https://muse.jhu.edu/article/675603/summary; and Philip Almond, 1987, pp. 391–406.

Citing various reasons pertaining to Britain, in *Of Many Heroes: An Indian Essay in Literary Historiography* G.N. Devy postulates that 'About half a century after Sir William Jones began his exploration of the Indian literary past, the British opinion of India's literary wealth had gone through a radical reversal' (1998, 80). It is not so. The European languages were engaged in translating the ancient Indian stories from each other's languages. Much before the upsurge of the Orientalist enthusiasm, the intellectual world, free from any imperialist or Orientalist agenda or patronage had already started looking at the migration of the ancient Indian tales with admiration, and the textual transaction among various cultures even led to very interesting religious developments.

After the initial Orientalist phase of the Asiatic Society, the translation of 'India's literary wealth' had a second phase during the second half of the nineteenth century when a number of Western scholar-translators, mostly patronised by Cambridge University and the Cambridge University Press turned their attention to ancient Indian literatures. It happened after the publication of Mary Eliza Isabella Frere's (1845–1911) *Old Deccan Days, or, Indian Fairy Legends* (1868). The appreciation of scholars like Max Müller (1823–1900), Sir George Christopher Molesworth Birdwood (1832–1917), Henry Wadsworth Longfellow (1807–1882), and others made this work very influential and the Western scholarship in no time started taking interest in the Indian tales and stories of all kinds. By the time of the publication of the third edition of *Old Deccan Days* in 1881, it had already been rendered in German, Hungarian, Danish as well as some of the Indian languages like Marathi, Hindi, and Gujarati. Besides, the works of Joseph Jacobs, Thomas William Rhys Davids (*Buddhist Birth-Stories [Jataka Tales]*, 1880), I.G.N. Keith-Falconer (*Kalila and*

Interestingly, the legend had its influence also on Western literature. In his Preface to *Barlaam and Josaphat*, Jacobs informs, 'As is well known, the *Caskets* story of the *Merchant of Venice* is ultimately derived from *Barlaam and Josaphat*' (1896, viii).

Dimna: Or the Fables of Bidpai, 1885), Hugh George Rawlinson (*Indian Historical Studies*, 1913), H.T. Francis and E.J. Thomas (*Jataka Tale*, 1916) and Dr R. Morris (*Folk-lore Journal*, vols. ii–v) were published after the 1880s.

In conclusion, I wish to say that translation has been a very interesting and significant part of India's cultural history and it is just not about colonial power-play. Associating it with colonialism will limit it to only one aspect of 'India in Translation'. The translation of our ancient texts in world languages which occurred roughly between the late years before Christ and the Medieval Age need to be looked at by our scholars because that will lead us towards 'discoveries' of many more kinds. The myth that India borrowed the forms of the short story and the novel from the West or that Indian literature was 'discovered' for the first time thanks to the imperial masters might need re-examination.

If the Orientalists believed that through them India was being "discovered" by the world, it was a great mistake. This, in fact, shows that *their* world was oblivious of the historiography of India in translation. While the Cambridge School of Historiography was championing imperialism and claiming that there was no colonialism in India, its scholars, under the patronage of Cambridge University itself were almost going in a parallel line making 're-discovery' of sorts. The world has been translating, appropriating and adapting Indian literature since the ancient times and a proper study of the historiography of *India in Translation* and *Translation in India* will surely have a benign influence on the postcolonial discourses on translation.

References

Almond, Philip, 'The Buddha of Christendom: A Review of *The Legend of Barlaam and Josaphat*', *Religious Studies*, Vol. 23, No. 3, pp. 391–406. Available at: https://www. cambridge.org/core/journals/religious-studies/ article/buddha-of-christendom-a-review-of-the-legend-of-barlaam-and-josaphat/8D638906A28D6C2CD3A3352BC4F2C920 (accessed 12 April 2018).

Andrews, Stefan, 'Through a Series of Mistranslated Texts, the Christian Church Unwittingly Accepted the Buddha as a Christian saint in the Middle Ages', *The Vintage News*, 20 March 2017. Available at: https://www.thevintagenews.com/2017/03/20/through-a-series-of-mistranslated-texts-the-christian-church-unwittingly-accepted-the-buddha-as-a-christian-saint-in-the-middle-ages/ (accessed 12 April 2018).

Benfey, Theodor, *Pantschatantra: fünf Bücher indischer Fabeln, Märchen und Erzählungen*, Leipzig, F.U. Bradhaus, 1859.

Das, Jagannath, *Srimad Bhagabata*, Odisha Sahitya Akademi, Bhubaneswar, 1989.

Deka, Kanak Chandra, *Sankaradeva: The Great Vaishanva Saint of India*, 1982, 2nd edn., Gauhati, Hemkos Printers, 1988.

Devy, G.N., *Of Many Heroes: An Indian Essay in Literary Historiography*, Bombay, Orient Longman, 1998.

Epitome of the Pali Canon, Chroniker Press Book, Lulu.com, 29 October 2012. Available at: https://books.google.co.in/books?id=3176AwAAQBAJ&dq=jataka+tales+%2B+bidpai&source=gbs_navlinks_s (accessed 29 October 2015).

Folena, Gianfranco, '*Volgarizzare e tradurre*', Turin, Einaudi, 1991.

Forlong, John G.R., *Encyclopedia of Religions*. Volume 1: A-D. 1906. Cosimo, Inc., 30 December 2008, pp. 255–56. Available at: https://books.google.co.in/books?id=LDoESlYRyMEC&dq=St.+Barlaam+teaches+St.+Josaphat+about+Buddhism+by+means+of+a+parable&q=Barlaam#v=snippet&q=Barlaam&f=false (accessed 12 April 2018).

Francis, H.T. and E.J. Thomas, *Jataka Tales: Selected and Edited with Introduction and Notes*, Cambridge, Cambridge University Press, 1916.

Gottheil, Richard, Review of *The Earliest English Version of the Fables of Bidpai, 'The Morall Philosophie of Doni,' by Sir Thomas North* by Joseph Jacobs. *Hebraica*, University of Chicago Press, Vol. 6, No. 1, October, 1889, pp. 67–69.

Holmstrom, Lakshmi, 'Let Poetry Win: The Translator as Writer—An Indian Perspective.' *The Translator as Writer*, edited by Susan Bassnett and Peter Bush, New York, Continuum/Bloomsbury Publishing, 2007, pp. 33–45.

Istrate, Maria Stanciu, 'A Legend Circulating through Time and Space: Barlaam and Josaphat', *Diacronia.ro,* RRL, LVIII, 2, 2013, 169–78. Available at: http://www.diacronia.ro/ro/indexing/details/A412/pdf (accessed 17 April 2018).

Jacobs, Joseph, *Barlaam and Josaphat: English Lives of Buddha*, edited and induced by Joseph Jacobs, London, David Nutt, 1896. Copy held at Robarts—University of Toronto, made available at: barlaamjosaphate00jacouoft (accessed 20 May 2016).

———, 'General Notes', *Complete Fairy Tales* (*Celtic Fairy Tales*, *Indian Fairy Tales*, *English Fairy Tales*, *More English Fairy Tales* in one *e*-book), edited by Joseph Jacobs, Osteon-Press, Aegitas, Digitised Text: 6 October 2015. Available at: https://books.google.co.in/ books?id=OT6wCgAAQBAJ&q=Jatakas&dq=Jacobs,+Joseph.+Complete+Fairy+Tales&source=gbs_word_cloud_r&cad=2#v=snippet&q=Jatakas&f=false. Available at: http://www.sacred-texts.com/hin/ift/ift31.htm (accessed 22 May 2016).

Keith-Falconer, I.G.N., *Kalila and Dimna: Or the Fables of Bidpai. Being an Account of Their Literary History, with an English Translation of the Later Syriac Version of the Same, and Notes*, Cambridge, Cambridge University Press, 1885.

Kiblinger, Kristin Beise, 'Review of *In Search of the Christian Buddha: How an Asian Sage Became a Medieval Saint* by Donald S. Lopez Jr. and Peggy McCracken', in *Buddhist-Christian Studies*, University of Hawai'i Press, Vol. 37, 2017, pp. 277–81. Available at: https://muse.jhu.edu/article/675603/summary (accessed 17 April 2018).

Lal, P., *Great Sanskrit Plays in Modern Translation*, Norfolk, CT, New Directions, 1964.

———, *Transcreation: Two Essays*, Kolkata, Writers Workshop, 1972.

Lang, D.M., '*The Life of the Blessed Iodasaph:* A New Oriental Christian Version of the Barlaam and Ioasaph Romance', *Bulletin of the School of Oriental and African Studies,* University of London, Vol. 20, No. 1/3, 1957, pp. 389–407, published online on 24 December 2009. Available at: https://doi.org/10.1017/S0041977X00061942 (accessed 12 April 2018).

Lopez Jr., Donald S. and Peggy McCracken, *In Search of the Christian Buddha: How an Asian Sage Became a Medieval Saint*, New York, W.W. Norton & Company, 2014.

Mukherjee, Meenakshi, 'Power and the Case of Horizontal Translation', *Translating Power: Stories, Essays, Criticism*, edited by Saugata Bhaduri, New Delhi, Katha, 2008, pp. 208–20.

Mund, Dr Subhendu, 'Travelling Tales: Migration, Translation, Adaptation and Appropriation of the *Jātaka Katha*', *Indian Births and Western Rebirths of The Jataka Tales,* dans 3, 2017, © *Publications numériques de l›ERIAC*, "Lectures du monde anglophone", No. 3, 2017. Available at: http://publis-shs.univ-rouen.fr/eriac/index.php?id=192.

North, Sir Thomas, *Fables of Bidpai: The Morall Philosophie of Doni*, London, David Nutt, 1570. Scholarly reissue edited by Joseph Jacobs with Preface, Introduction & Notes. Edinburgh and London: Ballantyne, Hanson & Co., 1888.

Pitkin, Annabella, 'How the Buddha Became St. Josaphat', review of *In Search of the Christian Buddha: How an Asian Sage Became a Medieval Saint* by *Donald S. Lopez, Jr. and Peggy McCracken, Lion's Roar: Buddhist Wisdom for Our Time.* 13 May 2014. Available at: https://www.lionsroar.com/reviews-how-the-buddha-became-st-josaphat/ (accessed 12 April 2018).

Satchidanandan, K., 'Do you Understand Me? Translation in India after the Classics'. *Translating Bharat, Reading India*, edited by Neeta Gupta, New Delhi, Yatra Books, 2017. *Scroll.in*. 15 May 2016. Available at: https://scroll.in/article/808155/do-you-understand-me-translation-in-india-after-the-classics (accessed 17 February 2018).

Trivedi, Harish, 'Translating Culture Vs. Cultural Translation', In *In Translation: Reflections, Refractions, Transformations*, edited by Paul St-Pierre & Prafulla C. Kar, Amsterdam, John Benjamins Publishing, 2007, pp. 277–87.

9

The Man of His Heart: Tagore's Kabir

Amitendu Bhattacharya

On the basis of Rabindranath Tagore's artistic and political preoccupations, it is possible to propose a set of postulates about how he viewed Kabir: (*a*) as a poet who represented the soul or ethos of India, (*b*) as his poetic predecessor and contemporary, (*c*) as a moral figure who could ameliorate the discord-laden scenario of a diverse Indian society, and (*d*) as a discourse, an affirmation of which would effectively counter colonial historiography's mendacious propaganda about Indian society and civilisation. If Tagore's writings and, by extension, translations, have any political value, it is in the element of dissent encoded in them. It was his disquiet about Indian social dynamics and colonial cultural politics that impelled him to translate Kabir. He worked his way backwards to Kabir through his long personal association with Baulism (the attitude and way of life of the Bauls) and Brahmoism, two extraordinary movements in the religio-cultural sphere of Bengal.

In the music and poetry of the Bauls, Tagore discovered the quintessence of Bengali culture and identity, indeed of Indian civilisation itself. His early engagement with Baul poetics and philosophy spurred the composition of many songs in the Baul style. He occasionally even identified himself as Rabindra Baul. Moreover, Baul philosophy was the fulcrum around which the future of his own social and cultural philosophy pivoted, as evidenced by his returning to the subject frequently in his later works such as *Creative Unity* (1922) and *The Religion of Man* (1931). Tagore commissioned the collation and compilation of the songs of the Bauls at Shantiniketan. His effort at preserving this oral tradition in Bengali culture enabled the translations of those songs into other languages, thereby securing a larger audience for them—the Bauls became extremely popular with the leading figures of the American counterculture, especially the Beat Generation.

The existence of the Bauls—a loosely-knit group of wandering minstrels and ascetics from both Hindu and Muslim communities—as a distinct religious sect can be traced to the sixteenth century. They are known for their emotive songs that often use a symbolic language. Strongly influenced by the Bhakti and Sufi movements that emphasised egalitarianism, a non-materialistic way of living, and an alternative path to spirituality, the Bauls embrace and preach emancipatory ideas and practices. They uphold secular values by rejecting religious dogmas, repudiate caste and gender hierarchies, espouse simple living and believe in a spiritual ideology that is akin to Unitarianism. A large population of Bengalis who are kept outside the mainstream of Hinduism and Islam and who often face persecution for their unconventional views on religion naturally gravitate towards the Baul way of life. Another distinguishing feature of the Bauls is the importance they attach to the human body and love as a route to knowledge. Thus, Jeanne Openshaw writes about the Bauls: 'They tend to reject the orthopraxies and orthodoxies of both religious traditions, including the worship of images and transcendent deities, the authority of scripture and indeed any other knowledge which is not one's own' (2002, 4). Consequently, in the mainstream Bengali society the Bauls are equally revered and reviled.

Tagore admired the Bauls for the very reasons for which they are reviled by the larger community, namely their alternative conceptualisation of religion, their independence from standard customs and practices, and their unique devotional songs and music. His sympathy for them may also have stemmed from a very personal grievance that made him regretfully aware of the rigidness of religious and caste barriers and of what it meant to be personae non gratae. The Tagore clan faced ostracism by orthodox Hindus who labelled them as 'Pirali Brahmins'. It is believed that sometime around the second half of the fifteenth century, one of the ancestors of the family was either deceived by a Muslim into catching a whiff of cooking beef or foolhardily entered matrimony with a Muslim girl. The high caste Kulin Brahmin family thus lost caste. The stigma of the incident stuck to the family even during Rabindranath Tagore's own lifetime. The Tagores, as Blair B. Kling observes, 'although in the secular world of the frontier metropolis ... could rise to the highest level of power and influence, in the Brahmanic world of social stratification based on pollution and pedigree they were irredeemable pariahs' (1976, 11).

It is a curious phenomenon that certain human thoughts and expressions that are often suppressed by the dominant social order sometimes get appropriated and celebrated by avant-garde artistic movements. Since its inception, the Bhakti movement (along with Sufism) has enthralled Indian creative practitioners. Many Anglophone Indian poets too turned to translating the works of some of the medieval religious and Bhakti poets. But no Bhakti poet has perhaps attracted as much attention from later-generation poets and scholars as the medieval saint-poet Kabir. And of all the distinguished translators of Kabir's songs into English—one thinks of Ezra Pound, Rabindranath Tagore, Robert Bly, Charlotte Vaudeville, Linda Hess, Shukdev Singh, Nirmal Dass, Vinay Dharwadker, Arvind Krishna Mehrotra and G.N. Das—it is Tagore who is widely regarded as one of the earlier and more influential poet-translators of Kabir. Therefore, within the complex history and praxis of translation in India, the circumstances and the thought processes that culminated in Tagore translating and publishing in 1915 *One Hundred Poems of Kabir* (hereafter *OHPK*) beg attention.

William Radice argues that 'Tagore was a radical...but there were strains of traditionalism in him' (1995, 21). The twin strands of radicalism and traditionalism are detectable in much of Tagore's creative and polemical writings and his translation of Kabir is no exception to this general propensity. Radicalism was enshrined in the Bengali tradition from the days of the 'Young Bengal' movement. The Brahmo faith in itself was a mixture of traditionalism and radicalism. As a reformist movement started by Rammohan Roy and led afterwards by both Tagore's grandfather and father, Brahmoism sought to liberate the Hindu religion from the clutches of cumbersome ritualism and take it back to its Upanishadic roots. Brahmoism was inspired as much by modern science as by the monotheistic movements in other religions. It intended to introduce to Indian society an inclusive and universal creed by combining the forward-looking aspects of Hinduism, Islam and Christianity. As a significant constituent of the larger discourse of the 'Bengal Renaissance', Brahmoism advocated a synthesis of the enlightened values of the 'East' and the 'West'. Its goal 'was to bring together the progressive forces within the bourgeois state that was then emerging to raise the cultural level of the country and to campaign for the abolition of caste, racial, religious and other barriers and for the reform of public education' (Judelson 1989, 83).

The Brahmos, like the Bauls, were regarded as heretics by conservative Hindus. While working on the Kabir translation project, Tagore might have reasoned that Brahmoism was not a one-off phenomenon in India's history and that the movement had a precursor in Kabir's conception of Bhakti. Bhakti was the bridge that connected Upanishadic precepts with Brahmoism and Baul philosophy. It ensured a smooth continuity of mysticism from ancient to modern times. Acknowledging that the progression of Indian philosophy from the Upanishads onwards had been accompanied all along by a mystical vein of thought, Ranade however highlights the differences between Upanishadic and medieval mysticism thus: 'The business of the mystic of the Middle Age consisted in mixing with the ordinary run of mankind, with sinners, with pariahs, with women, with people who cared not for the spiritual life, with people who had even mistaken notions about it' (1983, 1–2). In the nineteenth century, this need for 'practical devotional mysticism' led to the establishment of the Brahmo Samaj. Later in his life however, Tagore distanced himself from Adi Brahmo Samaj upon realising that it was turning out to be ritualistic, sectarian and unscientific (Bhattacharya 2011, 199).

Tagore may have distanced himself from the Samaj but the ideals espoused by Roy were hard to forget or unlearn. About Roy's lasting influence on Tagore, Radice remarks:

> The tenets of Rammohan Roy from which Tagore never moved throughout his life were: contempt for idolatry and externalized, ritualistic religion; a belief that the truth of Hinduism lay in the Vedanta philosophy of the Upanishads, with its recognition of only one true God; and a desire to bring the various religions of the world together, to extract their shared and quintessential meaning. Tagore's rationalism … was Rammohan's: it inspired in him the same hatred of intolerance and injustice and tyranny, and it also gave him a life-long interest in science. (1995, 23)

In view of Tagore's absorption of the message of the Brahmos and the Bauls, it can be said that it was both Kabir's mysticism and the anti-sectarian nature of his life and poetry that made him, in the eyes of his translator, the greatest and the most representative poet of India, a poet fit to be translated and projected onto the national and international literary and cultural landscapes.

The oral transmission of Kabir's verses has firmly established Kabir as a popular poet whose influence for centuries has cut across class, caste, gender, regional and religious divides. Literacy is not a precondition for the consumption and appreciation of his verses. Throughout northern India, especially in the Gangetic plains, Kabir is a household name. But then his origins are shrouded in mystery and whatever 'accounts' we have of his life and activities are apocryphal. It is also doubtful whether all the verses attributed to him were actually authored by him: the oral circulation of his verses over a substantially long period of time makes it unfeasible to separate the originals from the improvements, interpolations or distortions effected afterwards. Nevertheless, Kabir's verses have been recorded, compiled and preserved by many through the centuries. Many of his songs are included in the *Adi Granth*, the sacred scripture of the Sikhs. The other principal sources of Kabir's work are the *Bijak*, the sacred text of the followers of the Kabir Panth, the *Kabir Granthavali* and the *Anurag Sagar*. These textual compilations, in turn, contributed to the oral propagation of Kabir's *dohas* or couplets.

Hagiographies and legends claim that Kabir (1398–1518) lived in Kashi (Benaras) and that he was a foundling. His biological (Hindu?) mother abandoned him at birth and he was rescued by a childless Muslim couple. So, he was both Hindu and Muslim. He had no formal education and grew up to be a weaver. He took Ramanand as his spiritual mentor, prolifically composed verses in Purabia or Eastern Hindi dialect and propagated the message of his distinctive faith among the inhabitants of Kashi and its surrounding areas. Many believe that Kabir never really died as nobody saw him being buried or cremated. A perception accordingly formed that Kabir is beyond death. So, there is a certain timeless quality to the image of him in the popular imagination. His name has thus become a symbol and a myth.

Kabir's belligerent rationality and espousal of common speech in poetic language came long before the Protestant Reformation and the Age of Reason that swept through Europe and before Coleridge and Wordsworth's *Lyrical Ballads* was published. His efforts in harmonising, or rather obliterating, sectarian differences were not attempted by means of docile protestations but by scornful repudiation of the religious beliefs and performances of Hindus and Muslims alike. His devotees increased as he used a language which was in sharp contrast to the mumbo jumbo of the pandits and imams. He had a dim view of scholars and scholarship. He believed that formal education being always a means to protect and advance the vested interests of the dominant class, caste and religious groups was more restricting than liberating. Kabir and most of the Bhakti poets came from the marginalised sections of society and K. Satchidanandan categorises them as belonging to 'the *Sramana* tradition in Indian poetry that underlines the spiritual equality of all beings, and opposes all forms of religious and caste hierarchies as against the *brahmana* tradition that perpetuates inequality and hierarchy' (2008, 87).

The contrariness of Kabir and the continual relevance of his message of commonsensicality and freethinking have been a magnet for generations of Indian creative practitioners who share Kabir's free spirit and his rational and secular leanings. 'Then was neither vice nor virtue;/scriptures there were not, as the/Vedas and Puranas, nor as the/ Koran' (Kabir 1915, 87). Tagore, in spite of the Vedas and Puranas providing him lifelong spiritual sustenance, felt irresistibly drawn to the irreverence, or rather irreligiousness, of the saint. Self-reflexivity, Tagore thought, should be an integral component of religion and religion should not be abstract or ponderous—it should have practical sense to it. Besides, to be truly creative one must break free from all forms of societal and mental constraints. And Kabir had led the way in this process of breaking of the constraints in the cultural and intellectual realms, Tagore seemed to believe.

Kabir's tenacious stand against the normative notions of the sacred—organised religions, codified religious practices, valorisation of scriptures, idolatry, Brahminical supremacy, caste oppression and so forth—unmistakably enounce his *Nirguna* (attributeless) strain of Bhakti. He rejected external or visible manifestations of the divine being or devotion. The focus instead was on the internal aspects of piety: an indefinable and intense love for a personal, non-incarnated God who is devoid of any attributes. In this manner, according to Kabir divinity was not vested in any particular object or person but scattered in the whole of creation.

Rudyard Kipling was aware of Kabir's popularity among the 'natives' of India. 'A Song of Kabir' appears in *The Second Jungle Book* (1895). It is in Kipling that Kabir first finds mention in a canonical English literature text. According to Arvind Krishna Mehrotra, Kipling was not only familiar with the name of Kabir, but he also associated Kabir with religious tolerance (2011, xxviii). But neither Kabir's formidable status as a popular poet in India, nor his finding a mention in *The Jungle Books* served any purpose that the translation of his poems into English later sought to serve. This implies that, besides personal and artistic motivations, the Kabir translations by Tagore were carried out with a political purpose.

Many of Tagore's original Bengali writings have been translated into various Indian and foreign languages. Ironically, Tagore's own efforts at literary translation have received scant attention. The blame for this neglect need not be hoisted on Tagore scholars and translators alone. The problem of the 'ambiguous linguistic status of some of his texts' existed until in the 1990s Sisir Kumar Das edited three volumes of the English writings of Tagore for the Sahitya Akademi; that is to say, the books by Tagore that were in circulation in the English language earlier did not indicate 'what was the language he adorned as poet and playwright' (Mukherjee 2004, 125). But even if one considers the paltry research carried out on Tagore's own translations, one finds that most of it has tended to focus on his self-translations.

The autotranslations of his own poetry and the translations of the poems of Kabir comprise the bulk of Tagore's translation-literature in English. It is curious that while thinking of Tagore's literary productions we do not ordinarily remember that he did not translate any other poet or writer with as much concentration and enthusiasm as he did Kabir. A cursory glance at Tagore's translations into Bengali from European, Asian and Indian languages reveal that Tagore was an unmethodical and apathetic translator. Still, it was he who first elevated Kabir to the world stage with his English translations of the saint-poet, a project in which he was 'assisted' by Evelyn Underhill.

Even after Kipling, Kabir remained an obscure figure in the international literary circles. Ezra Pound translated Kabir through Kalimohan Ghose, a pupil of Tagore. In January 1913, 'Certain Poems of Kabir' by Pound appeared in *The Modern Review*, a leading English-language journal from Calcutta whose founder and editor was Ramananda Chatterjee, a close associate of Tagore. But why did Tagore choose to translate Kabir when some English translations of Kabir were already available? And, even if Tagore felt the urge to translate a medieval Indian devotional poet, why did he prefer to translate Kabir over other north Indian saint-poets like Ravidas, Nanak, Surdas, Mirabai or Tulsidas?

The answer is Kshitimohan Sen, one of the two individuals—the other being Ajit Kumar Chakravarty—who vitally contributed to Tagore's Kabir translation project. The two documents Tagore and Underhill relied on are Sen's Hindi text with Bengali translation of Kabir's poems and Chakravarty's manuscript of the English translation of 116 songs of Kabir based on Sen's text. Tagore did not have to look elsewhere since Sen's Bengali translations and commentaries of Kabir's songs were readily available to him, and he was greatly moved by their message. More than any other saint-poet, Tagore was impressed by the spiritual and political content of Kabir's compositions.

Sen's contribution to Tagore developing an abiding interest in the Bauls and the medieval Indian mystics cannot be gainsaid. The zeal to research on and collect the songs of the mystics took Sen to distant parts of India. Sen and Tagore together made Shantiniketan the foremost centre of scholarship in medieval Indian devotional poetry. Recording his appreciation of Sen, C.F. Andrews underscored the centrality of the mystic poets from different parts of India to Tagore's vision of the Indian nation:

> We see then at Shantiniketan ... two currents of Indian culture already meeting—Bengali and Hindi.... There is a Poets' corner there for Mirabai, side by side with Tulsidas and Tukaram, Nanak and Kabir, Rajjab and Jnanadas, on an equal footing with the poets of Bengal. Just as in Rabindranath's famous song of the Motherland he reveals his love for every part of India, so there is a place in his Asram for every true Indian culture. (2016, 227)

Sen's collection of the songs of Kabir in four volumes was published between 1910 and 1911. This collection was used as the source text by Kalimohan Ghose and Pound, Ajit Kumar Chakravarty and Tagore and Underhill for their translations of Kabir.

In his Introduction to the Bengali translation of Kabir, Sen explained the reason for undertaking the task of compilation. He contended that although many in Bengal were acquainted with the name of Kabir, very few knew of his euphonious compositions and that the currency in Bengali society of trashy and narrow sectarian *dohas* attributed to Kabir marred the stature of and the truth about the saint-poet (Sen 2015, 15). Tagore's translation of Kabir then was an act of carrying forward the mission of Sen into English—to give the readers a true sense of who Kabir was and what type of verses he composed.

Marvelling at the genius of Tagore, W.B. Yeats wrote in his Introduction to *Gitanjali*: 'At times I wonder if he has it from the literature of Bengal or from religion, and at other times … I find pleasure in thinking it hereditary, a mystery that was growing through the centuries…' (1953, xxi–xxii). In *OHPK*, Tagore seemed to be partly answering these questions. *OHPK* was brought out three years after the publication of *Gitanjali* (1912) and roughly two years after Tagore was awarded the Nobel Prize for literature (1913). Why did he introduce Kabir to an English-knowing audience when his own reputation in the West was growing spectacularly? Tagore became wildly popular in the West as 'the sage from the East' who possessed within himself vast reserves of Oriental spiritual wisdom. Rita Kothari suggests, 'Tagore personified to the West not only his poetry and his message, but also India' (2006, 22). Although there were no indications of it earlier in his literary career, it is evident that post-1913 Tagore nurtured the thought of being lionised in the West as the greatest poet from India and, by extension, the whole of Asia who made his mark on the world of English letters. Tagore's career as an international writer, though short-lived, was not an accident but a result of a far-sighted and well-orchestrated strategy. Sujit Mukherjee has shown how Tagore ceded to the temptation of being acknowledged as an 'English' poet (2004, 124–25). Subsequent to his winning the Nobel Prize, the demand for more books by him ensured that Tagore was being furiously translated and published into many Indian and foreign languages. Given this background, making Kabir into a competitor to his own unchallenged position as *the* poet of India or a claimant on the glory which was solely his would have amounted to a colossal pragmatic miscalculation. Still, Tagore translated Kabir. Kabir's reputation in India and outside grew parallelly with Tagore's due to the latter's translation. What connected Tagore to Kabir were mysticism and a burning urge to belong to a poetic tradition. *OHPK* abjures 'the anxiety of influence'.

Tagore navigated the world as a public figure. But he was a victim of his own public image which, rightly or wrongly, was that of a mystical poet. The imagery, the themes and the subject-matter of his poems reinforced that image. Various scholars have underscored the roles played by metropolitan poets and the colonial aesthetic politics in determining the idiom, style and content of the poems Tagore was translating into English. Drawing attention to the marked difference between the literal translation of the songs of *Gitanjali* from the original Bengali and Tagore's prose translation of them, Mahasweta Sengupta notes: 'These changes are conscious and deliberately adopted to suit the poetics of the target system, which Tagore does by altering tone, imagery and diction, and as a result, none of the lyrical qualities of the originals are carried over into the English translations' (Sengupta 1990, 57).

Tagore's translation of his Bengali poems into English compromised the spontaneity of the Bengali poems and made the English translations seem artificial—in other words, in translation the poems do not remain mere approximations of the originals but are distinct entities in their own right. Sengupta reads this phenomenon of Tagore recreating, or rather unmaking, his Bengali poems into English to meet the European aesthetic expectations from his poetry as a direct outcome of his warped understanding of English language and literature because of the colonial Indian education policy in the nineteenth century. She maintains: 'He fits perfectly into the stereotypical role that was familiar to the colonizer, a voice that not only spoke of the peace and tranquillity of a distant world, but also offered an escape from the materialism of the contemporary Western world' (Sengupta 1990, 58).

So far as the mystical contents of their poetry go, there are parallelisms in Kabir and Tagore's works. *OHPK* enhanced Tagore's image of being a mystical poet in the eyes of his Western admirers. In that respect, these translations are an extension of Tagore's own poems—one cannot regard *Gitanjali* and *OHPK* as mutually independent entities. Tagore's project may be viewed as a clever ploy to cater to the Westerners' perception of him and—in the vein of T.S. Eliot writing literary criticism to explain and defend his own poetics—a deliberate attempt at justifying the kind of poetry he himself wrote. Besides, it helped to prove that he was a true inheritor of the legacy of mysticism that flourished in India for centuries. The impression he seemed to be giving by taking Kabir outside the geographical confines of India was that though he was a poet in the modern world who wrote in a modern Indian language and himself translated his writings into English, he had not cut himself off from his artistic and intellectual roots. This was despite his appreciation, even joyful embracing of the literature and philosophy of other cultures and nations. The aim was to demonstrate that he embodied the thoughts of his poetic ancestors in India and through his own poetic compositions he was constantly improving upon and distilling those thoughts. From that viewpoint, it appears crucial that he should use a stilted, obscure, antiquated, flabby and unexperimental kind of 'hopeless' (Robert Bly's term) English in the translations of his own Bengali poems and those of Kabir when the currents of modernist poetry alongside which his own creative writings flowed insisted on precision in both thought and diction. While the lyrical, emotion-rich, moral, exotic-yet-universal, and 'automatic' nature of his writing initially endeared him to the giants of modernist literature like Yeats and Pound, the same factors precipitated his fall from grace from the charmed literary circles of the Western metropolises.

Arguably, Tagore desired to be favourably compared to the celebrated 'Oriental' poets like Omar Khayyam, Rumi and Hafiz. It is one thing to be well-versed with one's own cultural and intellectual traditions but quite another to be equalled with poets who came from other civilisations and times. Besides, being a writer of mystical poetry alone is not a sufficient qualification for favourable comparison or public acclaim. Edward FitzGerald's translation of Omar Khayyam—one also thinks of Edwin Arnold's translation of Indian classics—had enraptured the English-reading public and it is possible that Tagore wanted to replicate FitzGerald's success for himself by translating Kabir. Tagore's desire to be identified as a poet who was as rooted in the cultural traditions of his place of nativity as Omar Khayyam, Rumi and Hafiz were in theirs was perhaps also tinged with an impulse to usurp the high esteem FitzGerald enjoyed as Khayyam's translator in the eyes of the Western public. Thus, in the larger literary world Tagore sought for himself the status of a mystic, poet and translator all rolled into one—a poet who could not only contain or showcase in his work the 'wisdom' of his land but also, through his translations from his own work and from the work of others in his cultural milieu, carry that 'wisdom' to an eagerly awaiting audience outside his country without the aid of an intermediary, that too an intermediary who was an outsider to the source culture. Whether or not his 'ideas' of self-promotion succeeded in the long run is not a matter of speculation.

Most literary careers momentarily streak across the firmament of a culture only to sink permanently. It is more so in the case of the reputation of writers introduced into a particular literary tradition from other cultures and languages. Tagore's career as a writer outside Bengal was a product of the colonial aesthetic ideology that constructed the binaries of coloniser and colonised, West and East and self and other. His forays across these sharply-etched divisions were initially celebrated in the colonial metropolis, but no sooner this kind of pigeonholing received a severe jolt in the wake of the First World War and Tagore resisted Western typecasting of him than he was abandoned by and shut out of the same literary establishment (Snell-Hornby 2006, 94). In 1912, Yeats gushed about Tagore's prose translations as representing 'the work of a supreme culture' (1953, xiii) and as having 'stirred my blood as nothing has for years' (1953, vii). But in 1935, in an astounding volte-face, Yeats wrote in a letter to Rothenstein:

> Damn Tagore. We got out three good books … and then, because he thought it more important to see and know English than to be a great poet, he brought out sentimental rubbish and wrecked his reputation. Tagore does not know English, no Indian knows English. Nobody can write with music and style in a language not learnt in childhood and ever since the language of his thought. (quoted in Dutta and Robinson 1995, 4)

After Yeats' Introduction to *Gitanjali*, it was Underhill's turn to hold Tagore's hand when he again waded into the treacherous waters of the English literary market with his translation of Kabir's poems.

Underhill's Introduction to *OHPK* regurgitates at tedious length the pious legends about the life and work of Kabir and painstakingly expounds on the mysticism of Kabir. It is more an impediment than a clue to understand the politics behind Tagore's exercising the choice to translate Kabir. The main translator's studied silence too does not dispel the clouds of doubt surrounding the context of the translation.

In his Introduction to a 2003 reissue of *OHPK*, Sabyasachi Bhattacharya argues that 'mysticism is not an adequate explanation' for Tagore's attraction for Kabir and asserts that it is the 'this-worldly characteristic of the writings of Kabir—and not exclusively a commonality of a spiritual or other-worldly kind' that played a role (2003, 3). Tagore interpreted Kabir as 'one of the makers and symbols of India's unity' which is evident from the fact that Tagore intentionally selected the poems where 'Kabir's dissent from the established religion and rituals and obscurantism is the sharpest' (2003, 3). Bhattacharya also alerts us to the fact that Tagore was 'intellectually engaged fairly deeply with the issue of harmonizing different faiths and conflicting claims of primordial loyalties' at the time of preparing and publishing the translations of Kabir's poetry (2003, 4). The Partition of Bengal in 1905 made a resolute and sustained fight to overthrow the British from India inevitable. But it was a challenge to those in the driving seat of the nascent Indian nationalist movement to forge political unity among Indians divided along religious, caste, ethnic and regional lines.

To achieve political independence, it was important for Indians to cast away certain customs and practices that assaulted common sense and morality and to develop an attitude of tolerance towards each other by shedding sectarian prejudices, Tagore argued. To challenge boilerplate colonial portrayals of India as a land devoid of geographical, political, social and cultural unity, he tried to locate the unity of all Indians in India's past. It had to be the kind of unity and harmony that overrode all differences. He reminded:

> She [India] has tried to make an adjustment of races, to acknowledge the real differences between them where they exist, and yet seek for some basis of unity. This basis has come through our saints, like Nanak, Kabir, Chaitanya and others preaching one God to all races of India. (Tagore 2002, 107)

The atavistic nature of institutionalised religious and social practices which shackled Indian people and their mind had to be targeted and broken. For Tagore *dharma* or religion contained the message of liberation and *dharma-tantra* or religious establishment spelt enslavement (Bhattacharya 2003, 6). This religious establishment was the root cause of communal and social disharmony in India, he believed. It is in these circumstances that Tagore found Kabir's stance against religious and ritualistic excesses useful for his own polemic of Indian society. So that the wise discourses of India's ascetics and sages advocating love and tolerance did not escape the masses, it was essential to relay Kabir's message once more. Alternatively, this highlighting of the 'unity in diversity' aspect of Indian life in the historical context was crucial to not allowing the self-image of the Indians to suffer any more damage because of the manipulations and fabrications of Indian history at the hands of colonial historians and Orientalists. By catapulting Kabir to the international literary scene, Tagore was trying to prove that there existed a strong unifying and secular tradition in India long before the British arrived.

From the late eighteenth century onwards, translation from classical languages became a serious literary and pedagogical activity. The stated objective of this venture was to 'discover' the country's or the particular linguistic community's past. Being deeply interested in the idea of a borderless universe, Tagore, by translating Kabir, could well have been participating in this esteemed business of cultural exchange. But what set him apart from the European Orientalists was the fact that he, an Indian and a poet at that, was translating another Indian poet of the past. The knotty questions of authenticity, credibility and artistry were thus partially taken care of. It also demonstrated that the essentially mono-cultural or non-secular worlds of Sanskrit, Persian and Arabic classical texts that the Orientalists were translating did not present a true or holistic representation of the cultural pasts of those societies. These representations did not tally with the reality of a multi-ethnic, multi-religious and multilingual India of the early twentieth century. The texts translated by the European Orientalists did not adequately depict situations where people with different, even contrasting beliefs and worldviews were placed together. In between the demographically relatively sterile ancient world of India and the fecundity of its modern times, there was a time when India attempted a synthesis of races and religions and its poets and prophets emphasised secularity and tolerance.

Translation into English of legal, religious and literary texts was a political, administrative and economic imperative for the colonial regime. Texts were selected for translation that allowed the colonisers to perpetuate unequal relations of power, prejudice and domination. Projecting a distorted picture of the 'Orient', these translations heralded the British 'civilizing mission' in India. The avowed objective of the English Language Education Act of 1835 was to expose the 'natives' to the progressive and rational features of Western civilisation. But it actually sought to secure the mental subjugation of Indians through the study of English literature.

From the second half of the nineteenth century, some English-educated Indians disputed British contentions about the antiquity of Indian civilisation and the material benefits British rule brought to India. They began to rewrite Indian history from an indigenist perspective and reinterpreted the Indian epics for contemporary readers and translated them into English. But the impact of their writings was limited. It was not until the English translation of *Gitanjali* was published and Tagore won the Nobel Prize that Indians were deemed to be capable of creatively expressing themselves in a foreign tongue and of representing themselves and their country to the outside world.

Kothari asserts that Tagore translated into English 'for personal recognition, not to intervene in the colonial understanding of "Indian culture"' and that his translation(s) 'effectively reinforces Orientalist versions of India' (2006, 23). Tagore's ideas about cultural phenomena, expression and artefacts were moulded by the socio-political realities and the intellectual climate of nineteenth-century Bengal. But he still was aware of 'the deceptive nature of an identity that was constructed on the evidence of literary texts' (Sengupta 1998, 227). Tagore eventually wearied of the insistent onslaught of European rationalism and registered its negative impact on the indigenous languages of India, especially on Bengali: 'We do not conceive of any difference between England and Bengal, and to prove our point, we insist on calling a banyan tree an oak.... Our literature has become a world of echoes' (quoted in Sengupta 1998, 230–31).

Tagore diagnosed the problem of Western education in India thus: 'we have bought our spectacles at the expense of our eyesight' (Tagore 1922, 176). It is this erosion of the Indians' mental faculty in the wake of the introduction of English language education that made Tagore draw solace and inspiration from the sagacity and intellectual acuity of the reformist saint-poets who were mostly unlettered. Kabir, in all probability, did not know how to read or write. One is thus made aware of the difference between knowledge gained from life and learning acquired through formal education. But where does real learning lie? Kabir was learned without being 'educated'. For Indians, getting to know Kabir was more instructive than obtaining 'borrowed polish' from the colonial educational system. Moreover, the intuition and mystery in Kabir's poems nullified the overarching rationalism of Western education.

The dichotomy between an authentic Bengali Rabindranath and a falsified English Tagore, as articulated by Mukherjee, Sengupta and Kothari—although it may be relevant to Tagore's autotranslations—does not quite help in explaining the purpose of Tagore translating Kabir. Such a schema of translational reasoning obfuscates more than it illuminates the very political nature of all translation. That Tagore had the necessary cultural competence besides linguistic competence to translate Kabir is not a triviality. If *Gitanjali* indeed existed, as Kothari claims, 'in transcendental space, where it had no connection with other sides of Tagore's poetic and political career' (2006, 22), *OHPK* builds that bridge effectively. The compulsions that underlay Tagore's urge to translate intermittently is crisscrossed in *OHPK*. The translation betokens his resistance against unequal power dynamics and his succumbing to the allure of the centre. It is a complex text in that it both embraces and rejects the Orientalist representations of India. If the Orientalists were instrumental in creating a cultural hegemony, *OHPK* was positing a counterculture. Giving tradition a new lease of life, he was contributing to national cultural renewal. The fame and clout that Tagore achieved in the wake of his receiving the Nobel Prize afforded him the opportunity to introduce another poet from India who, though he belonged to the medieval times, had an important message to give to the people of the modern age both in India and abroad.

John Stratton Hawley in his Afterword to Robert Bly's *Kabir: Ecstatic Poems* traces the history of the translations by Bly to the New England Transcendentalists such as Emerson and Thoreau (2004, 77). Championing pro-nature, anti-industrial and socialist views, the American transcendentalists swam against the dominant thought currents of a scientific and technological modernity and capitalist society. Together with Romantic poets such as Robert Burns, Wordsworth, John Clare and Victorian writers such as Carlyle, Ruskin, Morris and Carpenter, the transcendentalists constituted the block of writers and thinkers that may be referred to as the 'dissident West'. Tagore was not unacquainted with the radical and redemptive energy of their writings. He read the social criticism of these writers to develop his own critique of the exploitative tendencies and territorial greed of the Western civilisation. It would, therefore, be an oversimplification to suggest that the intervention of nineteenth-century colonial education policy built in his mind an exaggerated regard for the English race or that his (auto)translations reinforced Orientalist stereotypes about India. Stressing on the stark difference between the moral content in the work of English writers and the rapacity of Western civilisation, Tagore wrote:

> We had been living in the atmosphere of the lyrical literature of poets like Shelley, Keats, Wordsworth, and we know what inspiration they had within them. And what it was for the rest of the world. There was an upheaval of idealism.... It was that atmosphere, that human aspect of the Western civilisation which appealed to us. It was the humanity of the West. It was not anything mechanical; it did not represent any physical or material quality. (Das 2006, 631)

Like Bly, Tagore perceived the congruity between the moral and spiritual content of Anglo-American literature and the literary and philosophical traditions of pre-colonial India. This literary socialisation and kinship between 'East' and 'West' activated in Tagore ideas of nonviolent, nonracist, non-sectarian, non-materialist and anti-colonial nationhood. *OHPK* is thus an attempt at critiquing, with the remembrance of dissident Western writings, the Eurocentric conceptions of literature, culture and civilization. It is an example of translation as re-territorialisation and re-storying—of staking claim to lost territory and recovering lost heritage.

Arvind Krishna Mehrotra's *Songs of Kabir* (2011) does not deviate from the idealistic vision of India as presented in Tagore's translation. But assessed together, the two texts are eye-openers in terms of the stylistic difference between 'Indian' and 'Western' models of translation. Complete with a preface by Wendy Doniger, an introduction and notes by the translator, a list of source texts and endorsements for the book by Amartya Sen, Eliot Weinberger and August Kleinzahler, Mehrotra's Kabir easily aligns itself with what might be called a Western conception of the translated text. In *OHPK* paratexts were seen as superfluous. *OHPK* does not influence the reader and keeps itself open to interpretation. In India, translations or transactions between languages have been a routine activity, and so translators are self-effacing. The Introduction by Underhill was the farthest Tagore could go in adhering to the Western notions of securing better marketing prospects for a translated text.

Tagore's taciturnity on the subject of the life and thought of Kabir or even on his own involvement in the translation is, again, a manifestation of his anti-colonial stance. It is as though he placed great confidence in the poem translations to find their way in the world and perform the work he expected them to. This silence can be attributed to his total rejection of the Western definition of 'history'. Obsessed with objective facts and sequential time, the Western model of history excludes myths which are rooted in memory and imagination. But in postcolonial societies myths reveal larger truths about the community, truths that are suppressed by the hegemonic narratives of the colonising powers. Myths challenge the entrenched social and political order and are potent tools of dissent and resistance. They are also a means to refer to and salvage the community's past. Tagore believed in the myth of Kabir. By being silent he was trying to simultaneously historicise and contemporise Kabir. The tradition, he seemed to suggest, was lively, living and concurrent. Yet, there was a threat that the ideals of the old tradition may be irretrievably lost because of colonialism-induced amnesia. The urgency of executing the translation was partly to allay that fear and partly to revive the tradition. In Tagore's hands, Kabir takes shape as an allegory to address issues of colonialism, secularism and Indian nationhood.

OHPK had far-reaching implications for Indian literature and the Indian nation. The 'idea of India' can make itself available only through translation (Nair 2002, 7). Assured of the spread of English language education to all parts of India, Tagore, through his translation, was trying to inoculate the non-Hindi-speaking Indians with the 'idea of India'. Besides making India comprehensible to people outside the country, Tagore was making India comprehensible to Indians. By translating what is essentially a secular text, he was breaking away from the established nineteenth-century practice of translating religious and mythological texts. From Kabir Indians could learn crucial lessons of secularity that would ensure the survival of India as a free nation. Moreover, in the tortuous and contested domain of colonial cultural politics, Tagore was positing the folk tradition of India against the logocentrism of the West. Again, translating Kabir aided in destabilising the hierarchical linguistic economy of India whereby the normative preference to translate from an elite and classical language like Sanskrit was replaced by the choice to translate from common speech. Sanskrit excluded a wide variety of Indian truths and experiences. 'Sanskrit learning does not exhaust all the elements of culture that exist in modern India', Tagore declared (Tagore, 1922, 192).

Perennially haunted by the spectre of violence in the lives of communities and nations, Tagore's philosophy of internationalism developed not just as a reaction against the two World Wars fought during his lifetime, but it was also an outcome of his revulsion to the man-made divisions and strife among the Indian populace. It is against this broad canvas that one must evaluate his translation of Kabir. Cultivation of human sympathy through the study of poetry was the antidote he propped up to stem the perpetuation of violence in society.

There is much more to Tagore translating Kabir than meets the eye. Kabir's *Nirguna* Bhakti resonated with Tagore and a common political ideology united them. Tagore regarded Kabir not only as his preceptor but also a national treasure. The project synthesised Tagore's aspiration to be a global poet with his dream to be a prophet of harmony at home. It augmented his mystical persona and gave credence to his internationalist outlook. By re-familiarising Indians with the trenchant thoughts of Kabir, Tagore was nudging Indian society towards greater unification and secularisation. A certain sense of history pervades *OHPK* and it can be read as a postcolonial text. It thwarted European rationalism by positing a discourse of intuition and mystery. It punctured the rhetoric of the assumed moral and cultural superiority of the British colonisers over the colonised Indians and tried to free Indian history and literature from the monopolist guardianship of European Orientalists. *OHPK* challenged the exalted status of English and Sanskrit in India and made a resolute move towards vernacularism. It also compels us to re-examine the concepts of 'orality', 'literacy' and 'textuality'.

References

Andrews, C.F., 'The Hindi Poets of the Middle Ages', *Patriots, Poets and Prisoners: Selections from Ramananda Chatterjee's The Modern Review, 1907–1947*, edited by Anikendra Sen, Devangshu Datta and Nilanjana S. Roy, Noida, HarperCollins, 2016, pp. 225–34.

Bhattacharya, Sabyasachi, 'Introduction', *One Hundred Poems of Kabir*, by Rabindranath Tagore, New Delhi, Chronicle Books, 2003, pp. 1–29.

———, *Rabindranath Tagore: An Interpretation*, New Delhi, Penguin, 2011.

Das, Sisir Kumar, ed. *The English Writings of Rabindranath Tagore, Volume 3: A Miscellany*, By Rabindranath Tagore, 1996, New Delhi, Sahitya Akademi, 2006.

Dutta, Krishna and Andrew Robinson, *Rabindranath Tagore: The Myriad-Minded Man*, London, Bloomsbury, 1995.

Hawley, John Stratton, 'Kabir and the Transcendental Bly', Afterword, *Kabir: Ecstatic Poems*, by Robert Bly, Boston, Beacon Press, 2004, pp. 77–102.

Judelson, Catherine, trans., *A Dictionary for Believers and Nonbelievers*, 1985, Moscow, Progress Publishers, 1989.

Kabir, *One Hundred Poems of Kabir*, translated by Rabindranath Tagore, London, Macmillan, 1915.

Kling, Blair B., *Partner in Empire: Dwarkanath Tagore and the Age of Enterprise in Eastern India*, Berkeley, University of California Press, 1976.

Kothari, Rita, *Translating India: The Cultural Politics of English*, New Delhi, Foundation Books, 2006.

Mehrotra, Arvind Krishna, trans., *Songs of Kabir*, Gurgaon, Hachette, 2011.

Mukherjee, Sujit, *Translation as Recovery*, Delhi, Pencraft International, 2004.

Nair, Rukmini Bhaya, ed. *Translation, Text and Theory: The Paradigm of India*, New Delhi, Sage Publications, 2002.

Openshaw, Jeanne, *Seeking Bauls of Bengal*, Cambridge, Cambridge University Press, 2002.

Pound, Ezra, 'Certain Poems of Kabir', *The Modern Review*, Vol. 13, No. 6, January 1913, pp. 611–13.

Radice, William, trans., *Selected Poems: Rabindranath Tagore*, New Delhi, Penguin, 1995.

Ranade, R.D., *Mysticism in India: The Poet-Saints of Maharashtra*, 1933, Albany, State University of New York Press, 1983.

Satchidanandan, K., *Indian Literature: Paradigms and Praxis*, New Delhi, Pencraft International, 2008.

Sen, Kshitimohan, *Kabir*, Calcutta, Ananda Publishers, 2015.

Sengupta, 'Translation, Colonialism and Poetics: Rabindranath Tagore in Two Worlds', *Translation, History and Culture*, edited by Susan Bassnett and André Lefevere, London, Pinter, 1990, pp. 56–63.

———, 'Literature for the Empire: Rabindranath Tagore Reads English', *Subject to Change: Teaching Literature in the Nineties*, edited by Susie Tharu, New Delhi, Orient Longman, 1998, pp. 219–37.

Snell-Hornby, Mary, *The Turns of Translation Studies*, Amsterdam, John Benjamins, 2006.

Tagore, Rabindranath, *Creative Unity*, London, Macmillan, 1922.

———, *Nationalism*, New Delhi, Rupa, 2002[1917].

Yeats, W.B., 'Introduction', *Gitanjali: Song Offerings*, by Rabindranath Tagore, 1913, London, Macmillan, 1953, pp. vii–xxii.

10

Transcending Borders, Bridging Cultures: Reading Faiz Ahmed Faiz[1]

Fatima Rizvi

People within a cultural tradition engage with their literary texts in a process of 'primary internalisation' whereby they interiorise literary capital in their collective consciousness. Authors and their texts, inclusive of metaphors, images and symbols, become part and parcel of a literary imagination. 'Secondary internalisation' requires people from different cultural domains to develop a level of familiarity with the linguistic practices, literary forms and styles of other cultural traditions. This makes serious demands upon readers. Only after striking the imagination of the new readers, can the new literary forms be accepted and subsequently internalised (Rahman 'Internalizing…'). Translation enables secondary internalisation by widening the scope of literary forms belonging to various literary and linguistic traditions. In the case of British Literature, translation decentralises its centrality by increasing the relevance of literatures belonging to other cultural and linguistic canons. It helps create liberal spaces of readership where acceptance of new texts and significance of different sensibilities becomes possible. It widens possibilities of reviewing and researching not only a text but also the

1 Faiz Ahmed adopted the *takhallus* (nom de plume) 'Faiz' which means munificence or bounty. The choice of Faiz is momentous as it upholds the view that art transcends geo-political borders and that ideas constituting India and Indian-ness are complex and composite.

culture of its location. Translational exercises are processes whereby the translator decodes semantic and syntactic codes of the source language along with the intangible and tangible cultural elements and recodes or appropriates them so as to blend with the target language and culture. Cross-cultural translational exercises are about understanding and interpreting cultural significations with a view to surmount both linguistic and cultural gaps. They involve a creative involvement with the source and the target languages. Familiarity with the cultural milieu of the two languages plays a significantly enabling role. This chapter reads poems of Faiz Ahmed Faiz (1911–1984) and their translations, as creative exercises, transcending borders and bridging cultures. It elucidates that translation is not merely 'a transaction between two languages … that literary texts [are] constituted not primarily of language but in fact culture, language being in effect a vehicle of culture' (Trivedi 2007, 278). It explicates that 'the task of the translator consists in finding the particular intention toward the target language which produces in that language the echo of the original' (Benjamin 2002, 258). The aim of translation is not to imitate the sense of the original, but to incorporate the original's way of meaning and thus make both the translation and the original recognisable as fragments of a greater language (Benjamin 2002, 260). The study comments on Faiz's assertiveness in having himself translated. It reads humanism in his poetry and goes on to read translators' engagements/conversations with the aesthetic and essence of Faiz's Urdu language poetry and its significations—both possibilities owing much to the availability of the translated Faiz.

During the nineteenth century, prose genres were popular, perhaps because they were better suited to express realism that was rapidly making inroads into the socio-cultural fabric of subcontinental India. Apart from this, the popularity of prose emanated from the fact that it was easy to grasp for readers who weren't from literary backgrounds, as also for those looking for the social change it was propagating. A similar preference for prose is visible in the choices the translators made with regard to what needed to be translated. Perso-Urdu poetry pinnacled accomplishment during this time but translations of poetry in English were scarce. Asaduddin notes that although European language translations of Urdu poetry were available as far back as 1825, few Urdu–English translations were available. He notes that though the early twentieth century saw individually undertaken translations of Altaf Husain Hali and Mohommad Iqbal in English, translators and publishing houses were indifferent to translations of Urdu poetry till the second half of the twentieth century (2001, 322–23).

It is thus against a prose-oriented translational culture that Faiz requested Victor Kiernan to translate his poetry.[2] Kiernan began translating Faiz in 1945—an exercise that began in colonial India and spanned over twelve years in the first instance. All selections for the resultant text were made by Faiz. Kiernan's translations were first published in 1958. Before this collection of the translated Faiz was brought out, Kiernan had translated Iqbal's poetry, and this was published as *Poems of Iqbal* in 1955, in London. Subsequently, Kiernan 'revised', 'polished', updated and included new/more translations in the 1971 edition. Faiz oversaw both the exercises, thereby participating in the translational process (Kiernan 2000, 9). Thus, contrary to Walter Benjamin's observation that 'important works of world literature never find their chosen translators, at the time of their origin' (254), Faiz found his translator(s) in his lifetime, even while he was composing. In fact, he welcomed translations of his verse (Kiernan 2000). Kiernan's observation points at a virile aspiration on the part of Faiz to see his poetry cross national borders and linguistic limitations, or, to ensure an 'afterlife' (Benjamin 2002, 254) for his oeuvre. This could have resulted from Faiz's perceptiveness of manoeuvrings in international politics,

2 Faiz's wife Alys George and Kiernan knew each other from their England days and perhaps this had to with Fiaz's request.

matched with an eagerness for global outreach. Moreover, this may be related to his participation (and non-participation) in the political affairs of Pakistan. That Faiz and his poetry have had a robust afterlife, and that he still captivates his readers, is indicated by the popularity of his Urdu language poetry as well as the fact that translations of his poetry are a worldwide phenomenon.

Many English language translations of Faiz's poetry are now available. This is a clear indicator of the fact that Faiz, internalised by Urdu readership, is also a product of secondary internalisation across cultures and this assures him a place in the larger canon of world literature. Since it is not possible to include all his translators in this study, a cross-section of multi-cultural and cross-cultural translational exercises covering approximately seventy-five years has been in this study.

Faiz and Humanism

Faiz is a canonical Urdu poet of the modern era, whose location in the composite Indo-Muslim political-cultural heritage of undivided India changed geo-politically, owing to the Partition in 1947. Nevertheless, the appeal of his poetry defies geo-political borders and spatio-temporal constraints, it commands both elitist, highbrow attention and immense popular support. Believed to stand next only to the nineteenth-century Perso-Urdu poet Mirza Asadullah Khan Ghalib[3] (1797–1869) and also influenced by him, Faiz's poetry is imbued with the zeitgeist of the twentieth century as Ghalib's is with that of the nineteenth. Ghalib experienced the turbulence of the 1857 Uprising and Faiz served the British Indian Army during World War II. Both wars impacted the two creative minds profoundly.

Professionally, Faiz was a lecturer at Oriental College, Lahore; at Mohammedan Anglo-Oriental College, Amritsar; and later, at Hailey

3 Mirza Asadullah Khan wrote under the *takhallus* 'Ghalib'. It means conqueror or the victorious.

College of Commerce, Lahore. He edited the progressive paper, *Adab-e Latīf* (Belles-Lettres) and later joined the British Indian Army as Captain during World War II, rising to the rank of Lieutenant Colonel; he was journalist and editor of the Roman-script *Fauji Akhbār* during his army days. In 1947 he resigned from military service to serve as the editor of the English language daily, *The Pakistan Times* and *Imroz*, both Left-wing papers. Faiz was a product of his times. He followed indigenous, nationalist politics closely through the freedom fighting and Partition years. Keenly perceptive of the rapidly changing world order, international politics, and the position of his country and countrymen within that order, Faiz made a lifelong tryst with politics. Influenced deeply by the Marxist socialist ideology, he aligned readily with the spirit and cause of the Progressive Writer's Movement[4] and in 1936 he became the secretary of the Punjab branch of the Progressive Writer's Association. In Pakistan, he was arrested in connection with the Rawalpindi Conspiracy Case.[5] Following his release in 1955, he returned to *The Pakistan Times*. After the palpable

4 The All India Progressive Writers' Movement was an avant-garde movement aimed at radicalising literature by foregrounding the zeitgeist by means of realistic narratives. Sponsored by the Communist Party of India, The All India Progressive Writers' Association (*Anjuman Tarraqui Pasand Mussanifin-e-Hind*) was the largest banner to homogenise literature under Communist principles and influence, over time, almost all Indian languages. Writers problematised socio-economic conditions of the masses and probed human psychology. Radical Progressive writers, towing the party line, were largely concerned with Marxist Socialist ideology, their texts highlighting the predicament of the working class and the peasants. Individualism led several writers to seek out a new order within the cultural construct of the existing one, simultaneously evolving a new aesthetic that comprised modernist stylistic and literary devices and experimental narrative techniques. These writers were ostensibly progressive but aesthetically and technically experimental, thereby ushering Modernism into Urdu literature.

5 The Rawalpindi Conspiracy case was an alleged attempt at a coup-d'ětat against the government of Prime Minister Liyaqat Ali Khan in 1951. Planned by army chief Major General Akbar Khan it was allegedly meant to bring Pakistan under Russian Communist government. Fifteen arrests were made including Faiz Ahmed Faiz, then editor of, *The Pakistan Times* and Sajjad Zaheer, then serving as the general secretary of the Communist Party of Pakistan. Trials were held in camera under strict secrecy. All conspirators were sentenced to varying terms of imprisonment. Faiz lived in solitary confinement (Central Jail, Lahore) under sentence of death by hanging. He and Zaheer (Machh Jail, Balochistan) served four years in prison. Zaheer completed his history of the AIPWA *Raushnai* (*The Light*, 1953) during incarceration.

crushing of the Pakistan Progressive Writers' Association by General Ayub Khan in 1958, Faiz's ideological alignment endured by means of engagement in a variety of artistic pursuits. The same year, Faiz was in prison again under the Safety Act[6] for a short period. After the General Zia-ul-Haq regime took over administration in a military coup, Faiz went into self-imposed exile in Beirut in 1978 for about four years. There he edited *Lotus, Journal of Afro-Asian Writers' Association.* Faiz brought out several collections of poetry which chart his evolution as a poet and stand testimony to his humanism, an enduring engagement with man in relation with his social and political environment. Faiz wrote in Punjabi, and translated the Turkish poet Nazim Hikmet and the Kazakh, Omar Ali Suleiman. He received the prestigious Lenin Peace Prize in 1962, the Lotus Award in 1976, and before his death in 1984 he was nominated for the Nobel Prize for Literature. In both, *Pravda* and *Izvestia*, Faiz is referred to as 'a famed poet of the struggling East'. Also,

> Faiz's poems as well as his entire tempestuous and heroic life are an inspiration in the struggle against colonialism and for freedom, peace and the brotherhood of all peoples. (Coppola 2017, 334)

Coppola notes that by this time Faiz had made a mark as a courageous and fighter poet and had been translated in several languages (2017, 334).

Faiz's poems exhibit a deep-seated realistic resolve to speak up against exploitation and orthodoxy at a global level and an equally robust will to give voice to the oppressed. He is a people's poet; a number of his poems are anti-establishment and confrontational, urging reaction against totalitarian governmental policies. Nevertheless, despite anger and disappointment, Faiz sang of hope and resolution in succinct and enigmatic verse.

---

6 The Safety and Security Acts originally constituted laws decreed by the British Indian government of colonial India, to check political dissent. They were opposed by the Congress Party and the Muslim League. In Pakistan, the Acts were further tightened under the newly formed government, to curb activities of supposed anti-state elements, particularly Communists.

Faiz had imbibed the traditions of Perso-Urdu poetry and knew that the traditional subject of poetry was the beloved. Nevertheless, social and political consciousness created dilemmas best expressed in '*Mauzū-e-Sukhan*' ('Subject of Poetry'). These led him to replace the image of the enchanting beloved with more enduring ideas embodying social commitment, best brought out in '*Mujh-sē pehlī sī mohobbat mērē mehbūb na māng*' ('Do not ask from me, my beloved, love like that former one'). Faiz rejects the 'first love', evidently the beloved, in preference for love of/commitment to social cause. Nevertheless, the romantic and the revolutionary/political are inextricably interlinked in Faiz's poetry, enriching it, obscuring it, and making it inspirational and enduring. As Agha Shahid Ali says in 'Homage to Faiz Ahmed Faiz', in his second dedication to the poet, in a series of three:

> ... you had redefined the cruel
> beloved, that figure who already
> was Friend, Woman, God? In your hands
> she was Revolution....
>
> (Ali 1987, l 4–7, *The Half-Inch Himalayas*, 31)

Referring to himself as a 'humanistic socialist' Faiz spawned confusion, debate and criticism, particularly among orthodox Islamic thinkers and politicians (Dryland 1993, 40). His oeuvre stands testimony to his life-long political-artistic-humanist commitment.

'*Yē shahr udās ...*' romanticises the past while accounting for the spiritual poverty and desolation of a city consumed by materialism and reeling under political and religious pressures.

> *gō sab kō baham sāġhar ō bāda tō nahīñ thā* 1
> *yē shahr udās itnā ziyāda tō nahīñ thā*
> *galiyoñ mēñ phirā kartē thē dō chār divānē* 2
> *har shaḳhs kā sad chāk labādā tō nahīñ thā*
> ...
> *vaa.iz sē rāh-o-rasm rahī rind sē sohbat* 5
> *farq in mēñ koī itnā ziyādā tō nahīñ thā* (Faiz 1991b, 702)

The Sad City

Though everyone didn't own a bar or plenty's horn
this city was never so melancholy and forlorn
Two or three loonies roamed the by-lanes, lost
but their garments were not hundred-patched or torn.

(Daruwalla 2018, 109)[7]

...

Known to me are the preacher and the drunk:
The chasm between them is neither deep nor long

(Daruwalla 2018)[8]

Some of Faiz's poems are exclusively political. '*Čand roz aur, mērī jān!*' was written shortly after the outbreak of World War II (1939) when the slogan of 'imperialist war' espousing non-cooperation with the Allies was declared and some progressive poets fell in line (Coppola 2017, 354). Faiz was serving the British Indian Army during this time. The poem centres Faiz's take on oppression and tyranny inflicted by foreign powers, particularly the British.[9]

Čand roz aur, mērī jān! Faqat čand-hī roz.
Zulm kī Čhā'oñ mēñ dum lēnē pē majbūr haiñ hum;
Aur kučh dēr sitam seh-lēñ, tadap lēñ, rō lēñ
...
Jism par qaid hai, jazbāt pē zanjirēñ haiñ
Fikr mahbūs hai, guftār pē ta'zīreñ haiñ (l 1–6 Faiz 1991b)

A few days more, my love, just a few days –
we are fated to live under tyranny's shadow.
Let's endure a little longer oppression, pain and tears.
...

7 Daruwalla translates this poem, because it has not attracted the attention of translators (email dated 27 April 2018).

8 Translated for the author (email dated 30 April 2018).

9 Shiv Kumar translates faithfully, retaining his rhythm but admits of difficulties in translating Faiz's 'thought, the rhythm of his words ... the evasive splendor of his images' (1553).

> Body imprisoned, emotions shackled
> thought chained and speech censored. (l 1–6 Kumar 1551)

Faiz's prison poems are steeped in a plethora of emotions ranging from anguish and loneliness to love and optimism. Torture, affliction, and execution loom large, yet Faiz exhorts, advises, and hopes for a better tomorrow. In '*Dāričā*' ('Window', 1954) Faiz employs the motif of the crucifix to illustrate that daily 'the spring cloud', 'the radiant moon', 'the morning breeze', and 'the trance-filled grove' are crucified at his prison window (Kiernan 2000, 205). Daily their bloodied, martyred bodies, visitations in his prison cell, desiring union with the Lord, are resurrected like the Messiah. In terms of language, form and content, '*Dāričā*' provides ample indication that modern Urdu poetry has disengaged from its traditional Perso-Arabic roots to adopt to Western/Catholic cultural motifs and relatively freerer linguistic habits (Rahman 1998, 165). In '*Qaid-i-Tanhāī*' ('Solitary Confinement', Lahore prison, March 1959) a lonely and frustrated Faiz writes of

> . . . disappointment of visiting day
> To drinking friends at home and in exile. (Coppola 2017, 393)

Faiz's composed *marsiyās*[10] for fellow comrades who were tortured and subsequently assassinated. In these poems, the executed become the speakers/narrators. This is Faiz's innovation, for traditionally, an omniscient narrator reports/conveys dialogic exchange between protagonists. '*Hum jō tārīk rāhoñ mēñ mārē gayē*' ('*We who were Executed*', Montgomery Jail, 15 May 1954, Faiz 1991a, 38–41), commemorates Julius and Ethel Rosenberg, assassinated in America for alleged espionage during World War II. Posthumously, the Rosenbergs sing of their mutual love, and herald a new tomorrow, rising from a continual striving for their popular cause.

10 An elegy commemorating the prophet's grandson Imam Husain and his family martyred in the battle of Karbala—could also be composed to mourn a loved one or a friend.

... Holding up our sorrows as banners,
new lovers will emerge
From the lanes where we were killed
And embark, in caravans, on those highways of desire.
(Ali 1987, 41)

Likewise, '*Khatm huī bārish-e-sang*' ('*The Rain of Stones is Finished*', November 1960) commemorates Hassan Nasir, Secretary General of the banned Communist Party of Pakistan, tortured to death in the Lahore Fort in 1959. In a fitting conclusion to his elegy, Faiz has the dead Nasir whip up the sentiment of the larger public, by means of a nuanced couplet borrowed from Ghalib:

Kaun hotā hai harīf-e-mai mard afġan-e-ishq
Hai muqarrar lab-e-saqī pē silā mērē bād (Ali 1987, 54)

Ali expands the couplet to convey the multi-layered meaning in Nasir's appeal to fellow comrades:

... "Who'll dare to drink this wine of love
that is blood and poison? Who?"
This is the cry in the tavern after I'm gone. (Ali 1987, 55)

Faiz's poems dealing with the Bangladesh war, replete with imagery of blood and gore, evoke horror and raise a cry against the futility of war. Conveyed also, is the harrowing psychological impact made by the war. Among a series expressing agony experienced in the aftermath of the Bangladesh war, '*Hazar karo mērē tan sē*' (March 1971, '*Stay Away from Me (Bangladesh I)*') discharges anguish of the common man surviving atrocious massacres. The poet persona's withered body becomes emblematic of psychological-emotional torment.

Mērē nāzār badan mēñ lahū hī kitna hai
Chirāgh hō koī raushan na koī jām bharē

There's almost no blood in my raw-boned body
and what's left
isn't enough to burn as oil in the lamp,
not enough to fill a wineglass. (l 4–7 Ali 1987, 75)

Explicating Faiz's Urdu Aesthetic and Its English Language Translations

Faiz's engagement with poetry is, to say the least, honest, sensitive, committed, and responsible. He explores a plethora of ideas and emotions in a poetic career spanning approximately fifty years. At *mushā'irās* (poetic symposia), Faiz had the felicity to mesmerise and surprise. Preferring to write (like most progressive poets) in the genre of the *nazm* over the *ġhazal*,[11] Faiz was experimental in both form and content; his content being current and his form evolving, without losing sight of the traditional. Over time, his poems became composite embodiments of his emotional-social-political-humanistic self, his diction cryptic, and imagery complex. Faiz had imbibed Perso-Urdu poetic traditions and appropriated them to suit his subject and his age. Traditional, romantic images in Faiz, and for that matter in most progressive poets, are employed to suit modernist, avant garde, or political intent. His employment of metre, rhyme and rhythm are both, conventional and innovative. This adaptability provides freedom to translators to negotiate his sentiment linguistically in terms of another cultural superstructure. Faiz's symbols and metaphors descend from a Perso-Arabic ancestry and are often nouns and/or adjectives compounded by means of

11 A *ġhazal* comprises end-stopped, thematically autonomous couplets (*misrās*) held together in a strict scheme of rhyme and metre. A *nazm* is a full-length poem elaborating a single subject or idea. By comparison with the traditional ġhazal, the nazm granted freedom in terms of form, subject, and rhyme, rhythm and metre. Rahman notes that the modern Urdu nazm has achieved a typical modernist stance. It has absorbed its own tradition and opened its frontiers to experiential variety and aesthetic dimensions available beyond its linguistic orbit (1998, 165).

the *izāfat* (-e-). This along with more involved poetic techniques, cultural nuances, and idiosyncratic usage, produces complexities which pose challenges to any translator. However, with an eye ever looking towards the West, Faiz was surely and steadily imbuing his poetry with the modernist impulse. Edward Said remarks that like Garcia Marquez, Faiz's

> ... major achievement—indeed it is unique in any language—was to have created a contrapuntal rhetoric and rhythm whereby he would use classical forms (*qasida, ghazal, masnavi, qita*) and transform them before his readers.... You could hear old and new together. His purity and precision were astonishing ... a poet whose poetry combined the sensuousness of Yeats with the power of Neruda.
>
> (Blurb to *The Rebel's Silhouette*, 1991a)

Any translational exercise of poetry is an intricate one, requiring a fine balance in the interpretation of the text and its rendition in another cultural idiom. A translator requires familiarity with the poetic traditions and the philosophical ideals within the cultural superstructure of the source language; he must take cognisance of inherent subtexts, explore the dynamics of subliminal consciousness, and strive to convey them in the target language or even conceive of a new poetic idiom. Absolute fidelity or faithfulness is a near impossibility or a myth but free translation and adaptation facilitate creative enterprise in translating Faiz's significations.

Victor Kiernan's translations of Faiz's poetry are careful exercises conducted in confidence with the writer. He concedes the problematic of translating Urdu poetry in a Western language, particularly English, owing to vastly different grammatical and syntactical structures as well as almost opposing cultural nuances and the complex metrical structures of Urdu poetry. He engages with Faiz literally and interpretively, providing two translated versions of every poem, since 'often some departure is unavoidable' (2000, 13). Kiernan aims at fidelity and faithfulness.

Agha Shahid Ali has Faiz's permission to adapt:

> Homage to Faiz Ahmed Faiz
> *(d. 20 November 1984)*
>
> 'You are welcome to make your
> adaptations of my poems'
>
> 1
>
> You wrote this from Beirut, two years before
> The Sabra-Shatila massacres . . .
>
> (l 1–2 *The Half-Inch Himalayas* 30)

In his Preface to *The Rebel's Silhouette*, Ali concedes to challenges encountered and adjustments made while translating Faiz whose genius lay in balancing politics with aesthetics. He also admits that he had to adjust the letter of Faiz's work and hopes that 'something may be borne across to English readers' by means of his translation—that if his 'translations manage to convey some of Faiz's magic and a fraction of the complexity that resulted from his political and cultural background [he] would consider [him]self as having managed to pay a modest tribute to his immense humanity.' Ali's translations are in fact, re-compositions or adaptations enriched with additional images, metaphors, and symbols—as if the English idiom falls short of capturing Faiz's sentiment. Ali also disrupts Faiz's line and length, inventing a befitting form to suit his own view of the poem while retaining the essence of the original. Ali's translations stand testimony to his own poetic impulse because he 'recognizes that all meanings are interwoven, just like calligraphy.'[12] This observation echoes Walter Benjamin's view that:

> ... all suprahistorical kinship between languages consists in this: in every one of them as a whole, one and the same thing is meant. Yet

12 This is Agha Shahid Ali's message to Saleem Kidwai, below the Translator's Dedication to Paru, *The Rebel's Silhouette*....

> this one thing is achievable not by any single language but only by the totality of their intentions supplementing one another; the pure language. (2002, 257)

Estelle Dryland undertook to write a Masters' dissertation on Faiz. Her translations form a part of the study. She observes at the onset that each poem was translated literally, comparisons were made, and that it was interpreted and reinterpreted in the process of its transmission from Urdu to English (1993, xii). She concedes that a 'traditional English-speaking background does not lend itself readily to translation of the rich and exotic literary heritage of the East' and that she encountered some 'almost insurmountable difficulties' (Dryland 1993, xii). Nevertheless, Dryland's transcreative style 'gives voice to the *intentio* of the original not as a reproduction but as harmony, as a supplement to the language in which it expresses itself, as its own kind of *intentio*' (Benjamin 2002, 260).

Carlo Coppola's translations of Faiz's poetry are part of a detailed study of the All India Progressive Writers' Movement. Along with translations of other progressive poets, they are meant to indicate 'what is progressive in the major works' of these poets, because each poet while he is regarded as a progressive, is known for a variety of other reasons (2007, xiv).

With regard to his translation exercises, Keki Daruwalla avers that he ensures correctness of rhyme and rhythm while making only austere departures from 'the purity of what the poet says' (email 4th March, 2018).

This section reads select poems from two published anthologies, *Naqsh-e-Faryādī* (*Complaining Image* 1942–1943) and *Dast-e-Sabā* (*Hand of the Breeze* 1952–1953)[13] and their translations comparatively. The poems are characteristic of Faiz's poetic realism, fusing the traditional with the modern and expressing robust politics and socialism in language steeped in romantic idiom.

---

13 The titles of Faiz's collections have been translated variously. *Complaining Image*—Kiernan; *Hand of the Breeze*—Dryland.

The *Ashār*[14] from *Naqsh-e-Faryādī* are essentially romantic in sensibility.

Ashār
Rāt yūn dil mēñ tērī khoī hūī yād a'ī
Jaisē vīrānē mēñ chupkē sē bahār ā-jā'ē
Jaisē sahrāon mēñ haulē sē čalē bād-e-nasīm
Jaisē bīmār kō bē-vajh qarār ā-jā'ē (Faiz in Kiernan 2000, 49)

Last Night
Last night your faded memory filled my heart
Like spring's calm advent in the wilderness,
Like the soft desert footfalls of the breeze,
Like peace somehow coming to one in sickness.
(Kiernan 2000, 49)

Last Night
At night my lost memory of you returned

And I was like the empty field where springtime,
Without being noticed, is bringing flowers;

I was like the desert over which
The breeze moves gently, with great care;

I was like the dying patient
Who, for no reason, smiles. (Ali 1987, 3)

Quatrains
Night found your lost memories and swept them in
Like spring alighting on scrub by stealth
Like the stir and rustle of cool desert winds,
Like a fevered brow cooling to sudden health.
(Daruwalla 2018, 111)[15]

---

14 Plural of *she'r* is couplet (*misrā).*

15 Daruwalla published several '*ashār*' under the title, 'Quatrains'.

The *Ashār* make few demands on the reader as regards the complexity of thought, diction, and syntax. '(M)emory' or '*yād*', introduced in the first line, is developed in the rest as a continuum. The poet persona is the lover rejuvenated by memories, in all likelihood, of the beloved. Faiz employs nature imagery to express romantic intent. Kiernan gives the *Ashār* a title, and is faithful to Faiz's images and their associations. Daruwalla's rendering is more or less similar. Both maintain syntactical and structural equivalence, beginning lines 2–4 with 'Like' for '*Jaisē*'. Ali recomposes Faiz, expanding the *Ashār* comprising four lines into seven, making them read like a full-length, slow-moving, evocative poem. Though he titles his piece 'Last Night', Ali begins with 'At night …' (l 1). He introduces the first person possessive pronoun 'my' in the first line, followed by the first person 'I' in the following lines, providing centrality to himself. He is like the 'empty field' (l 2); like the 'desert' (l 4), and like the 'dying patient' (l 6). Thus, Ali shifts the focus from memory, whereas in Faiz (and likewise in Kiernan) reminiscence is momentous. Ali's translated poem indicates his cultural hybridity, his sensitivity and his creative impulse which seek to stride the cadence of diverse languages. In Daruwalla, 'Night', finding lost memories, assumes the greater proportion. It is like 'spring' taking over the ambience by 'stealth' (l 2), then it cools the poet-persona's sensibilities, and finally becomes a balm for his 'fevered brow' (l 4). Ali and Daruwalla draw similitude in accordance with subjective interpretation. Kiernan and Daruwalla maintain Faiz's rhyme scheme abcb.

'*Bōl*', published in *Naqsh-e Faryādī* is stark in its simplicity.

Bōl, kē lab āzād haiñ tērē:
Bōl, zabān ab tak tērī hai,
Tērā sutwān jism hai tērā –
Bōl, kē jān ab tak tērī hai.

Dēkh ke āhañ-gar kī dukān mēñ
tund haiñ shu'lē, surkh hai āhan,
Khulnē-lagē quflōñ kē dahānē,
Phailā har ek zanjīr kā dāman.

Bōl, yē thoṛā waqt bahut hai,
Jism-o zabān kī maut sē pahlē;
Bōl, kē sach zindā hai ab tak –
Bōl, jō kuchh kahnā hai kah-lē! (Faiz)

SPEAK

Speak, for your two lips are free;
Speak, your tongue is still your own;
This straight body still is yours -
Speak, your life is still your own.

See how in the blacksmith's forge
Flames leap high and steel glows red
Padlocks opening wide their jaws,
Every chain's embrace outspread!

Time enough is this brief hour
Until body and tongue lie dead;
Speak for truth is living yet –
Speak whatever must be said. (Kiernan 2000, 88–89)

Speak, for your lips are free!
Speak! Your tongue,
Your body,
Your life are all still yours!
Look! In the blacksmith's shop
The flames are fierce, the iron red-hot;
The clutches of the locks break open,
Each chain-link is split wide.

Speak, for the time before the death of
body and tongue
Is short.
Speak, for truth lives!
Speak what must be said. (Coppola 2017, 352–53)

Victor Kiernan notes that the stylistic simplicity and directness of this poem have not since been reproduced either by Faiz or his imitators (2000, 283). It develops on the catchword '*bōl*'. Repeated throughout, it becomes an emphatic appeal for outrage. Faiz employs material/literal images such as '*lab*' (lips), '*zabān*' (tongue), '*jān*' (life), and '*dāman*' (skirt of a garment), which are also traditional and romantic, but his treatment of them is modernist and utilitarian. Images that are unconventional to traditional Urdu poetry seem to reflect the imagism and machine imagery common among the Pylon poets. The *āhañ-gar* (blacksmith), the *qufl* (padlocks), and *zangīr* (chains) depict fabrication and forgery, symbolizing employments of the working-class. Faiz deals with them in novel ways. Literally, his padlocks have jaws that gape wide open, the furnace smoulders red-hot and his chains have skirts which are spread wide like a garment. Kiernan maintains Faiz's line and length, his metre, and his rhyme-scheme (2000, 283). Contrarily, Carlo Coppola mostly employs monosyllables, appropriates the line and length of Faiz's short-line stanzas, and introduces the exclamation mark to recreate the charged, sloganeering effect. He treats of Faiz's images conservatively, thereby detracting somewhat from the element of surprise in the original. Compare, for instance, Kiernan's 'Every chain's embrace outspread!' (l 8) with Coppola's 'Each chain-link is split wide' (l 8). Kiernan's interpretive 'embrace outspread' maintains the effect of *dāman* while Coppola's 'chain-link' calls to mind the Anglophone reader's familiarity with links in/of a chain. Kiernan maintains Faiz's stanza structure rhythmic pattern.

Faiz's collection *Dast-e-Sabā* contains several pieces composed while he was serving term in prison for the Rawalpindi Conspiracy Case. '*Lauh-o-Qalam*' is a ġhazal where love and politics are inextricably interlinked. Its tone and tenor are challenging.

Lauh-o-qalam

Hum parwarash-e-lauh-o-qalam kartē rahēñgē 1
Jō dil pē guzartī hai raqam kartē rahēñgē

Asbāb-e-gham-e-ishq baham kartē rahēñgē 2
Vīrānī-e-daurāṇ̃ pē karam kartē rahēñgē

Hāñ talkhi-e-ayyām abhī aur baṛhē gī 3
Hāñ ahl-e-sitam mashq-e-sitam kartē rahēñgē

Manzūr yeh talkhi yeh sitam hum kō gawārā 4
Dam hai tō madāwa-e-alam kartē rahēñgē

Maikhānā salāmat hai tō hum surkhī-e-mai sē 5
Tazzīn-e-dar-o-bām-e-haram kartē raheñge

Bāqi hai lahū dil mēñ tō har ashk sē paida 6
Rang-e-lab-o-rukhsār-e-sanam kartē rahēñgē

Ek tarz-e-taġhāful hai sō woh unko mubārak 7
Ek arz-e-tamannā hai sō hum kartē rahēñgē (Faiz)

Tablet and Pen

I will go on cherishing the tablet and pen,
I will go on writing down what passes over the heart,
I will go on collecting the attributes of the grief of love,
I will go on pouring bounty on the desolation of the age.
Yes, the bitterness of the times will grow still greater;
Yes, the tyrant people will go on practicing tyranny;
This bitterness is accepted, this tyranny is acceptable to me,
While there is breath I will go on with the healing of pain.
While the wineshop is safe, with the red of wine
I will go on adorning the door and roof of the shrine;
While there is blood left in my heart, from each tear
I will go on creating colour for the lip and cheek of my idol.

There is a fashion of indifference; they are welcome to it –
There is an appeal of love's-demand, and this I will go on presenting.
(Kiernan 2000, 130–31)

We will go on nurturing the slate and pen; 1
We will continue to write about these things which happen to
the heart.
We shall gather reasons for the sorrows of love [i.e., give full
vent to our love] 2
And thus remove the desolateness of the times.
Indeed, the bitterness of days will now increase further; 3
Indeed the people of tyranny will continue their tyranny.
This bitterness is accepted; this tyranny is endurable to us; 4
As long as there is power, then we will go on providing cures
for sorrow.
As long as the wine shop is still standing, then with red
wine we 5
Will go on decorating the walls and doors of the mosque.
If blood remains in the heart, then we will make from every
tear 6
Colour for the lips and cheeks of the beloved.
A manner of deliberate neglect, so let her be happy with it; 7
A request for desire, and so we will continue to express it.
(Coppola 2017, 363)

Lauh-o-qalam indicates the advancement of Faiz's poetic imagination; his estimation of the idea of love, its complex state of being, and its employment in poetry, when compared with '*Muhjsē pehlī sī mohobbat . . .*'. Opening with the plural '*Hum*' ('We', l 1), Faiz asserts, in all likelihood, a collective will to continue nurturing destiny, *parwarash-e-lauh-o-qalam* (l 1) referring to the attempt/ power to write one's own destiny. Translated literally in terms of its material images, as 'tablet and pen' (Kiernan l 1), or 'slate and pen' (Coppola l 1), the surface idea of insistence upon writing what passes over the heart smoothly completes the couplet. However the larger assertion in the Urdu, to repeat acts of defiance in order to carve/rewrite destiny, despite what the heart (probably employed metonymically) suffers - the essential essence of the couplet, becomes subliminal when read along with the next couplet. This, second couplet elucidates that traditionally, love or the pain accompanying it make the world go round and so the assertion to continue inspiring men with the things that constitute love, thereby preventing aridity (l 3–4). In the Urdu, the torment sponsored by the state is concomitant with the anguish inflicted by the beloved and the poet-persona's declarations of persistence are, in fact, a robust intent to continue to hold fort against it (l 7–8).

Coppola's translation seems to overlook that love of the nation/ *watan* could also be connoted as love for the beloved/bride or that *ishq* (l 3)/*mohobbat* are subject to multiple interpretations in the cultural superstructure of traditional, Perso-Urdu poetry. Ideas associated with these emotions range from the bodily to the platonic and include love for the country, for life, or for cultural ethos. At a basic level, they may refer to romantic love, and may also indicate 'defiance, self-assertion or self-pity' (Kiernan 2000, 34).

His poet persona declares his intent to continue his professions of love in the couplet following the *matla* (opening couplet) and reiterates his intent in the *maqta* (final couplet) despite the odds against which he is pitched by the beloved. The genderless pronoun *unko* in the *maqta* (l 13) could have been translated as the gender neutral 'them' instead of the gendered 'her' (l 13) to capture the dual romantic/political sensibility in some measure. Coppola's choices seem inadequate, or are subject to debate—perhaps, due to the polysemy of Urdu. For instance, *haram* means sanctuary or sacred place and also wife, not the confining space of a 'mosque' (l 6); likewise, *sanam* could literally mean stone and connote the stone-hearted beloved and *dum* refers to life while Coppola translates it as 'power' (l 5).

Similarly, *maikhānā* (l 9; tavern, ale house) and *mai* (l 9; wine) can be interpreted as ideal states of being or in terms of grossness; rapture or ecstasy may also be interpreted variously. A *maikhānā* could connote material or non-material spaces of being, of habitation, and/or of experientialism—ideas which are not elucidated by 'wine shop' (employed by Kiernan and Coppola). Likewise, *mai* may connote intoxications, obsessions, and oblivions, not merely inebriation. In fact, there is play in Faiz's employment of *maikhānā* and *surkhī-e mai*, as there is on *haram*: 'Poetically, wine stood for exaltation, inspiration and the tavern was the abode of truly heart-felt spiritual experience as opposed to the formal creed of the mosque' (Kiernan 2000, 35). Faiz's semantic layering poses challenges to both his translators.

A reading of the first seven lines of '*Subh-e-Āzādi*' August 1947 ('The Dawn of Freedom' August 1947; *Dast-e-Sabā*) indicates that Faiz's idiom is romantic. He employs nature imagery to express disillusionment over the mayhem and carnage of Partition. While some images and associated ideas are lucid, some are elusive and obscure.

Yeh dāgh dāgh ujālā, yeh shab guzidā sahar
Woh intezār thā jiskā, yeh wō sahar tō nahīñ
Yeh woh sahar tō nahīñ, jis kī ārzū lekar
Čale thē yār kī mil jāyegi kahīñ na kahīñ
Falak kē dasht mēñ tāroñ kī ākhrī manzil
Kahīñ tō hogā shab-e-sust mauj kā sāhil
Kahīñ tō jā kē rukegā safīnā-e-ġham-e-dil (l 1–7 Faiz)

This stained light, this night-bitten dawn
This is not the dawn
we have awaited so long.
This is not the dawn our friends set out to find
believing that somewhere in heaven's great expanse

must lie the final destination of the stars;
that somewhere in the heaven of night's languorous swell
the ship of heartache would find deliverance.

(1 1–8 Dryland 1993, 58)

Dawn of Freedom (August 1947)
This stain-covered daybreak, this night bitten dawn,
This is not that dawn of which there was expectation;
This is not that dawn with longing for which
The friends set out, (convinced) that somewhere there would be met with,
In the desert of the sky, the final destination of the stars,
Somewhere there would be the shore of the sluggish wave of night,
Somewhere would go and halt the boat of the grief of pain.

(1 1–7 Kiernan 2000, 123–124)

This spotted dawn, this dawn bitten night;
Not the dawn which comrades wished for
When they set out to find, somewhere or other,
The final destination of the stars [i.e., dawn] in the desert of the sky.
At least somewhere then there should be a shore for lazy-waved night;
At least somewhere the ship of the heart's sorrow should dock.

(1 1–6 Coppola 2017, 219)

Estelle Dryland's translation conveys the sense of Faiz quite poetically. Her translations are mimetic exercises. Rhetorically combining adaptive, free, or literal modes, Her renderings are inspired by Faiz but suited to the English idiom. Her engagement with Faiz's *beher* (line) is her interpretation of his contemplation, philosophy, metaphor, or expression. At times she chooses enjambment over end-stopped lines; she adds to the number of lines and also converts long-line stanzas to shorter ones. She also appropriates stanza structures. In'*Subh-e-Āzādi*', Dryland converts the first two lines into three, introduces new phrases like 'heaven of night's languorous swell' (l 7); converts '*falak kē dasht mēñ*' (l 5) into 'heaven's great expanse' (l 5) and interprets '*jā kē rukegā*' (l 7) as 'would find deliverance' (l 8). Dryland's rendering of Faiz is almost as much about how she stratifies Faiz with her cultural experience as it is about rendering his thought into her linguistic and cultural superstructure. Incidentally, Kiernan, Dryland, and Coppola translate '*safīnā-e-gham-e-dil*' (l 7), a classic example of the use of *izāfat*, literally, as the boat/ship of heartache/pain/grief. While this compound noun serves well in Urdu, any rationalisation for compounding of the images and the metaphor and sensibility created thereof in the target language seems implausible and contrived. It is tricky to ascribe logical meaning to '*safīnā-e-ġham-e-dil*' which perhaps results from Faiz's idiosyncratic or modernist apprehension, or both—ironically, eluding equivalence, and compelling translators to resort to literalisms or reductive methods of translation. Interestingly, in Kiernan, the ship of heartache 'halts' (l 7), in Coppola it 'docks' (l 6) but in Dryland it hopes to 'find deliverance' (l 8).[16] Faiz's '*shab-e-sust mauj kā sāhil*' (l 6) is Dryland's adaptive '*night's languorous swell*' (l 7); Kiernan's literal '*sluggish wave of night*' (l 6); and Coppola's 'lazy-waved night' (l 5)—perhaps a modification of Kiernan. In Urdu poetry, '*yār*' (l 4) could connote beloved or friend or both, or like-minded people. The less nuanced 'friends' in Dryland and Kiernan (l 4) detracts from cultural

16 Qurratulain Hyder borrows the title of her novel *Safīnā-e-Ġham-e-Dil* from '*Subh-e Āzādi*'. Saleem Kidwai, who has translated the novel for Women Unlimited (forthcoming), feels that this hyphenated compound word is almost unworkable as a translated title. He has titled his text *Ship of Sorrows*, so as to have the plural '*Sorrows*' convey the essence of the text while ringing in the intertextuality with Faiz. This is only one of the ways translators engage with Faiz in multi-cultural/cross-cultural/multi-lingual contexts. Hyder transcreates '*Ākhir-e-shab kē humsafar*' (also borrowed from Faiz) - *Fireflies in the Mist*. *The Indian Quraterly* carries an introduction and an extract from *Ship of Sorrows* (vol. 7; issue 2; January–March 2019, pp. 92–96).

connotations but Coppola's 'comrades' (l 2) limits the sense of Faiz's usage to Marxist contemplation. The introduction of brackets, round in Kiernan and square in Coppola, points at the translators' keenness to convey Faiz's sentiment to Anglophone readership, despite, perhaps, a linguistic shortfall in expression or an inability to compress Faiz's thought to fit a single, end-stopped line. Dryland's translation is free of such constraints. This brings to mind Kiernan's observation that modern English is too overloaded with 'utilitarian burdens' to be capable of poetry, unlike Urdu, which might almost be a language made up by poets for their benefit (2000, 29).

'*Zin'dāñ kī ek Shām*' was first published in *Dast-e-Sabā*. The first seven lines have been studied.

Shām kē pech-o-kham sitāroñ sē
Zīnah zīnah utar rahī hai rāt
Yūn sabā pās sē guzartī hai
Jaisē keh dī kisīnē pyār kī bāt
Sahan-e zindāñ kē bewatan ashjār
Sar-niguñ mahv haiñ banānē mēñ
Dāman-e-āsmāñ pē naqsh-o-nigār (l 1–7 Faiz)

Prison Nightfall

Step by step, night slowly
descends a tortile stairway
of stars. Softly impeaching,
an intimate breeze
murmurs gentle words
of love.
The prison courtyard's
homeless trees immersed
in deep reflection,
sketching freedom's message
on the curtains of the sky. (l 1–11 Dryland 1993, 201)

A Prison Evening

Each star a rung,
night comes down the spiral
staircase of the evening.
The breeze passes by so very close
as if someone just happened to speak of love.
In the courtyard,
the trees are absorbed refugees
embroidering maps of return on the sky.

(l 1–8 Ali 1987, 19)

A Prison Evening

By evening's devious stars
Rung by rung night is coming down;
A breeze passes close by,
As if someone has spoken a word of love;
In the prison yard trees, with no native land,
Head drooping are absorbed in making
On the skirt of heaven images and pictures;

(l 1–7 Kiernan 2000, 189)

Faiz's images, the star-spangled night, the breeze, and the trees are all personified and invested with a sweet, sad, romantic sensibility that the poet persona experiences in prison. His translators express Faiz's sentiments according to individual interpretation. Dryland's translation is an estimation of her quest for an idiom that unites two divergent cultures. She devises a new adjectival image, 'tortile' (l 2) for Faiz's '*Zīnah zīnah*' (l 3, 'Step by step') to convey the slow coming of nightfall; Faiz's '*naqsh-o-nigār*' (l 7) become Dryland's 'freedom's message' (l 10) and his *Dāman-e-āsmāñ* (l 7) is her 'curtains of the sky' (l 11). Over and above, she adds to the number of Faiz's end-stopped lines and introduces enjambment to convey his essence and emotion. She also introduces the idea of 'an intimate breeze' that is 'softly impeaching' (l 3–4) to convey Faiz's sense of a gentle breeze that whispers words of love. Faiz's '*bewatan ashjār*' (l 5) open up possibilities of multiple interpretations also. They are 'homeless' trees (Dryland 1993, l 8), that have no 'native land' (Kiernan 2000, l 5), or even refugee status (Ali l 7). Dryland projects the idea of homelessness, Kiernan emphasises the need for belonging and Ali, a sense of refugee status. Perhaps, the subtext in Faiz is desolation. Kiernan retains Faiz's imagery and its associations but Ali appropriates Faiz's images establishing new ones. His rendering seeks to express the slowness of night's descent in the slowness of its happening. For him, each star is a rung of a 'spiral staircase' (l 2–3) down which night makes gradual descent. Faiz's '*Sahan-e-zindāñ kē bewatan ashjār*' (l 5) making '*naqsh-o-nigār*' on the '*Dāman-e-āsmāñ*' (l 7) are Ali's '... absorbed refugees/embroidering maps of return on the sky' (l 7–8). Ali's 'embroidering ... return' for '*naqsh-o-nigār*' evokes sensibilities outside of Faiz's poem yet it is connected to Faiz, perhaps in the possibility of his longing for return from exile. Perhaps Faiz's imagery captivates the diasporic exile in Ali, who like the trees in the courtyard hopes to map his return to his homeland. Ali and Dryland grasp the essence of Faiz's poem, 'touch[ing] the original lightly and only at the infinitely small point of the sense, thereupon pursuing [their] own course according to the laws of fidelity in the freedom of linguistic flux' (Benjamin 2002, 261). Thus, they are exercising in their translations, the 'experimental style' Faiz sought in his compositions accompanied by an 'open manner' and a 'more flexible imagery' (Kiernan 2000, 43).

Conclusion

Faiz has been internalised naturally in the collective literary consciousness of people sharing his cultural tradition. As a poet, Faiz sought to transcend borders by universalising both his art and his political-humanist-socialist concerns, thereby making a mark as a global poet. Faiz bridges cultures by expanding the Perso-Arabic/Indo-Muslim base of his poetry to include Western cultural and literary ethics, thereby making it more inclusive and modernist. Imbued with robust political consciousness, Faiz expresses humanism by means of socialist and political posturing, in a language steeped in exotic, romantic idiom and adapted to the zeitgeist. Crusading against oppressive political systems, he projects human suffering as a global phenomenon. Despite anarchy, he sings of hope and optimism. Perhaps these qualities, propelled by his initial venture and keenness for transmission in more languages, spur more and more translations.

Translation of Faiz's poetry is a serious exercise demanding dual linguistic and literary engagement. Victor Kiernan's translation of Faiz's poetry, at Faiz's request, beginning in colonial India, against the larger tradition of prose translations, indicates a robust instinct on the part of the poet to challenge the traditional—an instinct evident also in his breaking away from traditional forms and content of Urdu poetry. Faiz hopes to transcend borders or bridge cultures and civilisations by expanding readership—a concerted effort made by a colonial subject in reaching out to an Anglophone, international readership. As Faiz's earliest translator, Kiernan assumes archetypal eminence. Agha Shahid Ali shares Faiz's literary tradition and is familiar with his Urdu oeuvre. His renderings are sensitive exercises flavoured with his own poetic sensibility. In Ali, Faiz's felicity in Urdu meets with his poetic felicity in English. Estelle Dryland's translations imbibe the essence of Faiz in an idiom well-matched with the location of its culture and express his thought in an idiom that seeks to stride two diametrically divergent cultures. Daruwalla's translations, imbued with the spirit of Faiz, maintain his form and rhythm. Carlo Coppola's exercises are undertaken from the point of view of a progressive historian. The translations presented in this study indicate that while form may be retained, meaning may be translated, but the metre, rhythm and nuances in the tradition bound ghazal may pose serious challenges.

The nazm, lending itself to formalistic and linguistic experimentation provides greater scope for translators to experiment also.

Faiz's English language translators engage with his poetry in various ways so as to transmit the philosophy, the cultural ethos and expression integral to his compositions but admit to complications and inadequacies. Nevertheless, their translations echo Faiz. Adaptation, free translation and transcreativity employed extensively indicate several ways of inter-cultural and multi-cultural engagement. Moreover, multiple versions of Faiz's translated English language poetry alone, indicate popularity and multiple kinds of readership. However, for the bilingual reader, the translated Faiz is Faiz transcreated, Faiz adapted, Faiz transformed or Faiz under erasure.

References

Ali, Agha Shahid, *The Half-Inch Himalayas*, Middletown, Connecticut, Wesleyan University Press, 1987.

Asaduddin, M., 'Poetry in Translation: The Case of Urdu', *Indian Poetry: Modernism and After*, edited by T. Satchitanandan, New Delhi, Sahitya Akademi, 2001, pp. 322–38.

Benjamin, Walter, 'The Task of the Translator', *Selected Writings 1913–1926*, edited by Marcus Bullock and Michael W. Jennings, Vol. 1, Cambridge, Massachusetts, London, England, Harvard University Press, 2002, pp. 253–63.

Coppola, Carlo, *Urdu Poetry, 1935–1970: The Progressive Episode*, Karachi, Oxford University Press, 2017.

Daruwalla, Keki N., *Nishapur and Babylon: Poems (2005–2017)*, New Delhi, Speaking Tiger, 2018.

———, Message to the Author, 4 March 2018, e-mail.

———, Message to the Author, 27 April 2018, e-mail.

———, Message to the Author, 30 April 2018, e-mail.

Dryland, Estelle, *Faiz Ahmed Faiz (1911–1984): Urdu Poet of Social Realism*, Lahore, Pakistan, Vanguard Books, 1993.

Faiz, Faiz Ahmed, *Naqsh-e-Faryadi: The Rebel's Silhouette: Faiz Ahmed Faiz*, translated by Agha Shahid Ali, Salt Lake City, Layton, Utah, Peregrine Smith Books, 1991a.

Faiz, Faiz Ahmed, *Nuskha Hai Wafa*, Delhi, Educational Publishing House, 1991b. Available at: https://www.rekhta.org/ebooks/nuskha-e-haa-e-wafa-faiz-ahmad-faiz-ebooks (accessed 10 February 2019).

———, *Poems by Faiz: Faiz Ahmed Faiz*, 2nd edition, translated and introduced by V.G. Kiernan, New Delhi, Oxford India Paperbacks, 2000.

Kidwai, Saleem, Personal interview, 20 April 2018.

Kumar, Shiv K., 'The Poetry of Faiz Ahmed Faiz', *Masterpieces of Indian Literature*, Director and Chief Editor Dr K.M. George, Vol. 2, New Delhi, National Book Trust India, 1997, pp. 1551–53.

———, 'On Translating Modern Urdu Poetry', *Indian Literature*, Vol. 42, No. 3(185) (May–June 1998), Sahitya Akademi, pp. 163–176. Available at: https://www.jstor.org/stable/23338504 (accessed 10 October 2018).

———, 'Internalizing Faiz Ahmad Faiz: Problematic of Impact and Response'. Available at: https://www.sahapedia.org/internalizing-faiz-ahmad-faiz (accessed 2 November 2018).

Trivedi, Harish, 'Translating Culture vs. Cultural Translation', in *Translation: Reflections, Refractions, Transformations*, edited by Paul St. Pierre and Prafulla C. Kar, Philadelphia, John Benjamin's Publishing Company, 2007, pp. 277–84.

11

Resisting Voices or the Allure of the Centre: French Fiction in Hindi Translation

Nipun Nutan

Arrival of French Literature in India

The systematic arrival of European literature and the development of the publishing industry in the Indian subcontinent started in the first half of the nineteenth century (Shaw 2013, 159). This period also witnessed the arrival of British education (1835) and the establishment of libraries in India (Ngurtinkhuma 2010, 26–27). In the same year (1835) the colonial law on publishing was also relaxed, thus giving an opportunity to Indian publishers to enter the publishing sector. These three initiatives led to the establishment of two markets in India. On the one hand, a market for school manuals in English was established, and, on the other hand, it initiated the publication of works in Indian regional languages. By the 1850s, I see the rise of the British publishing house Macmillan (Joshi 2004a, 20–21) and over 1,000 works were published through lithography in India (Shaw 2013, 160). Meanwhile, French literature in English translation arrived in India along with British literature under the garb of European literature, however in a limited capacity through the British established libraries (Joshi 2004b, 308). Thus the same readership consumed both English as well as French literature.

In the second half of the nineteenth century due to colonial policy changes, European literature started arriving in the Indian regional languages. The translation of European literature into Indian regional languages saw momentum after the Wood's Despatch and subsequent Vernacular Education Act of the year 1854 (Vedalankar 1969, 164). In this second policy change, it was decided that vernacular languages of India will be enriched with European knowledge. Consequently, the second half of the nineteenth century witnessed the growth of press in regional languages and also publication of school books in English as well as Indian languages. These publications should be seen through the concept of demand and supply. A demand was created for these works under the influence of British policies and consequently, the publishers started supplying them. I can conclude two things, firstly during the second half of nineteenth century there was the business of import of English books and secondly, the publishing market in the Indian languages was flourishing due to the development of the education sector both in English as well as the Indian languages. The growth of education had developed in favour of written rather than oral languages, which was again a result of colonial policies (Devy 2017, 278) that had already created a readership for English works. Now this readership extended to Indian regional languages as well.

The study of catalogues of various Indian libraries undertaken by Priya Joshi demonstrates that besides British authors certain French authors also found place in most of the libraries here. For example, Alexandre Dumas was present in all the fourteen libraries studied by Priya Joshi (Joshi 2004b, 306–07). Besides, the reading patterns of Indians during the second half of nineteenth century demonstrates that libraries were forced to make their selections according to the choice of the readers or else they had to face decline in membership (Joshi 2004b, 298). The choice of British authors by the Indian readership was not the same as those famous in Britain. The most famous British author that the Indian libraries had to keep was G.W.M. Reynolds. While G.W.M. Reynolds and other British authors famous among the readers in India were little known in Britain (Harikrishnan 2004), French authors like Alexandre Dumas, Victor Hugo and Jules Verne, on the other hand, were eminent authors of the time, not only in France but also in other parts of the world. Though the most successful British publishers in India such as Macmillan and Keagan Paul were not actively introducing French authors, yet they arrived and created a space for themselves. This could be apprehended as the outcome of their acquired symbolic capital.[1] This popularity and repute of French authors forced Macmillan to include them in its Colonial Catalogues of Literatures in English at a later stage (first addition in 1880 and later in 1896) (Joshi 2004a, 49).

French Literature in Indian Languages

When I move from the English literary domain in India to Indian languages, I find that among the ten non-British authors translated into major Indian languages five were French. And there were particular works of these French authors which were translated across Indian languages. These included Alexandre Dumas's *Le Compte de Monte Cristo*, Victor Hugo's *Les Miserables*, Jules Verne's *Twenty Thousand Leagues under the Sea* and *Around the World in Eighty Days*, Eugène Sue's *The Mysteries of Paris* (Joshi 2004b, 310). Joshi's research also shows that other works of these authors were also present in different proportions in several Indian languages (Joshi 2004b, 310).

Meanwhile, when I went through the sources of these studies carried out by Joshi I found that the Indian languages which had received the works of British as well as French authors were Telugu and Tamil (Madras Presidency), Marathi and Gujrati (Bombay Presidency), Bengali, Oriya and Assamese (Calcutta Presidency) and Hindustani, that is, Urdu (Joshi 2004b, 311). Through this observation I can deduce that by the turn of the century the Indian languages close to British presence got introduced to the French authors through indirect translations done from English versions of their works.

1 Here 'Symbolic Capital' is being used in Bourdieusian sense that is 'the value of any form of capital depends, in part, upon social recognition' (Crossley 2008, 88).

When these already established languages, which had developed between the twelfth and sixteenth century (Bubenik 2017), were witnessing these new interactions with the European World, Hindi in Devnagari script was in its nascent stage. Thus, at the time when these languages were getting enriched, Hindi did not have a large readership. A profitable readership in Hindi got established through Babu Devaki Nandan Khatri's *Chandrakanta* published in 1892. It was a super success and remained in continuous print for a long period. Many people learned Hindi with the sole motive of reading this novel (Rai 2005, 70). From this last decade of the nineteenth century started the commercial phase of publishing in Hindi. Also, this commercial period witnessed the rise of popular literature[2] as the most read genre.

Through this preliminary discussion I conclude that during the nineteenth century Hindi in Devnagari script was in its nascent stage and thus in comparison to other Indian languages did not receive large volumes of non-Indian literatures. However, it was by the beginning of the twentieth century that the conditions changed and became viable for the arrival of French literature in Hindi.

Translation of French Literature into Hindi

Having established the patterns of translational activity during the nineteenth century, I come to my primary study that is the translation of French works into Hindi. The motives behind the translation of French works in India have been described through various perspectives. In Harish Trivedi's opinion, 'The reception of French literature in India may not always have carried a whiff of subversion against English literature, but it has nearly always provided a necessary and salutary supplementarity to it …' (Trivedi 1997, 414). Alternatively,

2 Britannica Encyclopedia defines 'Popular Literature' as 'writings intended for the masses and those that find favour with large audiences. It can be distinguished from artistic literature in that it is designed primarily to entertain.

Shanta Ramakrishna after studying two famous translations of the period views these translations as attempts to 'change the terms of Cultural Transmission' (Ramakrishna 2000, 91).

Anthony Pym argues against the selection of isolated translations as the representative of a historical period. This in his terms could lead to a false hypothesis. He suggests that in the case of translation history one should always start with the compilation of bibliographical lists of translations (or in other cases, translators, places of publication, translation theories and so forth) (Pym 1998, 38–39). In my opinion, this approach of starting with an exhaustive catalogue of translations is rational. I posit this because this approach will present us with the holistic scenario of a period with its booms and break points. The first French work which I could locate being translated into Hindi was in 1910.[3] To understand the development of French to Hindi literary translation I plotted the works translated on a line graph (Figure 11.1). Since per year production of translations was very less and was difficult to analyse, thus I plotted a decade-wise distribution of translations.

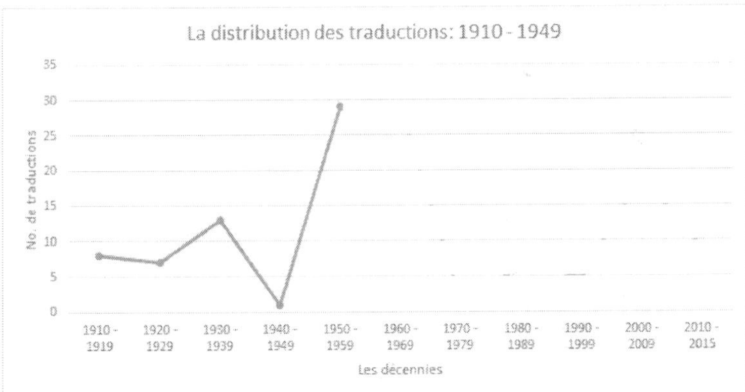

Figure 11.1: ***Distribution of Translation of French Works into Hindi: 1910–1949.***

Source: Created by the author.

3 We discovered one in 1900 too, however we could not establish whether it was a translation or an original work.

In Figure 11.1, we can very well observe that the translations (of French prose works into Hindi) during the pre-independence period was a phase which comes to an end in the 1940s (the last appearing in 1946). And the subsequent translations restart not before the 1950s. Since this first phase of French to Hindi translations coincides exactly with a phase in Indian history and comes to end with the Independence of Indian Subcontinent, thus we can infer that various political, social or economic factors had a role in defining the conditions under which these translations were taking place.

Having established that the pre-independence period was a particular phase in the history of French to Hindi translations, I entered inside this period to understand further nuances such as which authors were being translated.

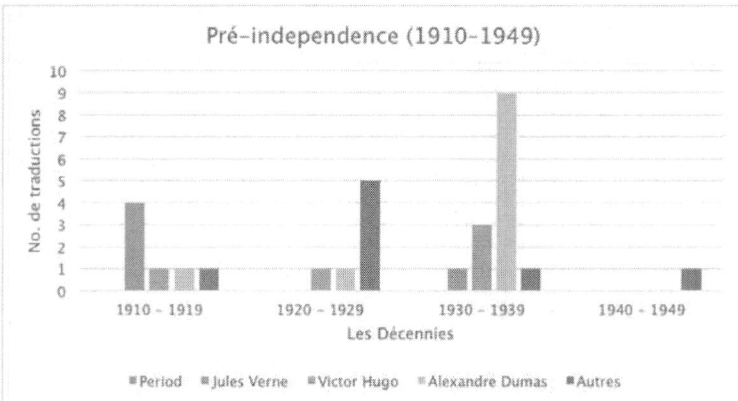

Figure 11.2: ***Decade-wise distribution of French authors translated into Hindi: 1910–1949.***

Source: Created by the author.

In Figure 11.2, I have represented the leading authors by individual columns. By leading authors I mean whose more than one work was translated in a decade. The French authors whose only one work appears in a decade are clubbed under the column *Autres* (or Others).

I plotted the distribution of the works of these authors across the decades. Now, this distribution revealed to us interesting facts, as discussed further.

The first French work which got translated into Hindi was in 1910 and the first decade is marked with the dominance of Jules Verne. In the second decade, we see a rise in the category of '*Autres*' which means non-leading authors, thus the choice of works is exploratory. In the third decade, we see a steep rise in Alexandre Dumas translations. And during the last decade, there is a steep decline with only one translation appearing. This graph gives us a preliminary pattern in the translational activity happening during the period.

In this preliminary analysis we can see that the leading French authors being translated belong to popular fiction and melodrama, which was the most read category at the time. Secondly, as we have studied earlier, these three authors—Dumas, Verne and Hugo—had already created a space for themselves among Indian languages. Thus, this preliminary analysis seems to accomplish that it was the symbolic capital that lead these authors to be rendered into Hindi.

In this chapter I argue that since popular literature was in vogue and established a market in Hindi, it had become profit driven; thus, translation of French works in Hindi was done with the motive to harness the symbolic capital of the French authors.

For this analysis I have created three categories of the motives (Table 11.1) based on which the translators were taking up the translation activity. These are firstly the category which is largely refuted by previous authors, that is, the motive was 'resistance against British dominance'; secondly, the category which Shanta Ramakrishna has deduced on studying the two Hindi translations which is 'Changing the terms of Cultural Transmission' and finally the category which I have assumed through preliminary analysis that is 'Harnessing the Symbolic Capital of French works and authors'.

I define these categories as given further:

Table 11.1: ***Possible motives or intents behind the translation of French works into Hindi.***

'Resistance against British Dominance'	'Changing the Terms of Cultural Transmission'	'Harnessing the Symbolic Capital' of French Works and Authors
If the motive of the agents of translation is to make conscious choices in order to: a. subvert British actions b. instigate revolutionary ideas c. address any social issue	If the motive of the agents of translation is to: a. Introduce new cultural and literary elements from non-British literatures, besides or along with British elements.	If the motive of the agents of translation is to: a. Gain economic benefits from the repute of the French authors. b. Translating the genre or category that people want to read. c. Enhance personal stature by translating a French author. d. Using translation as a learning process

Source: Created by the author.

Through an in-depth study of the movement of works, translators and publishing houses I will try to establish the individual reasons behind the choice of works translated.

1910–1919

When I observe the first decade of French–Hindi translations, it is basically the decade of Jules Verne. The first work, one of Jules Verne's, was published in Bombay by Sri Venkateshwar Steam Press. Now, the first page of the book explicitly mentions that this translation was ordered by 'Khemraj Shrikrishnadass' (the owner of the Press) and was done by the English clerk of the *Maharajdhiraj* of Indore from its Marathi version into Hindi (Gopal Vinayak 1910, Book Cover). In the choice of this translation the central role is of the owner of the Press. Owning a steam press during that time of history meant that the press was among the biggest publishing houses (Stark 2013, 220). Thus, this work undertaken by Khemraj could be considered as a trend setter in this field which other publishers would eventually follow.

Secondly, publishing a Hindi work from Marathi in Bombay could be justified through the fact that Khemraj Shrikrishnadass is what Anthony Pym calls an 'interculture'. An interculture is someone or something at the intersection of two cultures (Pym 1998, 177). Khemraj Shrikrishnadass belonged to a business community of Churu district in Rajasthan. His press was known for publishing the literature that was actually making a profit at the time, that is, the Hindu religious works (Mukul 2015, 11). Moreover, the community itself of the Marwaris in Bombay should be looked at as an interculture community. Akshaya Mukul describes this community as: '... Bombay in 1919 was a huge network of intellectuals, political leaders and philanthropists; also a new Marwari world less closed than that in Calcutta owning to its new found wealth from industry and interaction with the wider world' (Mukul 2015, 47).

It shows that they were at the intersection of Indian as well as foreign cultures. Venketaswar Press through this translation was acting as an interculture between the Hindi world and the wider world. However, the choice of Jules Verne for translation could be considered as being based on the reputation of Jules Verne in the intercultural milieu of Bombay and hence as a new profit-making venture.

Paul De Kock was a French author with a short-lived stature but was very highly celebrated (Olivier-Martin 1980, 49). He was the author of popular literature which people used to read for entertainment and then used to forget. He was more famous in other countries than in France (Kock 1920). I could not locate the original work of De Kock which was translated; however, its translation was undertaken by *Bharat Jeevan Press* (Sethi 1981, 232) situated in Banaras, which was linked to the Hindi propagation movement (Das 2015). Thus, this could be considered as another act for the enrichment and propagation of Hindi. Author/translator Jainendra Kishore had already published four original novels in a span of fifteen years before undertaking this translation. The themes of his original works have been love stories, principles of Jain religion and conduct of an ideal wife, thus largely conservative in nature (Goyal 2001, 325–26). The choice (if made by the translator) of a popular literature author such as Paul de Kock appears to be based on its success. Moreover, since I do not know which translation was published earlier, thus, this could also be the pioneer effort in Hindi. Through this effort, the publisher is trying to introduce new literature to change the terms of cultural transmission; however, the choice of the author for translation is not conscious but is based on its popularity around the world which could have been a sort of symbolic capital in the Indian context and probably also due to its conformation to pre-independence Indian readers' taste.

The next work of Jules Verne was translated by Girija Kumar Ghosh. He was the editor of one of the most famous Hindi magazines of the period *Saraswati Patrika*. This is not an early career translation. The translator is already known to have introduced Rabindra Nath Tagore in Hindi (Yayavar n.d., 46). Thus, he is an established translator. This leads us to assert that the choice of the work is made by Girija Kumar Ghosh and not by the publishing house. The choice of Jules Verne for translation seems to be based again on his reputation and its commercial value.

Then came two important translations of this decade. The translation of Victor Hugo's *Les Miserables* and Alexandre Dumas's *Le Compte de Monte Cristo*. These two translations have been undertaken by Durga Prasad Khatri, the son of Babu Devaki Nandan Khatri who is known to have established the commercial market for fiction in Hindi. Since Babu Devaki Nandan Khatri had established a press to publish his works, consequently his son had inherited that press. Hence, as in this case, the publisher and translator are one and the same; as a consequence, the choice of work for translation is a personal decision of Durga Prasad Khatri. The interesting part is that Durga Prasad Khatri finished his education in 1912 and same year published *Jagat Yantra Dekhiye*. This novel was written when his father the legendary Devaki Nandan Khatri was alive. His independent career seems to start around 1914, that is, after Devaki Nandan Khatri passed away in 1913. The works undertaken were these two translations. *Les Miserables* was published in five volumes during 1914–1915 and *Le Compte de Monte Cristo* was published as a serial between 1914 and 1921 (first part being translated by Chunni Lal Khatri) (Goyal 2001, 343–48). These two French works are the most famous works of these authors and according to Priya Joshi were already present in more than four Indian languages (Joshi 2004b, 310). Hence, this choice firstly can be an early career attempt, thus an act of learning through the works of these authors; secondly, since Lahiri press and the Khatri family had a reputation of their own, thus these famous authors and their equally famous works should come through them, again an attempt to harness the symbolic capital of these French authors.

In 1918 came another translation of Jules Verne. This translation was undertaken by another Hindi writer Shiv Sahay Chaturvedi. He is primarily known for his research on folk literature of Bundelkhand. He also established a Braj Bhasha Academy in 1940 (Narayan 2013, 331). The point to be noted is that this research on folk literature of Bundelkhand is undertaken between 1940 and 1950. During the period from 1910 to 1920, he has undertaken translations of two Bengali works into Hindi, a story based on a theme borrowed from the *Mahabharat* and this work of Jules Verne (Goyal 2001, 812). Thus, the choice of this French work for translation can be taken as an early career learning attempt. Since he translated other works from Bengali, there is a great probability that the French work was also translated from its Bengali version.

The details of the last two works could not be established except that it was published in Calcutta and not in the Hindi region. The translator has not mentioned his/her name and had used the pseudonym *Ek Hindi Sevak* (a Hindi servant). The reason behind this choice for translation could be again the reputation of the author and the popular genre that was in vogue in this period.

Thus, I can conclude that the first decade of French to Hindi translations is marked with the translation of popular literature which could be easily translated and will be profitable in the market. Moreover, I also witness many early career translational behaviour in this phase.

1920–1929

The 1920s is the most interesting decade of this first phase of French to Hindi translations. As during this decade, it was not popular literature which formed the main content for translation, but it was the social novels which were mostly translated. The second important finding of the period is that two (of the total three) contemporary French authors were translated in this decade. This infers that translators which were mostly authors of the period were not following blindly the trends and were engaging consciously with French literature.

The first two works of this period were published in 1922. These were a translation of Victor Hugo's *Ninety-Three* and another translation of a work by Maurice Leblanc. Maurice Leblanc's original work could not be identified; however, he is known as the creator of a character *Arsène Lupin*, a gentleman thief, who is considered the French equivalent of the British Sherlock Holmes (*Encyclopedia Britannica*). Thus, Leblanc had a reputation of his own during the period. And this was the period of apogee for Maurice Leblanc. Its translation in Hindi was undertaken by a School Book Depot in Lucknow. No details could be found about the translator (except the name). The choice seems to be based on the popularity of the original author.

The second translation is one among the most discussed translations from French into Hindi. Victor Hugo's *Ninety-Three* was translated by Ganesh Shankar Vidyarthi. Ganesh Shankar Vidyarthi was a revolutionary journalist, freedom fighter, a leader of the Indian National Congress and a writer in Hindi (Salil 1998, 11–16). This translation was published through 'Pratap Press' (Sethi 1981,

238), which was his own venture (Salil 1998, 22). Thus, the choice of the work for translation was based totally on the intellectual level of Ganesh Shankar Vidyarthi. He had already studied languages like Urdu, Persian and English during his formal education. And personally, he had studied authors like Victor Hugo, Bernard Shaw, Shelley, J.S. Mill, Rousseau, Mazzini and many more (Goyal 2001, 356–58; Salil 1998, 12). Thus, the choice was not an influence of the trend but a conscious one. Moreover, he had manipulated the work to highlight the theme of sacrifice that was needed at the time of the freedom movement and, therefore, his motives seem actually to use non-British literature against British hegemony.

During the same decade, we witness the publication of three translations of French works through the *Saraswati Press*. These were Anatole France's *Thais*, Théophile Gautier's *Avatar*, and Alexandre Dumas's *Joseph Balsamo*. Saraswati Press belonged to the most renowned Hindi writer Munshi Premchand (Goyanka 1988, 52–53). The first translation in 1923 was undertaken by Premchand himself. This was the translation of the contemporary French author Anatole France's *Thais*; to understand this choice of Premchand, one needs to understand the life of Premchand. Premchand was very fond of reading Western literature and looked towards them for inspiration (Agarwal 1971, 86–87). One of his favourite works was *Pickwick Papers* of Charles Dickens (Agarwal 1971, 86). Before undertaking this translation, he had already translated twenty-three stories of Leo Tolstoy and published them under the title 'Prem Prabhakar' (1916–1917) (Rai 1982, 388; Agarwal 1971, 86; Shailendra 2016, 259). He had read *Les Miserables* and wished to translate it into Urdu as well (Agarwal 1971, 87). According to Bharat Bhushan Agarwal, a renowned Hindi scholar, Premchand's choice of works was based on his creative and innovative nature. He further adds that the choice of *Thais* for translation was also in the same league (1971, 87).

The other two translations which appeared during this period from Saraswati Press were *Avatar* written by Theophile Gautier and *Joseph*

Balsamo written by Alexandre Dumas. The translation of *Avatar* is an interesting case. I could not find much information about the translator. However, the interesting fact is that it was translated from its Bengali version.[4] And this Bengali version was actually translated directly from the French by Jyotindra Nath Thakur, the brother of Rabindra Nath Thakur (Thakur 1922, 1). The Bengali version specifies that at the time when it was translated into Bengali it was not yet rendered into English (Thakur 1922, 3). Hence, this fact might be considered one of the reasons which attracted the translator to take up the task. If a translator is basing his/her decision on the non-selection of English language, this could be considered as an act of resistance.

Another ignored but important translation is of Balzac's *The Elixir of Life*. This translation was undertaken by a translator with the name Raghupati Sahay. When I looked deeper, I found that Raghupati Sahay is the original name of none other than the legendary Urdu figure Firaq Gorakhpuri (Shauq 1992, vii). His work spans across Urdu, English and also Hindi. He translated this work during the early phase of his literary career. He left his job at the ICS and joined the freedom movement in 1920 (Shauq 1992, xxviii–xxix). This was also the period when he was undergoing a financial crisis and was forced to slowly sell his inherited assets (Shauq 1992, xxxii). This translation comes at this phase of his life when he is learning from literatures as well as life.

Joseph Balsamo written by Alexandre Dumas could not be located, and neither was sufficient information found about its translator Shashi Shekhar Gupt. However, since it was translated through Saraswati Press therefore the impact of Premchand's idea that 'translations from foreign literature are the means of enriching Hindi' (Avadhesh 2016, 135) is undeniable.

Thus, this phase can be considered as a period when some of the most recognised figures or to be known figures of Hindi literature

4 A fact established by undertaking a comparative study of the two versions.

got involved with French literature and chose the serious, social literatures for translation.

1930–1939

The very next decade was marked with the dominance of Alexandre Dumas. Out of twelve works translated during the period, nine belonged to Alexandre Dumas.

The first translation of the period comes from a place away from the dominating Hindi literary circles (Ajmer, Rajasthan). It is the translation of Victor Hugo's *Le dernier jour d'un condamné* (The Last Day of a Condemned). This is a social novel and elaborates the idea, thoughts and emotions of a man about to face capital punishment. The publishing house 'Sasta Sahitya Mandal' was created under the patronage of Mahatma Gandhi and thus to move forward the idea of the national movement against British rule;[5] thus, this translation is a conscious choice by the publisher. This translation should be seen in the backdrop of the Defence of India Regulations, which authorised the British government to setup special tribunals which even had the powers to award death penalties to Indians, without giving them the option of appealing against such sentences (Horniman 1984, 44–45). The translation in its preface mentions that this book will be read by those whose hands are red with the blood of many innocent people (Hugo 1931). Thus, this translation should be considered as an open act of resistance.

The second translation of the period appeared from Calcutta; an unidentified work of Dumas published by the Hindi Pustak Agency (Sethi 1981, 233). The owners of the Hindi Pustak Agency had a considerable history of working in the literary domain. Mahavir Prasad Poddar, the owner of the press, had worked in the publishing industry

5 'About Us.' *Sasta Sahitya Mandal.* Available at: http://www.sastasahityamandal.org/about-us (accessed 13 April 2018).

in Kanpur, where he edited the translation of *Uncle Tom's Cabin* (Stowe 1916, 'Preface'). He also worked at the Gita Press, Gorakhpur, for some years (Mukul 2015, 120). Thereafter, he established the publishing house Hindi Pustak Agency at Gorakhpur and later shifted its head office to Calcutta. It was this publication which published the first collection of Hindi short stories of Premchand (Gopal 1964, 122). Various scholars have mentioned Mahavir Poddar's good terms with Munshi Premchand (Bandhopadhyay 1996, Chapter III; Chishti 2016; Sigi 2006, 94–95). Thus, Mahavir Prasad Poddar even though situated in Calcutta at the time of this translation had active links with the literary developments of the Hindi heartland. In my opinion, this translation falls under the same trend of translations as discussed earlier.

Four works out of the nine Dumas translations of this decade are translated by a celebrated author of Hindi, Rishabhcharan Jain. The Preface of one of the works explains the reason why Rishabhcharan undertook the translation of Dumas. He states: 'I consider Dumas as the greatest novelist of the World; and I not at all doubt this belief of mine. In the tongue of Delhi, Dumas is my *dilruba* [beloved] and I am his *ashiq* [lover].... His novels can still teach the middle aged authors of Hindi how to write for at least twenty years' (Jain 1948, 6). Whether this was true or a marketing gimmick, in both cases these words explain that Rishabhcharan Jain was highly influenced by the works of Dumas. The choice of works to translate was made by him as he published these translations through his own publication in Delhi. Thus, these attempts are again based on the symbolic capital of the original author.

Retranslations

Meanwhile, another interesting fact of the period is that two of the works of Dumas witnessed retranslations during the same period. *Le Chevalier de Maison Rouge* was translated in Delhi by Rishabhcharan

Jain and two years later was published in Calcutta through the Hindi Pustak Agency. Similarly, two translations of *Les Trois Mousquetaires* appeared in the year 1937; and both were done at Lucknow. Since the Atmaram Sethi's catalogue (Sethi 1981, 234) mentions different translators' name, thus, there is less probability that the two versions are one and the same.

According to Anthony Pym, a retranslation can be either passive (when they are periodic in nature that are retranslated according to the differences of time and geography) or active (when they are sharing the same cultural location or generation) (Pym 1998, 82–83). In the above mentioned two cases, the first retranslation appears from a different geographic region, and thus could be considered a passive retranslation. However, the second case when the two translations appear from the same region and in the same year, an in-depth study needs to be undertaken to unearth the underlying causes for such acts of translations. However, the overall reason for all these Dumas translations and retranslations seem to be related to the popularity they carry with themselves.

The translation of Dumas's *The Fourty Four Guardsmen* was undertaken by Raj Bahadur Singh. Raj Bahadur Singh had already translated *The Diaries of Leo Tolstoy* in 1932, a year earlier. And his subsequent works which were on the themes of history and biography came after the translation of Alexandre Dumas (Goyal 2001, 628–29). Thus, this could be an attempt to learn as well as to gain from the symbolic capital that Alexandre Dumas translations have accumulated during the period.

The only social novel during the period was translated from Banaras by Jyotiprasad Mishra. It is *Une Vie* of Guy de Maupassant and is based on the life experiences of women. This translation seems to be again chosen with a conscious mind. Two years earlier, in 1931, the author had written a work *Stri Kavi Kaumudi*, which were critical notes on the life and works of women authors along with examples of their poetry (Goyal 2001, 329). Two years later, the translator translates this work based again on the theme of the life of women. This presents the choice of this work for translation as a conscious and informed one and an act of addressing the social issues of the time.

1940–1949

The last decade of the pre-independence period witnessed only one translation of French works. This was a translation of an unidentified work of Maurice Dekobra who was one of the most famous authors between 1920s and 1930s. And his works were translated into 77 languages (Radio France 2003). He was famous for his detective and crime novels. Thus, the choice of the author was based on the trend of the period. Moreover, the first original novel as well as this translated work of the author/translator Arun both appear in 1946 (Goyal 2001, 39–41). Thus, this is the early career phase of the translator. Hence, there is again an attempt to exploit the popularity and success of the author.

Conclusion

In this chapter, through this case by case analysis of the translations of French fiction into Hindi, I can conclude that the majority of the translators were choosing the works for translation based on the symbolic capital of the French authors, that is, on their success in English, other regional languages, or in the international literary space. Their choice of translating certain French authors was linked with firstly the availability of these authors which is again linked to their reputation; secondly, the importance such translation might have on their personal career growth, and thirdly, whether it will render them economic gains and thus was linked to market demands. On the other hand, we also have certain authors of repute as well as people engaged with the nationalist movement who made conscious choices to translate among the available literature to address the concerns of the Hindi language or to address the political or social issues that the Indian subcontinent was facing. They used French literature as a way to put forward their resistance or to introduce innovative ideas alongside the systematically introduced British ideas. However, the market had an upper hand over the resistance or reform.

References

Agarwal, Bharat Bhushan, *Hindi Upanyas par Pashchatya Prabhav*, Delhi, R.C. Jain, 1971.

Bandhopadhyay, Manohar, *Premchand: Life and Works*, Delhi, Publication Division, 1996. Available at: https://books.google.co.in/books?id=cYs-DwAAQBAJ&printsec=frontcover&source=gbs_ge_summary_r&cad=0#v=onepage&q=mahavir%20prasad%20poddar&f=false (accessed 20 April 2018).

Bubenik, Vit, 'Historical Developments from Middle to Early New Indo-Aryan', Oxford Research Encyclopedias, March 2017. Available at: http://linguistics.oxfordre.com/view/10.1093/acrefore/9780199384655.001.0001/acrefore-9780199384655-e-290?result=1&rskey=vPNrun (accessed 20 April 2018).

Chishti, Anees, 'A Literary Genius talks of his Mentor', *Mainstream Weekly*, 7 November 2016. Available at: http://www.mainstreamweekly.net/article6807.html (accessed 11 April 2018).

Crossley, Nick, 'Social Class', *Pierre Bourdieu: Key Concepts*, edited by Michael Grenfell, Durham, Acumen Publishing, 2008, pp. 87–100.

Das, Arvind, 'Communal Agenda and Hindi Press in a Globalizing India', *Twocircles.net*, 4 August 2015. Available at: http://twocircles.net/2015aug04/1438676393.html (accessed on 11 April 2018).

Devy Ganesh N., 'The Oral, the Written and Memory: A History of Indian Aphasia', *Literary Culture and Translation: New Aspects of Comparative Literature*, edited by Dorothy M. Figueira and Chandra Mohan, New Delhi, Primus Books, 2017, pp. 274–83.

Hugo, Victor, *Fansi*, Ajmer, Sasta Sahitya Mandal, 1931 (Hindi Translation of 'The Last Day of a Condemned Man').

Gopal, Madan, *Munshi Premchand: A Literary Biography*, New Delhi, Criterion Publications, 1st ed. 1964.

Gopal, Vinayak, translator, *Chandralok ki Yatra* by Jules Verne, Bombay, Shri Venkateshwar Steam Press, 1910.

Goyal, Santosh, Usha Kasturiya and Umesh Mathur, *Hindi Upanyas-kosh 1870–1980*, Vol. I, II and III, Delhi, B.R. Publishing Corporation, 2001.

Goyanka, Kamal Kishore, ed. *Premchand ka Aprapya Sahitya*, Vol. I, New Delhi, Bhartiya Gyanpeeth Prakashan, 1988.

Harikrishnan, Charmy, 'Author Priya Joshi Muses about Indian Readers of 19th Century', *India Today*, 29 March 2004. Available at: https://www.indiatoday.in/magazine/society-the-arts/books/story/20040329-author-priya-joshi-muses-about-indian-readers-of-19th-century-790193-2004-03-29 (accessed 12 April 2018).

Horniman, B.G., *British Administration and the Amritsar Massacre*, Delhi, Mittal Publications, 1984.

Jain, Rishabhcharan, translator, *Quaidi* by Alexandre Dumas, Lucknow, Ganga Pustakmala Karyala, 1948, 2nd ed. (Hindi translation of *Black Tulip*).

Joshi, Priya, 'Trading Places: The Novel, the Colonial Library, and India', *Print Areas: Book History in India*, edited by Abhijit Gupta and Swapan Chakravorty, Delhi, Permanent Black, 2004a, pp. 17–64.

———, 'Reading in the Public Eye: The Circulation of Fiction in Indian Libraries, c. 1835–1901', *India's Literary History: Essays on the Nineteenth Century*, edited by Stuart Blackburn and Vasudha Dalmia, Delhi, Permanent Black, 2004b, pp. 280–326.

Kock, Charles Paul de, *The Encyclopedia Americana*, 1920. Available at: https://en.wikisource.org/wiki/The_Encyclopedia_Americana_(1920)/Kock,_Charles_Paul_de (accessed 12 April 2018).

Mukul, Akshaya, *Gita Press and the Making of Hindu India*, Noida, HarperCollins, 2015.

Narayan, Badri, 'Documenting Dissent', *Life as a Dalit: Views from the Bottom on a Caste in India*, edited by Subhadra Mitra Channa and Joan P. Mencher, New Delhi, Sage Publications, 2013, pp. 316–39.

Ngurtinkhuma, R.K., 'An Assessment of Role of State and District Libraries in the Socio-cultural and Educational Development of Mizoram', Unpublished PhD Thesis, Mizoram University, 2010.

Olivier-Martin, Yves, *Histoire du Roman Populaire en France de 1840 à 1980*, Paris, Albin Michel, 1980.

'Popular Literature', *Encyclopaedia Britannica*. Available at: https://www.britannica.com/art/popular-art#ref236490 (accessed 20 April 2018).

Pym, Anthony, *Method in Translation History*, London and New York, Routledge, 1998.

Radio France Broadcast on Maurice Dekobra, 2003. Available at: https://web.archive.org/web/20051107065803/http://www.radiofrance.fr/chaines/france-culture2/emissions/vie_oeuvre/fiche.php?diffusion_id=16927 (accessed 11 April 2018).

Rai, Amrit, *Premchand: A Life*, translated by Harish Trivedi, Delhi: People's Publishing House, 1982.

Rai, Gopal, *Hindi Upanyas ka Itihas*, Delhi, Rajkamal Prakashan, 1st ed., 2005, 4th ed. 2014.

Ramakrishna, Shanta, 'Culture Transmission through Translation: An Indian Perspective', in *Changing the Terms of Cultural Transmission: Translating in the Postcolonial Era*, edited by Sherry Simon and Paul St. Pierre, Ottawa, University of Ottawa Press, 2000, pp. 87–100.

Salil, Suresh, *Ganesh Shankar Vidyarthi Sanchayan*, Delhi, Sahitya Akademi, 1998.

Sethi, Atmaram, *Anudit Hindi Sahitya: Vishishth Granth Soochi (1875–1975)*, Gurgaon, Indian Documentation Service, 1981.

Shauq, Sumat Prakash, *Thus Spoke Firaq…: A Collection of Interviews (1959 to 1976)*, New Delhi, Allied Publishers Limited, 1992.

Shaw, Graham, 'Calcutta: Birthplace of the Indian Lithographed Book', *The History of Book in South Asia*, edited by Francesca Orsini, Farnham, Ashgate, 2013, pp. 159–81.

Sigi, Rekha, *Munshi Prem Chand*, New Delhi, Diamond Pocket Books, 2006.

Singh, Avadhesh Kumar, 'Premchand on/in Translation', *Premchand in World Languages: Translation, Reception and Cinematic Representations*, edited by M. Asaduddin, London and Newyork, Routledge, 2016, pp. 129–43.

Singh, Shailendra Kumar, 'Demystifying the Sanctity of the Village Council: "Ghareeb ki Haye" as a Counter-narrative to "Panch Parmeshwar"', *Premchand in World Languages: Translation, Reception and Cinematic Representations*, edited by M. Asaduddin, London and New York, Routledge, 2016.

Stark, Ulrike, 'The Coming of the Book in Hindi and Urdu', *The History of Book in South Asia*, edited by Francesca Orsini, Farnham, Ashgate, 2013, pp. 183–240.

Stowe, Harriet, *Tom Kaka ki Kutiya*, Kanpur, Pavitra Vastu Pracharak Company, 1916. (Hindi translation of *Uncle Tom's Cabin*).

Thakur, Jyotindra Nath, translator. *Avatar* by Théophile Gautier, Hugli, Sri Lalbehari Baral, 1922.

Trivedi, Harish, *India, England, France: A (Post-) Colonial Translational Triangle*, in *Meta*, Vol. 42, No. 2, 1997, pp. 407–15.

Vedalankar, Shardadevi, *The Development of Hindi Prose Literature in the Early Nineteenth Century (1800–1856 A.D.)*, Allahabad, Lokbharti Prakashan, 1969.

Yayavar, Bharat, *Purkhon ke Kothar se*, Bhopal, Prerna Publication. Available at: Google Books, https://books.google.co.in/books?id=

JjQEDAAAQBAJ&printsec=frontcover&source=gbs_ge_summary_r&cad=0#v=onepage&q&f=false (accessed on 20 April 2018).

Encyclopedia Britannica. Available at: https://www.britannica.com/biography/Maurice-Leblanc (accessed 11 April 2018).

दुर्गा_प्रसाद_खत्री (Durga Prasad Khatri). Available at: http://bharatdiscovery.org/india/दुर्गा_प्रसाद_खत्री (accessed 11 April 2018).

12

The Kafkaesque in Urdu: Naiyer Masud and the Essence of Translation

Huzaifa Omair Siddiqi

In his early work in the 1980s, the Italian philosopher Giorgio Agamben asked what seems to be on the surface, a simple question: Is there a human voice as such? In that period the French philosopher Jacques Derrida's deconstruction of the privilege of the voice over writing in Western metaphysics had opened up new areas of study in both language and literature. Yet what Agamben unearthed in a seminar titled *Language and Death* is a puzzle embedded at the very heart of the deconstructive project. What Agamben asked Derrida was a simple question: What is the voice as such? A voice 'that is the voice of man as the chirp is the voice of the cricket or the bray is the voice of the donkey?' (Agamben 1993, 3). A voice that is essentially the *human* voice, a 'Voice (which we now capitalise to distinguish it from voice as mere sound) enjoys the status of a no-longer (voice) and not-yet (meaning)' (Agamben 2007, 35)? In this chapter I will use the Voice only in the sense developed by Agamben as mentioned previously, as a suspension between two negations: no longer mere sound, and not yet with a full meaning. Can we ever come upon a situation where we can hear this Voice in its enigmatic resonance?

I have a hypothesis, that this problem is one that can be seen to be concerned with the originality of translation. The Voice, that which is not a mere sound but does not yet have a meaning, is first encountered in infancy, according to Agamben (1993, 3). But is it also not encountered when we hear a language we do not know, or know very faintly? What we hear in that singular situation is not simply mere sound, since we are after all listening to another human being. Yet what is heard does not also have any meaning yet. In this situation the Voice finds itself infinitely suspended: and this is quintessentially the experience that calls upon the possibility of translation. This transitional zone, in which we encounter once again our infancy, is the space of our openness to a primordial and incessant translation where what is already under the sign of negation, the Voice, is heard in its negativity. It is, perhaps, this Voice that signals the very possibility of translatability as such, the possibility of the passage from sound to meaning. What I am concerned with is this originary translatability which in itself though resisting translation, is the very ground and condition of all translations. Like Agamben I wish to ask, is there a human voice? And if we do hear it, especially at the moment when we hear a language we do not know, this makes it essentially a problem of translation. This is the paradigm within which I want to consider Naiyer Masud's early translations of Franz Kafka, published as *Kafka Ke Afsaney* in 1978—as being concerned with finding a *habit* for this Voice in translation. This is a task that must necessarily involve explicitly exposing the essence of translation in a translated work.

Naiyer Masud, the famous Urdu writer of short stories, passed away in his home in Lucknow in 2017. Though Masud received the Saraswati Samman, the Sahitya Akademi's highest literary award in 2007, his recent popularity is due to the translations of his works into English done by Muhammad Umar Memon. Masud's stories are written in a very different tenor than most of Urdu literature and they are usually noticeable for a style which as Memon says, is both orderly and neat,

> terse and highly clipped prose … one that shuns even the slightest trace of hollow rhetoric, so stark in its suppression of qualifiers that it unsettles the mind. No or few idioms, no verbal pyrotechnics of any kind. It is Urdu all right, but it does not read like ordinary

> Urdu. Attenuated but overlain with invisible density and evocative of absence. (Memon 1997, 2)

Masud was not just a writer but also a translator. While it has often been claimed that his stories are eerily similar in style and content to those of Kafka's, it is not as well known that he was the first to translate the latter's shorter stories into Urdu in 1978. Translation played an important part in his conception of writing. In an interview with Sagaree Sengupta published in *The Annual of Urdu Studies*, Masud provided an interesting anecdote regarding his first published short stories. Since his stories had been rejected by many journals for being too strange and obscure, he had to pass them off as translations: 'I had liked a Persian short story that I had read and had translated into Urdu. I put a false name on it, saying this was the name I found on it—I didn't know what the original language of composition had been, but I had read it in Persian translation and then had translated it into Urdu' (Sengupta 1997, 138).

The questions that I thus want to raise in this chapter are primarily the conventional ones we must ask when regarding a translation project: Why does Masud choose to translate Kafka? And what does his translation wish to achieve? My hypothesis is that Masud's desire to translate Kafka arises from his recognition that the latter is a writer who presents the experience of the Voice in his stories. In his translation of Kafka, Masud wishes to project translation as the *habit* of this Voice; for him the task of translation is to manifest that transitional site where the Voice is no longer mere sound and does not have any meaning yet.

Masud's style of writing, as had been remarked previously by Memon, is a product of intense work and effort. It's very decorum and neatness predispose the reader to believe that it has been translated into Urdu from some foreign language, an effect that Masud says is perhaps deliberate. In his interview with Sengupta, Masud quite clearly expresses that his very lack of a distinctive 'Urdu' style driven by a desire to efface the identity of the author, is perhaps what leads many to believe his stories are actually translations:

> And as far as suspicions of these being translation, I don't use language tagged with straightforward [cultural] identity to the extent that one could.... Because of this, the language seems a bit strange, and some people have gotten the idea that it's translation. (Sengupta 1997, 141)

This deliberate stylistic intention to present an original piece of fiction as if it was a translation is not simply a literary quirk on Masud's part. In fact, it can be understood as his desire to foreground the significance of translatability as such: the primordial translation of sound into meaning which is always virtual, already in the past at the very instant language is voiced. In effect, we must understand Masud's translation project very differently from how we conventionally think it to be. When translating from one language to another, most translation projects proceed with one of two alternatives: either by bringing the source text closer to the target, by which the process of translation undergone is effaced, and the text can be enjoyed without any mediation, or by foregrounding the work of translation itself, by which the text retains its identity as having been translated and presents an element of foreignness. In theory, these are the basic paradigms that most translators have to choose between, though the final product in most cases can turn out to be neither here nor there, which is not necessarily a bad thing. However, most translators have to decide the politics of their project at the outset itself and try to stick to it consistently throughout, whether to efface foreignness or preserve it. However, what is preserved is still only an incidental sense of alienation, one which proceeds from the relative cultural and linguistic distance between the two languages. What Kafka manifests is a kind of integral foreignness even when he is writing in standard German—for Kafka is as Gilles Deleuze says a 'foreigner in one's own language' (Deleuze and Parnet 2007, 4). How is a translator to translate that foreignness of expression? Would the two basic models of translating work in this case, where foreignness is an integral, and not incidental, aspect of the work to be translated? Masud's project does not attempt to simply carry across this integral foreignness but also to explore what is it that makes one a foreigner in one's own language. To experience one's own language as utterly foreign is already a way to open up the problem of the Voice, of the suspension between mere sound and meaning. Can this be considered as Masud's real literary project?

In his Introduction to the translations of *Kafka Ke Afsaney*, Masud writes that 'Reading Dostoevsky's stories the reader feels that he himself has changed. Reading Kafka's stories, he sees that the world itself has changed' (2009, 14).[1] This distinction that Masud draws here is a very fine one indeed. The question of how it is possible for literature to change the world is founded on the problem of *meaning*. If we read Masud correctly, then the meaning that the world bears for us changes after reading Kafka. For the meaning of the world to change implies that the world itself has changed. But what is this enigmatic power of meaning, which through the medium of something immaterial like language can wholly transform the material world? The real puzzle that motivates what we call the Kafkaesque lies in the fact that of all the strange and mysterious things that occur the strangest is the residual precipitation of meaning amongst, and in spite of, the meaningless. Kafka's stories posit the survival of order, but what is lost, however, is the key to this order. It remains an encrypted order; like a code without its cipher, this order is both meaningless and yet already potentially full of meaning. As Masud says in his introduction, Kafka's stories are like a '*khwab pareshan*' (troubled dream) and 'when the reader returns to his own familiar world he feels that he has entered a new *khwab pareshan* but this dream is not one of chaos but under some

---

1 All references from the 'Introduction' to *Kafka ke Afsaney* have been translated into English by me.

encrypted order under which all things are integrated' (2009, 14). There is an order to the world, but what remains extremely puzzling is that no one can say what exactly is this 'encrypted order' that is felt but not understood.

The challenge that Masud thus confronts is monumental because he is not just translating a text from one language to another. What confronts him is this cryptic problem that is translatability itself. It is not simply about translating the cultural milieu of Kafka's Prague into Urdu. In a way it can be said that Masud hardly considers this at all. The very first story he translates is titled '*Shikari Gracchus*' which is a translation of Kafka's '*The Hunter Gracchus*'. This story in the original German is about a boat which arrives at a riverside port carrying the long dead Hunter Gracchus. Gracchus meets the mayor of the town and tells him about his fate which is to wander eternally across the seas and rivers. This story references many things like the Ancient Greek myth of the River Styx, the boatman who ferries souls across and other myths which most people educated in Europe would have an idea of. But this idea has no equivalent in either Indian or larger Islamicate cultures and Masud does not even make the slightest effort to explain it via a footnote or an introduction to the story. He is completely unconcerned with this aspect of cultural translation.

But then this is not to claim that he wants to create an air of vague mystery, of foreignness just for its own sake. What Masud wants to evoke is his (which is also Kafka's own) surprise: that there is meaning after all! How is it even possible that mere sounds, under the influence of some encrypted order whose provenance remains concealed, can become meaning? To truly comprehend this transition means manifesting a space between the two negativities of no longer sound and not yet meaning. This space is for Masud none other than that of translation itself. What he wants to retain in his translation is that experience of the Voice. That is why of all writers Masud chooses Kafka, because he understands that in him he finds a kindred soul, someone who shares the same project. Masud's literary project is to manifest this Voice in its utter nudity: a certain limit where language is not mere sound but not yet, not wholly, has meaning. And that of course complicates his project entirely. How does one present the Voice? One can argue that every propositional statement also carries within it, implicitly, this reference to the Voice; every utterance as Agamben says, is primarily the voicing of the existence of language (Agamben 1999, 42). However, in most utterances this is always implicit, as Hegel would say, in-itself, and not explicitly manifested. To manifest this explicitly means an utterance which is not just the garment for the non-linguistic presupposition 'there is language' but also its dwelling place. This is Masud's challenge: to find the *habit* of this Voice. The word 'habit' neatly encapsulates the two requirements for this manifestation because it means both dwelling place (as in habitat, inhabit) and also garment. Literary language can be thought as the garment of the Voice, but it is the effect of integral foreignness generated in translation that is truly both the garment and the dwelling place of the Voice. Thus, Masud translates Kafka in his own enigmatic way, retaining that trace of utterly integral foreignness in one's own language. It is in his translations that the Voice is made explicit and finds its habit in translation. The stories chosen by Masud all reflect a careful method which is premised on discovering the habit of the Voice. Most of them are extremely short stories, some not more than a paragraph, even two or three lines. The stories, like '*Red Indian Hone ki Khwahish*', '*Libaas*', '*Darakht*', '*Agla Gaon*', '*Paas se Guzarne Wale*', '*Be-Khayali mein Khirki se Dekhna*', '*Ek Choti Si Kahani*' all are about, in some way or form, about the play of appearances. '*Darakht*' and '*Agla Gaon*' express this quite well:

> *Darakht*
>
> *Aisa hai ke hum barf mein darakhton ki tawon ki tarah hain. Dekhne mein wo dheele dhale pare hote hain aur ek halka sa dhakka unhein larkhane ke liye kaafi hona chahiye. Nahin, aisa nahin kiya jaa sakta.*

> *Is liye ke wo zameen mein bainthe hue hain. Magar dekhe na, khud ye bhi dikhawa hi toh hai.*[2] (Masud 2009, 56)
>
> *Agla Gaon*
> *Mere dada kaha karte the:*
>
> *zindagi hairat khez had tak mukhtasar hai. Main toh jab apne zindagi par nazar karta huun toh ye itni qaleel maalum hoti hai ke misaal ki taur mere samajh mein nahi aata ke koi naujawan is andeshe ke beghair agle gaaon ko rawana hone ka irada kis tarah kar sakta hai ke aisi safar mein jitna waqt darkaar hoga us ke liye—haadson se qatah nazar—ek puuri khush o kharam tabihi zindagi middat bhi kam par sakti hai.*[3] (Masud 2009, 59)

Both of the above translations try to manifest the habit of the Voice. What is carried across by Masud in his translation is the 'encrypted order' (Masud 2009, 14) which he finds in Kafka, where the literary is the habit of the Voice suspended between the no longer sound and not yet meaning. What appears to be true, as in '*Darakht*', is not: the stumps of the trees cannot be unseated from the ground as easily as they seem to be. But even this truth is ultimately nothing more than an appearance. Suspended between two negativities, no longer real and not yet appearance, the effect of the story is to foreground the paradox of an 'encrypted order'. Masud's translation of Kafka's stories thus unveils an integral and incessantly oscillating alienation where one feels like a

---

2 Edwin and Willa Muir's English translation of this story goes like this:
The Trees
'For we are like tree trunks in the snow. In appearance they lie sleekly and a light push should be enough to set them rolling. No, it can't be done, for they are firmly wedded to the ground. But see, even that is only appearance.'

3 Another English translation by Edwin and Willa Muir:
The Next Village
'My grandfather used to say: 'Life is astoundingly short. To me, looking back over it, life seems so foreshortened that I scarcely understand, for instance, how a young man can decide to ride over to the next village without being afraid that—not to mention accidents—even the span of a normal happy life may fall far short of the time needed for such a journey.'

foreigner in one's own language. Translation is, thus, not a secondary, or derived project for Masud, but an endless task whose goal is to incessantly manifest the suspension between no longer sound and not yet meaning. In that very rigorous sense, translation is an arduous task which is even more original and literary than writing one's own stories for Masud. A style of translation can only be successful in this manifestation of the experience of the Voice when even an original work can be mistaken for a translation. Masud's translations of Kafka, then, should not be restricted to this little book but perhaps can be extended to all his short stories. One can hear Masud saying of all his stories: 'I didn't know what the original language of composition had been, but I had read it in Persian translation and then had translated it into Urdu' (Sengupta 1997, 138). However, Masud in his interview denied that he was primarily a translator of Kafka:

> when I began to write short stories, I hadn't even read Kafka. But it did seem to me that the language he used was of the sort I liked, it seemed to be just right. It could be translated into similar language in Urdu. That's why it began to seem like both things were written by the same person. (Sengupta 1997, 154)

In this case we have to understand his impetus as not one concerned with the translation of the 'Kafkaesque' into an 'Indian' vocabulary but to manifest the Voice in the habit of translation, which for Masud would be the highest literary goal. The Kafkaesque is chosen by him as a vehicle because it is also occupied with this puzzle of the Voice, this problem of an untranslatable translatability. Masud's work is thus not a 'translation' as such but a work in parallel with that of Kafka. For both of them this work of translation, wherein the Voice finds itself in its habit, is an unending task. It is both incalculable and unprogrammatic. The task of the translator does not lie in producing a finished work which stays true to the original, but on the contrary to manifest the condition of translatability itself, to let the human Voice be heard even as it remains suspended between two negativities. Thus when we speak of 'Translation in India' and 'India in Translation' we would do well to suspend ourselves in the caesura that separates the two phrases, and so remember Masud's profound words: '*Lekin Hindostaan tak ka raasta koi nahi bata sakta, koi bhi nahi*' (2009, 57).[4]

References

Agamben, Giorgio, *Infancy and History: Essays on the Destruction of Experience*, translated by Liz Heron, New York, Verso, 1993.

———, *Potentialities: Collected Essays in Philosophy*, translated by Daniel Heller-Roazen, Stanford, Stanford University Press, 1999.

———, *Language and Death: The Place of Negativity*, translated by Michael Hardt, London, University of Minnesota Press, 2007.

Deleuze, Gilles and Claire Parnet, *Dialogues II*, New York, Columbia University Press, 2007.

Masud, Naiyer, *Kafka Ke Afsaney,* Karachi, Aaj Ki Kitabein Publishers, 2009.

Memon, Muhammad Umar, 'Naiyer Masud: A Prefatory Note', *The Annual of Urdu Studies*, Vol. 12, 1997, pp. 1–8.

Muir, Edwin and Willa Muir, *Collected Stories of Franz Kafka*, New York, Schocken Books, 1971.

Sengupta, Sagaree, 'An Interview with Naiyer Masud', *The Annual of Urdu Studies*, Vol. 12, 1997, pp. 123–60.

4 Edwin and Willa Muir's translation goes: 'But no one, no one can lead us to India'.

13

Translating Gramsci in Bengali: Redefining the Buddhijibi[1] *in Post-Liberalisation Bengal*

Shinjini Basu

For Bengalis growing up in the 1990s, Marxist political literature used to be a significant part of their cultural milieu. To use the term 'Bengali' without any class/caste-qualifier is not to celebrate 'The Bengali' as a homogenous and purely culturally defined entity. It is simply to observe that the dissemination of Marxist literature could overcome the contingencies of class, caste, community and region in Bengal and their availability in Bengali translation had a significant role to play in that.

The Marxist praxis in India itself is often seen as an act of translation of a political thought born in the West and translated to analyse and act upon a very different social setting. Sudipta Kaviraj goes to the extent of calling it an instance of the failure of translation that could not accommodate specific socio-cultural denominators such as caste in its frame of reference (Kaviraj 2009, 173).[2] However, more specific

---

1 'Buddhijibi' is the commonly used Bengali term for 'intellectual', though there are variations which would be discussed in the course of this chapter.

2 While at it one must also mention the rejoinder of Aditya Nigam where he discusses the methodological problem of looking at Indian Marxism merely as an act of translation of a Western thought—it does not take into account the intermediate displacements Marxism had already gone through, particularly in Russia, and its specific exigency in colonial and post-colonial subcontinental society and politics. Nigam also points out that before being completely overtaken by the officially sanctioned Stalinist overhauling, Marxism 'was perceived to be a political doctrine. It was not a whole new 'world-view' that sought to control every part of the believer's being' (Nigam, Web).

instances of translation of Marxist literature in local languages have had a significant impact on the organised Left movement in India. Juned Shaikh, for example, has examined the role of the Marathi translation of the *Communist Manifesto* titled *Kamyunista Jahirnama* published in 1931 in the context of the workers' movement in Bombay in the 1930s and has argued that it helped to create a 'workers' public' that could enter in a conversation with the 'elite public sphere' (Shaikh 2011, 65).

In Bengal, the history of critical engagement with Marxist and Leninist literature goes back to the time of the Bolshevik Revolution with the writings of people like Soumendranath Tagore and M.N. Roy. Soumendranath Tagore was the first translator of *The Communist Manifesto* in Bengali. This translation of *The Communist Manifesto*, arguably the first in any Indian language, was published in the journal *Langal* edited by Kazi Nazrul Islam. M.N. Roy translated parts of the *Eighteenth Brumaire of Louis Napoleon* in Bengali. In 1925, when the Communist Party of India was being formed in Kanpur, Muzaffar Ahmad translated a few texts of Marx. Translations of smaller texts, essays and pamphlets by Marx, Engels or Lenin were published from time to time in the four journals—*Dhumketu*, *Langal*, *Ganabani* and *Arani*. After the division of the Party, and then the further splintering in the form of the Naxalbari movement, Bengali translations proliferated and started including not only Soviet thinkers but important Chinese names such as Mao Tse-tung and Lu Xun as well. Saroj Dutta, a major ideologue of the Naxalbari movement, translated Soviet literary texts along with theoretical writings.

Continental Marxist thinkers would strike as a conspicuous absence from this body of translated works. This absence has a lot to do with the fact that much of such translation work used to be carried out through different cultural and organisational platforms or individual translators working within the broader paradigm of what could be considered the official Left in Bengal. Apart from the foundational texts of Marxism–Leninism, writers from either the Soviet or the Chinese block were thought to be of more practical value as far as capturing and sustaining state power is concerned, even as the diversion and subsequent conflict of the Soviet and Chinese lines that shaped the politics of the 1970s continued to influence the intellectual landscape. Though by the late 1980s the political capital of the Left Front Government in West Bengal had consolidated into social capital; the dramatic changes in global and national politics around this time demanded a re-examination of the available cultural capital of the Left. This chapter will try to look at the rediscovery of Antonio Gramsci not only in Bengal but across the world in this context.[3] The disillusionment with state communism and its gradual dismantling are obvious and decisive factors behind this intellectual churning. Looking at *Buddhijibi o Shiksha* (1991), a translation with commentaries of 'On the Intellectuals' and 'On Education' from Gramsci's *Prison Notebooks*, part of a translation project undertaken by three well-known Marxist intellectuals from Bengal, one would argue that this translation responds to the need for new critical models and in the process tries to contextualise the role of the intellectual in the face of a unipolar world order.

Samik Bandyopadhyay, Sobhanlal Datta Gupta and Sourin Bhattacharya started working on what Bandyopadhyay calls a body of '*pramanya*' or authoritative translations of Gramsci's writings in 1989–1990. As a result of that endeavour a series of translated texts were published: *Antonio Gramsci: Nirbachita Rachanasangraha, Pratham Khanda* (1993), *Antonio Gramsci: Bichar Bisleshan* (1993, 2000), and *Antonio Gramsci: Chithi-Patra* (1997). The first among

3 The extent of celebrations of the fiftieth anniversary of Gramsci's death in 1987 and his birth centenary in 1991 is indicative of his continued, in fact reinvigorated intellectual influence worldwide. In a commemorative issue published in 1987 Eric Hobsbawm refers to a survey that lists Gramsci among the 250 most frequently cited authors (Buttigieg 1994, 98).

these books is *Buddhijibi o Shiksha*, edited and translated by Bandyopadhyay and Bhattacharya. According to Bandyopadhyay, on its first publication the response of the readers was lukewarm, forcing the translators as well as the publisher to abandon the project midway having translated only a fraction of Gramsci's complete body of work (Bandyopadhyay 2014, 'Preface'). The slim volume that the present chapter intends to engage with was republished in 2014 by a different publisher.

If one turns to the tradition of Marxist theoretical developments within Bengal one would find that it mostly runs parallel to the organisational developments and divisions within the Party and then the radical break in the form of the Naxalbari movement of the 1970s. Apart from intra-party documents, exchanges in the public sphere took place through journals such as *Quest* and *Frontier* in English, and *Natun Sahitya* and *Parichay* in Bengali. Debiprasad Chattopadhyay, Satindranath Chakraborty, Achyut Goswami, Samar Sen, Susobhan Sarkar and many others actively participated in creating a dialogue between international Marxist discursive practices and the Marxist praxis in Bengal. The events from the fall of the Berlin Wall in 1989 to the final dissolution of the Soviet Union in 1991 serve as a break in that continuity, often captured through a language of doom. Sourin Bhattacharya writes, 'The Cold War is over, a unilateral decree has been served. The long standing soldier, well known as Marxism has been vanquished. His effigy is being burnt worldwide' (Bhattacharya 2005, 86, translation mine). He also feels the need to look back and reassess our own engagement with it: 'Were the seeds of domination latent in our Marxist thinking, its expression and theorisation? Did we take Marxism for granted as the singular key to open all doors? Was our Marxist thought way too influenced by the regimentation of international Marxist establishment?' (Bhattacharya 2011, 26, translation mine). This was a moment of crisis in the broader consensus between the carefully calibrated Left public sphere and the state machinery. At this moment of internal turmoil, one could turn to those thinkers who did not quite fit the codes of the regime.

At this crucial historical turning point, Sobhanlal Datta Gupta refers to the 'ever-expanding Gramsciana' (Datta Gupta 1988, 1620) on which much of the present-day critique of capitalism thrives. Gramsci, as one of the earliest observers of the Bolshevik Revolution, terms it 'a revolution against Marx's Capital', a moment when 'events overcame ideology', also a moment that proves that 'the laws of historical materialism are not as set in stone, as one may think, or one may have thought previously' (Gramsci 1917). In the post-Cold War world gratuitously announcing the end of ideology, such pronouncements could serve a very different purpose—of providing an alternative interpretative framework to comprehend events that seemed to overwhelm ideology once again. Gramsci opens up possibilities of more contemporary and contextual engagement with Marxism. However, the altered geopolitical circumstances of re-engagement with Gramsci also run the risk of appropriating Gramsci, turning him into a revisionist figure, a caution articulated by Perry Anderson as early as 1977. Anderson discusses how the sole ascription of the term hegemony on Gramsci strategically conceals its long history within the workers' movement in Russia. In fact, 'the hegemony of the proletariat in the bourgeois revolution was a common inheritance for Bolsheviks and Mensheviks alike…', at some point espoused by Lenin himself but became redundant in the advent of a socialist revolution (Anderson 1977, 16–17). Anderson fears that this dehistoricisation of Gramscian terminology and the 'simple location of hegemony within civil society and the attribution of primacy to civil society over the State' (Anderson 1977, 26) would blunt the revolutionary edge of Marxist political discourse, trying to assimilate it within social democracy—a possibility that Datta Gupta too is acutely aware of: 'Gramsci … is an outsider who does not belong to the orbit of classical Marxism's universe…. The echoes of this interpretation are felt at once; Gramsci is stripped off his revolutionary potential and explosive possibilities and this has the transformatory effect of reducing Gramsci, the Communist, to Gramsci, the intellectual' (Datta Gupta 1988, 1620). In fact, Gramsci, the Communist and Gramsci, the intellectual are often pitted against each other.

Any 'authoritative' translation of Gramsci has to be aware of this appropriative atmosphere. The fact that out of the three translators of this series Samik Bandyopadhyay is from the background of literature, Sobhanlal Datta Gupta from political science and Sourin Bhattacharya is from philosophy indicates that the translation project is aware of the broader and interdisciplinary range of Gramsci's formulations. In any case, to a great extent, *Buddhijibi o Shiksha* is a translation of a translation as it treats the 1971 English translation of the *Prison Notebooks* by Quentin Hoare and Geoffrey Nowell Smith as its source text. Before that there was the 1957 translation by Louis Marks. Both the English translations were published before the complete critical edition of the *Prison Notebooks* became available in Italian in 1975 and are based on a preliminary edition containing the bulk of Gramsci's writings brought out in six volumes between 1948 and 1951 from Turin under the editorship of Felice Platone. Clearly then, the equivalence of meaning was going to remain a problem, though the three translators in Bengali did learn Italian and went back to the Italian original in case of any confusion in deciphering the meaning. Such confusions are already embedded in the fragmentary structure of the *Prison Notebooks*, written under conditions of strict censorship. Another, but related, problem is what Nowell Smith calls 'the uncertain status of the Notebooks in Gramsci's intentions' (Nowell Smith 1971, 15). Soon after his arrest by Mussolini's police, Gramsci, in a letter to his sister-in-law Tatiana, expresses his desire to write something 'forever', something that would 'give a focus to his inner life' (Nowell Smith 1971, 15). The conditions of his prison—Mussolini dictated that he be given all kinds of reading material except for any contemporary book, journal or newspaper—makes this 'forever' the only possible reader for him to address. For critics such as Anderson, these restrictions leave inevitable limitation in Gramsci's theory. But for translators/interpreters such as Samik Bandyopadhyay, it makes for an open-ended text from which 'forever' can draw its own sustenance. Bandyopadhyay writes in the Preface to his translation: 'We understood what Gramsci was writing amid all the restrictions of the prison was not meant for immediate publication, rather it was meant as draft to be written later, at a distance, with more assurance' (Bandyopadhyay 2014, translation mine).

Equipped with the vantage point of an assured distance, Bandyopadhyay contextualises Gramsci in the intellectual history of Italy and of continental Europe, on one end of which is the Italian classical age, and on the other the aestheticism of Benedetto Croce, a contemporary of Gramsci. In the process he also looks at the history of the intellectual across the world. But the theoretical legacy of the Soviet Union remains a significant oversight, considering that Gramsci did spend a year in post-Revolution Russia and came in direct contact with the Russian revolutionaries. Also, while discussing the concept of hegemony, Bandyopadhyay does not mention its evolution in the Comintern resolutions of the times (Anderson 1977, 17–18), especially since Gramsci participated in the Fourth World Congress held in 1922. Instead, he discusses how the Gramscian model can be used to understand the changing role of Black intellectuals vis-à-vis Black people in the US or intellectuals in Latin America. One wonders if this is an attempt to shift the goalpost of the revolution from a worldwide dictatorship of the proletariat to more localised, contingent political scenarios. This shift can also be seen in the context of the socio-political developments in India at that time with the beginning of economic liberalisation in 1991 and the Ram Janmabhumi movement showing the initial signs of a proto-Fascistic political force. The political significance of the intellectual needed to be reaffirmed but also redefined in the face of emerging realities that made people think over not only the means, but also the ends of the Revolution.

The intellectual has been translated in the text as '*buddhijibi*', a word which has widespread, if contested, currency in Bengali.[4] Samar Sen, in his discussion of Stephen Spender's 'Forward from Liberalism', published in *Parichay* in 1961 says that '"Forward From Liberalism" has been written mainly for the class between the capitalist and the labour. The *buddhijibi* belongs to this class' and the same 'reactionary class is the life force of Fascism' (Sen 2011, 110, translation mine). When Susobhan Sarkar proposes the term '*buddhibaadi*', or on a later date Amlan Dutta floats the term 'Chintak' (Bandyopadhyay 2014, 13), they try to assign certain benignity to the term as a classless entity. The suffix 'baadi' is associated with 'baad' meaning '-ism'. The 'buddhibadi' then is the one for whom intellect is a matter of ideals, not of profession. 'Chintak' would simply mean anyone who can think, again obscuring the specific class-identity of the intellectual. But the translators do not intend to obfuscate the class-location of the intellectual, which is why they stick to a term that locates the functions of intellect within the circuit of production.

However, the concept of 'class' itself is ambiguous as far as Gramsci is concerned. In order to avoid censorship even when Gramsci uses the term 'class' he never does so in its Marxist sense, instead using a range of terms open to interpretation. For example, Nowell Smith mentions that while listing various forms of the intellectual Gramsci uses the word '*ceti*' in Italian, which he has translated as 'strata' for

4 The suffix 'jibi' is linked to the word 'jibika' meaning profession. 'Buddhijibi' then is the one for whom intellect is a means of profession, directly locating her/him in class dynamics.

lack of alternatives. Sometimes, 'group' serves as a euphemism for class, but sometimes it does not: 'to avoid ambiguity Gramsci uses the phrase 'fundamental social group' while referring to one or the other major social classes (bourgeois, proletariat) defined in strict Marxist terms…' (Nowell Smith 1971, 134). Bandyopadhyay and Bhattacharya use '*goshthi*', '*sreni*' and '*bargo*' as roughly equivalent to 'group', 'class' and 'stratum' respectively.

Compared to the more generalised use of 'class' in the 1971 English translation, they use '*sreni*' in its more overtly Marxist meaning. For example, in one place, 'social group' has been translated as '*samajik gosthi*' but in the same passage 'one or more strata of intellectuals' is translated as '*buddhijibi srenir ek ba ekadhik bargo*' (Gramsci 2014, 25). Or even before that the sentence 'does every social group have its own particular specialized category of intellectuals' (Gramsci 1971, 134) has been translated as '*na ki pratyek samajik gosthir modhyei ache tar nijaswa buddhijibir bishista ek sreni?*' (Gramsci 2014, 25). Clearly then, the Bengali translators feel freer than their predecessors in the English version to use the word 'class'. Samik Bandyopadhyay claims in his Introduction that even though Gramsci could not use the term 'class', 'closer reading makes clear its actual signification' (Bandyopadhyay 2014, 15). In their frequent use of the Bengali version of 'class', that is 'sreni' with clear Marxist intonations, these translators are actually closer to the 1957 edition. With this conscious choice to apply an intentionality to Gramsci otherwise latent in his writings, the translators try to resist the critical reductionism that Gramsci may be subjected to; simultaneously they also want to unambiguously state the class character of the '*buddhijibi*'.

Another critically important but ambiguous term in the Italian text is '*dirigente*'. It may mean leadership; in that sense '*classe dirigente*' becomes the ruling class. However, in certain cases Nowell Smith says that he has translated it as 'directive' 'in order to preserve what for Gramsci is a crucial conceptual distinction, between power based on "domination" and the exercise of "direction" or hegemony' (Nowell Smith 1971, 19–20). In this later sense, the Bengali translators use '*agraganya*' (Gramsci 2014, 82), literally meaning forward, as if to position the term firmly vis-à-vis the subaltern.

In original Italian, Gramsci uses '*classi subalterne*' and '*classi subordinate*' interchangeably with '*classi strumentali*' keeping them open to interpretation (Hoare and Nowell Smith 1971, 166). In the next piece, '*Shiksha Prosonge*', that is, 'On Education', while discussing classical and vocational education the English translation reads 'the vocational school for the instrumental classes, the classical school for the dominant classes and intellectuals' (Gramsci 1971, 165–66). The Bengali translation uses '*adhastano sreni*' for 'instrumental classes' and '*pradhan sreni*' for 'dominant classes' (Gramsci 2014, 80). The use of the word 'adhastana' for 'subaltern' is interesting. By this time the subaltern history group had gained critical significance by using the Gramscian framework. Subaltern history as an academic discipline is almost unanimously translated as 'nimnabarger itihaas' and not as 'adhastana srenir itihaas'. 'Itihaas' is 'history'; 'sreni', as one has already clarified, is the word used for class whereas 'bargo' is simply 'social group'. Both 'nimno' and 'adhastan' mean 'subordinate' but while 'adhastana sreni' clearly identifies the subaltern as a class, the word 'nimnobargo' treats them as a social group. By giving primacy to '*sreni*' over '*bargo*' there is a clear attempt at distancing from the subaltern school, a difference reinforced by the use of Marxist terminology. Two other Gramscian terms made into extensive use by subaltern historiography are 'dominance' and 'hegemony', translated as '*pradhanya*' and '*adhipatya*' respectively. The translators clearly relate hegemony to '*adhikar*', that is, ownership, and by default to means of production, undercutting the revisionist claim that hegemony is located solely in the superstructure.

In *Buddhijibi o Shiksha* one finds two apparently contradictory strategies at work. On the one hand, the translators try to position

Gramsci at a critical distance from the institutionalised Marxist hagiography. On the other hand, there is an attempt to use a terminology that is unapologetically Marxist in order to reclaim his revolutionary legacy without its institutional baggage. One should not look at it as a purely linguistic recuperative measure. Ranabir Samaddar writes in an article in *The Statesman* on 29 January 1993 that,

> The New Right, with its "monolithic perception of Hindu power", is a response to the crisis of liberalization in a post-colonial society. Only a New Left can be the answer to the New Right. The official Left and the secularist stopped the clock on December 6, 1992. (Samaddar 2013, 41)

The nuanced and open texture of the Gramscian formulation, capable of retaining contradictions without compromising on radicalism, could provide an alternative template for the New Left. The '*buddhijibi*' of post-liberalisation Bengal, shakily positioned over the haloed terrain of the so-called Bengal Renaissance, the much mythologised legacy of radical politics, and the dystopia of industrial decline trying to cover the fractures of her quotidian life did need to recognise the precariousness of her position in order to recalibrate her public function as intellectual.

References

Anderson, Perry, 'The Antinomies of Antonio Gramsci', *New Left Review*, No. 100, November 1976–January 1977, pp. 5–78.

Bandyopadhyay, Samik, 'Preface', 'Mukhobandhyo' and 'Buddhijibi Sreni', in *Antonio Gramsci: Buddhijibi o Shiksha* (1991), Kolkata, Anushtup, 2014, pp. 13–24.

Bhattacharya, Sourin, *Pathaker Garaj*, Kolkata, Anushtup, 2005.

———, '*Marxbaadi Bangali: Nirbachita Rachana Sankalan 1*', edited by Sourin Bhattacharya, Kolkata, Talpata, 2011, pp. 5–26.

Buttigieg, Joseph A., 'Philology and Politics: Returning to the Text of Antonio Gramsci's *Prison Notebooks*', *Boundary 2*, Vol. 21, No. 2, Summer, 1994, pp. 98–138. Available at: http://www.jstor.org/stable/303191 (accessed 1 March 2018).

Datta Gupta, Sobhanlal, 'Understanding Gramsci: Some Exploratory Observations', *Economic and Political Weekly*, Vol. 23, No. 32, 6 August 1988, pp. 1620–22.

Gramsci, Antonio, *Selections from the Prison Notebooks*, edited and translated by Quintin Hoare and Geoffrey Nowell Smith, London, Lawrence and Wishart, 1971.

———, *Buddhijibi o Shiksha* (1991), edited and translated by Samik Bandyopadhyay and Sourin Bhattacharya, Kolkata, Anushtup, 2014.

———, 'The Revolution Against *Capital*' (1917). Available at: https://www.marxists.org/archive/gramsci/1917/12/revolution-against-capital.htm (accessed 20 April 2018).

Kaviraj, Sudipta, 'Marxism in Translation: Critical Reflections on Indian Political Thought', in *Political Judgment: Essays in Honour of John Dunn*, edited by Reymond Geuss and Richard Bourke, Cambridge, Cambridge University Press, 2009, pp. 172–200.

Nigam, Aditya, 'Reflections on Sudipta Kaviraj's "Marxism in Translation"', 2 March 2011. Available at: https://criticalencounters.net/2011/03/02/reflections-on-sudipta-kaviraj-marxism/ (accessed 20 April 2018).

Nowell Smith, Geoffrey, 'Preface', *Selections from the Prison Notebooks*, London, Lawrence and Wishart, 1971.

Samaddar, Ranabir, *Passive Revolution in West Bengal 1977–2011*, New Delhi: Sage Publications, 2013.

Sen, Samar, '*Udarneetibaad Prasange*', in *Marxbaadi Bangali: Nirbachita Rachana Sankalan 1*, edited by Sourin Bhattacharya, Kolkata, Talpata, 2011, pp. 109–15.

Shaikh, Juned, 'Translating Marx: Mavali, Dalit and the Making of Mumbai's Working Class 1928–1935', *Economic and Political Weekly*, Vol. 46, No. 31, 30 July–5 August 2011, pp. 65–73.

14

India through a Translation Anthology: An Evolving Perspective

Runjhun Verma

In her essay 'India Mirrored in Contemporary French Writings', Radha Sharma states:

> From exotic myth to sordid tale, from the sublime to the squalid, from paradise to festering canker, the range of avatars that India seems capable of assuming is seemingly elastic enough, seemingly ambivalent enough to accommodate an entire range of contradictory representations. (Sharma 2009, 56)

India has been written about and cast in many shapes, images and shades in different kinds of French writings such as memoirs, travelogues, poems, novels, stories, articles and, of course, translations. Translations have always served as bridges between two cultures by discovering and linking them.

The literary exchanges between India and France date back to ancient times. However, the colonial conquest by the European countries, France in this case, marked a different approach to these exchanges. The rediscovery of India through the translation of certain ancient works into European languages created a rather biased image of India. In the late eighteenth century, when the translation of Indian works into European languages began, the *Bhagavada Gita* was one of the first works to be translated into French via English.[1]

1 *Bhagavada Gita* translated from English (Charles Wilkins) into French by Foucher d'Obsonville as mentioned by Castaing (2005, 316).

Soon followed other Sanskrit classics like *Bagavadam* translated from Tamil into French as *Doctrine divine, Ouvrage indien, canonique; Sur l'Être suprême, les dieux, les géants, les hommes, les diverses parties de l'Univers* (Divine Doctrine, Indian Canonical Work; On the Supreme Being, the Gods, the Giants, the Men and the Universe). The choice of certain works, writers, themes and genres played a huge role in creating India for the French reader. The idea which motivated these images was to reinforce the oriental imagery associated with India and to justify colonialism. The choice of works to be translated from ancient languages such as Sanskrit and Tamil and that of religious works led to the imagination of India as a land of great wisdom but also that of poverty and chaos.

According to Pierre Bourdieu, the French sociologist, all international exchanges are creators and transporters of misunderstandings (Bourdieu 2002, 3). It is interesting to observe that the choice of ancient languages and religious works for translation continued well into the twentieth century and even after India's independence from the British colonisation. If the works translated from Indian languages in the 1950s are to be taken into account, almost all the works translated from various languages into French were either classics or religious in nature including the ones published by UNESCO and, barring a few exceptions, such as works of some of the contemporary authors from a few selected languages.[2] These works reflect a certain choice of authors, languages, texts and themes which were instrumental in constructing an image of India which was still reminiscent of its past glory, divinity and spirituality as N. Kamala remarks in her article on translating India:

2 The other works non-religious in nature were the works of Premchand in Hindi, Bankim Chandra Chatterji, Sharat Chandra Chatterji and Rabindranath Tagore in Bengali, who was already widely read among the Europeans (Connaissance de l'orient, collections UNESCO d'œuvres représentatives, Gallimard). Cf. Anne Castaing (2005). Also cf. UNESCO, available at: unesdoc.unesco.org/images/0014/001414/141456eb

> If patronage is to be considered as a factor which exerts influence on the literary outlook of a country, then it can be said without hesitation that UNESCO has created the image of an India which is mystical, religious and essentially rich in ancient literature. (Kamala 2014, 113)

As mentioned earlier, patronage is one among the many factors that determine the global literary exchanges today. Pascale Casanova explains that translation is no longer considered as a simple and horizontal linguistic transfer as it does not concern itself just with textual distortions and differences in two languages. On the contrary, given the hierarchies and inequalities that operate in the global market, literary translation can only be seen as a disproportionate activity (Casanova 2002, 7). It is in this view of translation as a sociological object and a study of cultures that we aim to study the construction of the image of India through a translation anthology *Littératures de l'Inde* published as an edition of the literary journal *Europe* in the year 2001.

The cultural turn in the Translation Studies in the 1980s laid emphasis on studying the source culture(s) and asserting the identity of the translated culture. A literary translation was earlier said to serve as a bridge to link diverse cultures. Now, with the cultural turn in Translation Studies, questions were raised about such bridges, their interpretation by the translators and the purpose they served. Translations were seen as conscious efforts to study the differences between cultures and to shape the political and cultural identities of people around the globe. The arrival of the postcolonial writing/approach on the international translation scene registered postcolonial translation as an enabling category identified with self-assertion, registering resistance and negotiating strategies of representation (Guttal and Mathur 2013, ix). It highlighted the unequal power equations between the cultures and how these affect translation.

On the one hand, there were texts increasingly talking about 'post-colony' (Guttal and Mathur 2013, ix) without glossing and/or stereotyping it, and on the other, these 'post-colonies' were consciously (re)presented to foreign readers not only by translators but also by editors, patrons and other agents of translation. The translated text now reflected the viewpoint of translators and agents of translation along with that of the author.

The politics of translation which facilitates the making of the finished product raises a pertinent question in the choice of translation of Indian literary works into French in terms of languages, genres, themes, authors and works chosen to be translated. Among various works translated into French from India, the number of Sanskrit classics tops the list followed by Bengali, Hindi, Tamil and now Indian English.[3] First, what are the criteria for choosing works to be translated from (a) certain language(s)? Second, how many works are chosen/have been chosen from (a) particular language(s)? How does this impact the image of multilingual India to a foreign reader?

Within India, translations serve two main purposes; first is nation-building by enriching various languages and strengthening them and second is that of connecting people from different parts of the country and establishing a common identity for a foreign reader. It is seen that in order to accomplish this objective of establishing a collective national identity, translation becomes an indispensable and often a manipulative tool when it homogenises the regional differences to make it 'Indian' and the politics of translation comes into play in the

3 Among the works translated various Indian languages into French, Sanskrit seemed to be the premier choice as a lot of classics and religious texts were translated during the colonial times. This trend was repeated with several Bengali works figuring among translations into French partly because of Tagore's wide recognition. In the later years, works from Hindi were translated, mostly classics like works of Premchand, Jay Shankar Prasad and the likes. Indian English now seems to have taken over with a lot of works being translated of writers of Indian origin living abroad. Cf. N. Kamala (2014, 111–24).

choice of authors, texts, languages and the time period of the works chosen along with the translators. What captures our attention is the purpose translation serves in an international context for the foreign reader. Does it just reflect and (re)present Indian culture and society? If yes, then how do the translated texts put across the 'Indian' for a foreign reader? Or do translators construct the 'Indian' in the texts by putting together the diverse literatures of India?

Against this background, the central question that motivates our study is the emergence of postcolonial translation that constructs or has slowly constructed India's image for a Western audience, in this case French. The translated texts reflect certain choices such as the choice of language from the Indian subcontinent, the choice of authors, works and of the presentation of India which become even more evident when several translated works are compiled together in an anthology. Collections of Indian works translated in French such as *Indiennes*, *Rudali et autres nouvelles* and *Anthologie de la poésie bengalie* (Devi 2004; Mukherjee 1991) are examples of a compilation of a particular genre often elaborating works by one author and one language respectively. The selection and ordering principles of the content in an anthology play an important role in constructing a certain image of the culture(s)/literature(s) represented. Whereas the monolingual anthologies (can) represent a partial image of the nation through a deliberate choice of texts and authors, the multilingual anthologies come up with more diverse and varied aspects of India as a nation where the multiple identities created by literatures from different Indian languages are juxtaposed. In such works, translation constructs a certain identity instead of just representing it.

The conscious choice of works, authors and genres for translation and compilation in an anthology reveals a certain objective/principle to establish literary reputations and a national culture more visible than in isolated translated works. It is at this juncture that the politics of translation plays a powerful role in the kind of texts that are chosen to represent a culture/nation/country. The politics of translation is largely defined by the flow of cultural traffic and market needs. The presentation of an anthology in terms of the number of pages, content and languages chosen is not a natural given (Lefevere 1992, 124).

Against this background, this chapter wishes to explore the anthology *Littératures de l'Inde* published in the year 2001. In order to do so, I would start by looking at the paratextual elements of the collection which establish the first contact of the readers with the text. I will then move on to the languages represented in this anthology and consequently, to the writers and themes presented. The last section of this chapter would deal with the role of the agents of translation in the construction of a translation anthology.

Littératures de l'Inde

Generally, the anthologies of translation of Indian literary works consist of works or texts from a single genre.[4] *Littératures de l'Inde* is an exceptional case as it presents short stories as well as poems. Published in 2001 as an edition of the journal *Europe*, it is an anthology which is prospective as well as retrospective;[5] certain poets have been presented to the French readers for the first time whereas others have been published before in different anthologies and individual works.

The journal *Europe* publishes in general literary works from across the world, concentrating in particular on the peripheral and lesser-known literatures. It has already published editions on South East Asian literatures including works from Thailand, Laos, Burma and Cambodia. The relation between this journal and India goes a long

4 *Les nouvelles contemporaines* publiée en 1985, *Littératures de l'Inde, Anthologie de nouvelles contemporaines* published in 1987 and *Anthologie de la poésie bengalie* are some of the generic anthologies.

5 Armin Paul Frank and Helga Essmann (1990) establish the difference between different types of anthologies: retrospective, introductive, generic, thematic and chronological in their article (Harshvardhan 1999, 74).

way to 1923 when Romain Rolland published serially an essay on Gandhi. It has since then published an edition on *Literatures of India* in 1981 and then in 2001. Jean-Baptiste Para, the editor of this last edition on India, states that the *Literatures of India* published in 2001 is twice more important than the one published in 1981 in terms of number of pages, number of translated authors and much more in terms of the languages translated and represented. And this is why we shall be concentrating on this latest edition of the journal published in 2001.

Image 14.1: *'A Muslin Ghagra', Cover Page of the Journal.*

Courtesy: Photo by Samar Singh Jodha, Jaipur City Palace Museum, Europe, 2001.

The editor Jean-Baptiste Para describes India as a modern country; nonetheless, it is India's past with its rich literary traditions that has been glorified in the Introduction. The theme of modernity has been treated sceptically. For example, the cover of the book evokes the colonial past of India by choosing a photo (Image 14.1) of the nineteenth-century gold embroidered *ghagra* displayed at the Jaipur city museum. The anthology further has four photos placed every 100 pages approximately. The first photo depicts the bank of a river in Thanjavur whereas the second photo presents a crowded street in Delhi with a Hindi film poster in the background. The third photo is from a village courtyard with a woman sitting with her head covered as is the tradition in the villages. The last photo is a silhouette of two women walking somewhere. None of the photos have been dated except one which has been taken in 1989 but they all seem to be from the recent past and they create an impression of the Other; the antithesis of the West. The image of contemporary India has been presented in contrast to that of its grand past.

Para's introductory lines to present India in the journal *Europe: Littératures de l'Inde* published at the beginning of this century, in 2001, are an admission that,

> India fascinates as well as confuses a western traveler. It shakes our beliefs, troubles our thoughts, swinging us between astonishment and awe, joy and uneasiness, enthusiasm and dizziness. (Para 2001, 3)

Para justifies the above-mentioned introductory phrases by presenting India that is old and new and rich and poor at the same time. The idea seems to be to establish the then socio-political and socio-economic situation in order to help the reader situate the context of the works presented in the collection. In the second part of the Introduction, the readers are introduced to the ancient and medieval literary traditions of the country. Para makes an effort to choose a few well-known poets from across the Indian languages and present some excerpts of their works: Lal Ded, Kabir, Tukaram, Tiruvalluvar and Sarvajna. The last part of the Introduction concentrates on the two centuries of British colonisation and the development of modern Indian literature. It is at this juncture that the editor clarifies the objective of the present collection, which is to fill in the void in the publishing of works from different Indian languages into French that occurred post Tagore's work and the overwhelming presence of Indian English literary works post the 1980s.

The collection presents a microcosm of the literatures of India. The usage of the term 'literatures' in the plural indicates the diversity of the languages and cultures that exist in this country. The editor highlights the presence of more than 1,600 languages and dialects that exist in India with the help of a linguistic map of India to situate the languages geographically. Works from all the 18 official languages at the time have been included in this anthology. It presents more than 50 authors/poets from 18 Indian languages from Kashmir to Kanyakumari and from Gujarat to Manipur which covers most of literary India. However, there is one language from the Tibeto-Burman language in the book, that is, Manipuri, and no language from the Austro-Asiatic family of languages.

The book contains 16 stories by Indian authors and more than 60 odd poems presented over 100 pages. The stories have been taken from Malayalam, Odia, Bengali, Urdu, Hindi, Tamil, Kannada, Punjabi, Marathi, Konkani and Manipuri respectively, whereas we do not find stories in Indian English. The editor explains this omission by saying that the stories or literary works in general are published in abundance in the international literary market and it is the works in regional languages or other Indian languages that the readers ought to know better. Nonetheless, he has included quite a few poems from Indian English poets citing their minimal presence as a genre. The poems have been taken from Telugu, Hindi, Kashmiri,

Punjabi, English, Sindhi, Bengali, Malayalam, Assamese, Gujarati, Dogri and Marathi respectively. It is to be noted that more poems have been chosen from a more varied group of languages than in the case of short stories. This, of course, underlines the space accorded to a particular language/author or a work of fiction. The works have been presented in a chronological order according to the date of birth of authors/poets; the hegemony of certain languages over others is evident. It is not a question of place given to a certain language but to the number of works chosen from it. As seen in Table 14.1, Hindi remains in a position of power with the maximum number of stories and there are no stories from Bengali.

Table 14.1: *Stories translated per language.*

Languages Represented		Number of Stories Translated
i.	Malayalam	2
ii.	Odia	2
iii.	Bengali	1
iv.	Urdu	1
v.	Hindi	3
vi.	Tamil	2
vii.	Kannada	1
viii.	Punjabi	1
ix.	Marathi	1
x.	Konkani	1
xi.	Manipuri	1

In the case of poems (Table 14.2), there are more than 60 poems translated from different languages. The difference as explained by the editor is: 'We have accorded all the privilege to the poets as compared to novelists as they are seldom translated and do not enjoy a stupendous recognition on the international literary scene'.[6]

6 Para, Jean-Baptiste, Email Interview, 17 February 2017.

Table 14.2: *Poems translated per language.*

Languages Represented		Number of Poems Translated*
i.	Dogri	1
ii.	Kashmiri	1
iii.	Punjabi	2 poems of the same poet.
iv.	Telugu	9 poems overall. Many poems of the same poet sometimes.
v.	Gujarati	3
vi.	English	9 poems overall. Many poems of the same poet sometimes.
vii.	Sindhi	1
viii.	Bengali	10 poems overall. Many poems of the same poet sometimes.
ix.	Hindi	19 poems overall. Many poems of the same poet sometimes.
x.	Malayalam	5 poems of the same poet.
xi.	Assamese	2 poems of the same poet.
xii.	Marathi	5 poems overall. Many poems of the same poet sometimes.

* The data include the poems published by the same poets.

Among the 12 languages represented, Hindi poems occupy the first position followed by English and Telugu. So, instead of including more poets from one language, the hierarchy has been imposed by more poems from one language and often by same poets such as three poems by Amrita Pritam in Punjabi, three poems by Nissim Ezekiel in English, Lokenath Bhattacharya in Bengali and Raghuvir Sahay in Hindi.

In the postface of the collection, the editor states that apart from two of the works; the short story in Malayalam by O.V. Vijayan and one of the poems by A.K. Ramanujan, all the others have never been published in French before. The double hegemony comes into play when the choice of writers and the space they have been assigned are taken into account. Writers such as Nirmal Verma, Krishna Baldev Vaid and Lokenath Bhattacharya are already well known in France and they find their positions reinforced by an increased number of their works in translation as well as the publication of their interviews.

The choice of authors/poets depends on their status in the given language as well at the national level. All the writers chosen here have been recipients of literary awards such as the one given by the Sahitya Akademi and other such government bodies. It is also evident that canonical works are chosen to be translated. The anthologies of translation create in effect new literary canons in their attempt to preserve one.

According to the editor, India is a country of contrasts where one half of the population does not get enough to eat and the other half goes to slimming centres. The works chosen for this collection weave India as a modern country with all the challenges that it faces. It clearly seems to be a departure from the earlier multilingual anthologies published in French which stressed on the spiritual nature of the country and glorified its rich ancient past. The stories and the poems presented in this collection deal with a range of themes: from the common mundane life of urban middle class to the prevalent socio-political and socio-economical issues such as Dalit identities and tribal and women rights. Given the fact that *Europe* published an issue on Literatures of India in 1981, it is only in this issue twenty years later that we see the works of the poets Namdeo Dhasal and Jyoti Lajewar. Dhasal's poems were first published in the 1970s and the Dalit movement had gained a considerable momentum by the end of that decade. However, stories and poems dealing with such issues started coming to the fore much later.

In an anthology of translated works, sometimes an extract takes the place of the text and that of the work as well as that of the whole literature itself. In fact, most of the time, this extract becomes the only point of contact between the readers and that particular literature/culture (Everett and Marcotte 2010, 11). Taking this into account, the role of the agents of translation becomes pertinent in the construction of an image of a given culture. The international exchanges are facilitated by a group/network of people and institutions which influence implicitly or explicitly the final product. In this case, it becomes important to observe that the journal *Europe* becomes an agent of translation as it publishes the lesser known literatures from across the world into French. The editor then assumes a significant task to choose the works and the authors and hence create or present his image of the country/culture/literature to the readers. Jean-Baptiste Para is a writer and a translator who has a significant amount of works to his name. For the publication of this collection, Para made it a point to do a thorough background research on literatures of India. His major source was the Sahitya Akademi in New Delhi where he systematically consulted the journal *Indian Literature* published by the academy. So, the vision of a government body of India was imprinted on the choice of works for this collection. He also got in touch with the network of Alliance Française in India to verify the works he had chosen. It is here that he found the translators for these works which shows that the people he chose had first-hand experience of cultures of India. Translations have been done in a team of two people; an expert of the Indian language and an expert of the French language except for a few languages like Odia and Malayalam which have been translated through a filter language, English. The translators play a very important role in the reception of a text in the target culture. Translations done in a Franco-Indian team reflects that the editor of the anthology has made efforts to study both the cultures.

Since the first true contact between India and France during the colonial era, the image of India has definitely evolved for the French readers. It does not symbolise anymore a spiritual country with a glorious past but its image is one of the modern thriving country that has its own challenges and beauty. Having said this, the nostalgia of the colonial past still forms the background of most of the literary translations from India into any European language, French in this case. Translations have had an indispensable role in the construction of the image of India through many centuries and it has mediated this image through the choice of languages, genres, themes, writers and even that of a translator.

Published in the 1980s for the first time in India, the anthologies of translation have presented a new perspective in the representation of plurality of the country. The multitude of works, of languages, of writers and so forth has helped in creating a multilingual and multicultural character of the country in the target language. Translation in such anthologies has become an act of rewriting and reconstruction of many Indian identities. It is in this light that the *Litteratures de l'Inde* presents a comprehensive image of the country.

It presents 85 literary works—short stories and poems in 18 different Indian languages. The languages like Manipuri, Sindhi and Dogri have been included for the first time and presented to the French reader. We find, nonetheless, that a lot of other dialects and languages have been left out. Having said this, the peripheral languages like Dogri, Sindhi and Manipuri remain at the periphery even in the target culture in terms of the space accorded to them. In this anthology, the languages of power like Bengali, Hindi, and Indian English have retained their positions in the target culture as well.

The multilingual anthologies present a varied and diverse image of the country, but the politics of translation might create or recreates the hierarchies and hegemonies of certain writers/languages among other factors even for the target language readers. The presentation of the anthology therefore creates/asserts and reaffirms the image of a country as Teresa Seruya says while comparing anthologies to museums,

> Anthologies and collections can do for texts what museums do for artefacts and objects serve and considered of cultural importance:

preserve and exhibit them, by selecting and arranging the exhibits, project an interpretation of a given field, make relations and values visible, maybe educate taste. (Seruya, D'hulst, Rosa and Moniz, 2013, 1)

References

Armin, Paul Frank and Helga Essmann, 'Translation Anthologies: A Paradigmatic Medium of International Literary Transfer', *American Studies (Amst.)*, Vol. 35, No. 1, 1990, pp. 21–34.

Bourdieu, Pierre. 'Les conditions sociales de la circulation internationale des idées'. *Actes de la recherche en sciences sociales*, Vol. 5, No. 145, December 2002, pp. 3–8.

Casanova, Pascale, 'Consécration et accumulation de capital littéraire. La traduction comme échange inégal'. *Actes de la recherche en sciences sociales*, Vol. 144, Traductions: les échanges littéraires internationaux, September, 2002, pp. 7–20.

Castaing, Anne, ed. *Ragmala. Les Littératures en langues indiennes traduites en français, Anthologie*, Paris, Langues & Mondes-L'Asiathèque, 2005.

Devi, Mahasweta, *Indiennes: Rudali et autres nouvelles*, Arles, Actes Sud, 2004.

Everett, Jane and Sophie Marcotte, 'De l'anthologie', *Voix et Images*, Vol. 35, No. 2, 2010, pp. 7–15.

Guttal, Vijaya and Suchitra Mathur, eds. *Translation and Postcolonialities, Transactions across Languages and Cultures*, Hyderabad, Orient Blackswan, 2013.

Harshvardhan, Chitra, 'Bridging Differences? Translation Anthologies: Constructing the Other', in *Encountering the Indian, Contemporary European Images of India*, edited by Vibha Maurya, New Delhi, Aryan Books International, 1999, pp. 74–92.

Kamala, N., 'Traduire l'Inde: Texte, contexte, image', *Rencontre avec l'Inde*, Vol. 43, No. 1, 2014, pp. 111–24.

Lefevere, André, *Translation, Rewriting and the Manipulation of Literary Fame*, London and New York, Routledge, 1992.

Maurya, Vijaya, ed. *Encountering the Indian, Contemporary European Images of India*, New Delhi, Aryan Books International, 1999.

Mukherjee, Prithwindra, *Anthologie de la poésie bengalie*, Paris, Noël Blandin, 1991.

Para, Jean-Baptiste, ed. *Littératures de l'Inde*, Paris, Europe, revue littéraire mensuelle, 2001.

Seruya, Teresa, Lieven D'hulst, Alexandra Assis Rosa and Maria Lin Moniz, eds, *Translation in Anthologies and Collections, 19th and 20th Centuries*, Amsterdam/Philadelphia, John Benjamins Publishing Company, 2013.

Sharma, Radha, 'India Mirrored in Contemporary French Writings', in *Encountering the Indian. Contemporary European Images of India*, edited by Vibha Maurya, Delhi, Aryan Books International, 2009, pp. 56–73.

Von, Herausgegeben and Harald Kittel, eds. *International Anthologies of Literature in Translation*, Berlin, Erich Schmidt Verlag, 1995.

15

*Translating Beckett into Indian Language/s: Towards World-building**

Samudranil Gupta

Samuel Beckett and Self-translation

Samuel Beckett did not write in one language. While on the one hand, it can be argued that Beckett felt least at home in any language that he spoke or wrote in, on the other hand, his fluency in English, French and German—the three languages that he extensively wrote in—not only contradicts the former hypothesis but also reveals a paradox that plays a vital role in determining the Beckettian principle: 'that there is nothing to express, nothing with which to express ... together with the obligation to express' (Beckett 1984, 139). This paradox of expressing that which cannot be expressed or expressing at the limit of expression lies at the heart of Beckettian philosophy and hence this paradox also plays out at the level of Beckett's use of various languages. According to Beckett, to use language at its best is to put it in misuse or abuse.[1] Throughout his lifetime as a writer, Beckett seemed to have left no

* Acknowledgements: I would like to express my affectionate gratitude to Malay Bera, who is pursuing an M.A. in Linguistics at Jawaharlal Nehru University, New Delhi, for helping me to understand various linguistic terms and concepts that have been referred to in this chapter. Any mistake is mine.

1 See Beckett's letter to Axel Kaun, 9 July 1937, edited by Fehsenfeld and Overbeck, 2011, pp. 512–20. The letter, originally written in German was earlier collected in *Disjecta*, an anthology of miscellaneous writings by Beckett edited by Ruby Cohn along with Martin Esslin's translation from German to English.

stone unturned to 'drill one hole after another' into language in order to dissolve the 'arbitrary materiality of the word'. In his famous 1937 letter to Axel Kaun, he had already anticipated a method of creating what he conceptualised as 'literature of the unword'[2]—and it can be argued that self-translation was one of the many ways that led towards putting language into perpetual uncertainty.

Samuel Beckett confirmed that he wrote in English up until 1945.[3] The poem 'Whoroscope' was published in 1930, an essay on Proust was published in 1931, *More Pricks than Kicks* in 1934, *Echo's Bones & Other Precipitates* in 1935, *Murphy* was published in 1938, and *Watt* was written in between 1942 and 1945 and was eventually published in 1953.[4] It was after this that he turned to French and began writing *En attendant Godot* in 1948, and finished composing the play in January 1949. In this context, Ruby Cohn notes,

> Once the war was over, re-established in a Paris that had lost Joyce and many of his entourage, Beckett shifted from his native English to French for fiction and drama. At the same time he began his series of unprecedented self-translations which are unique in the history of literature. (1961, 613)

For instance, as Cohn further reminds us, he will soon begin to translate Murphy into French, and then many other texts back into English.

We should not overlook the fact that Beckett while translating his own writing was not translating a foreign text into what can be called 'his' language since Beckett never probably had any language that

2 While in the latest translation edited by Fehsenfeld and Overbeck, 'Literatur des Unwort' is translated as 'literature of the non-word', I have taken the liberty of retaining Esslin's translation of the phrase as 'literature of the unword' since the word 'unword' comes closer to the Beckettian idea of undoing language. However, any other reference to this letter has followed the latest translation edited by Fehsenfeld and Overbeck.

3 See Beckett's letter to Hans Naumann, 17 February 1954 in Beckett (2011), pp. 460–66.

4 Beckett (2011).

he could, in a very Derridean vein,[5] have called his own. Although he said at one point that English indeed was his language, he openly announced his disdain for the language—and for that matter, disdain for language in general. That could possibly be one of the more crucial reasons why he was writing and continuously translating his own texts into another language—either from English to French or vice versa in order to corrupt or disrupt language itself as James McGuire has very aptly suggested.[6] Therefore, as a self-translator, Beckett, I would like to think, was not trying to domesticate the text—which, according to Lawrence Venuti, can happen in case of any translation, as he states in one of his essays called 'Translation, Community, Utopia' that,

> Translation never communicates in an untroubled fashion because the translator negotiates the linguistic and cultural differences of the foreign text by reducing them and supplying another set of differences, basically domestic, drawn from the receiving language and culture to enable the foreign to be received there. (2004, 468)

However, in the case of Beckett, it was exactly the opposite because by writing in and translating his own works into different languages, and oftentimes with persistent anxiety despite his eloquence, Beckett was (*a*) trying to escape writing in English, a language which he found increasingly difficult to write in, and (*b*) trying to occupy an unfamiliarity in relation to language so that he could reveal the precarious, unhomely nature of language itself.

We can look at one of his letters in this connection that he wrote to Hans Naumann, who was a translator and editor of French and Irish Literature, in response to what Naumann asked Beckett. In his letter, Naumann wrote to Beckett,

> Given the impossibility of launching an Irish-language work beyond the borders of that small country, you find yourself forced to choose

5 Derrida's famous statement (1998) 'Yes, I only have one language, yet it is not mine', p. 2.

6 James McGuire (1990, pp. 258–63).

> a foreign language: either French or English; you choose French. But there must all the same be a deeper reason. Do you think that French culture is a more adequate base for your work? (Beckett 2011, 466)

In his reply on 17 February 1954, Beckett said:

> Since 1945 I have written only in French. Why this change? It was not deliberate. It was in order to change, to see, nothing more complicated than that, in appearance at least. In any case nothing to do with the reasons you suggest. I do not consider English a foreign language, it is my language. If there is one that is really foreign to me, it is Gaelic. You may put me in the dismal category of those who, if they had to act in full awareness of what they were doing, would never act. Which does not preclude there being urgent reasons, for this change. I myself can half make out several, now that it is too late to go back. But I prefer to let them stay in the half-light. I will all the same give you one clue: the need to be ill equipped. (Beckett 2011, 464)

It is interesting to observe how Beckett uses the phrase '*mal armé*' in the letter, originally written in French, which is translated as 'ill equipped' by the latest translators of Beckett's letters. As Thirthankar Chakraborty (2017) has pointed out that the intelligent pun not only invokes the name of the French poet Mallarmé but also the idea that literary writing is only possible when one is ill-equipped to use a language. The ill-equipped-ness may occur only when one claims the unfamiliarity in relation to language that further facilitates putting language into misuse, abuse and eventually leaving it undone.

Unfortunately, therefore, one who might not know either French or German cannot read Beckett's self-translations in order to compare the exclusions and inclusions that are carried out in the process of writing and rewriting. In this context, we can turn to Ruby Cohn's comment on the French translation of *Murphy*:

> Most of the changes that Beckett incorporates into the French translation of *Murphy*—incorporations, deletions, and bare-faced emendations—serve to heighten its comic tone. Although the English *Murphy* is already a funny novel, there are more additions than deletions, the latter being restricted to extraneous, non-comic

> detail and to word-play for which Beckett was evidently unable to find a satisfactory equivalent. (Cohn 1961, 614)

Hence, as it is evident from Cohn's reading, for a multilingual or bilingual reader these translations should serve as parallel texts. Thus, we can argue that it is impossible to read Beckett in his entirety without having consulted and read the translations since these translations should be considered as re-creation of the same text, rewritten in a different language, with changes and improvisations rather than multiple mimetic reproductions of the same in different languages.

Possibilities of Translating Beckett into Indian Languages

The problems of translation include difficulties in retaining various characteristics of the source language in the receiving language or the target language—like dialect, cultural specificities and traditional conventions. These problems vary from one language to another in relation to the target language into which the text is being translated. For instance, translation taking place in between two adjacent linguistic communities is relatively easier than when the target language and the source language belong to different linguistic territory without any prior cultural communication or similarity. In light of this argument, we can posit that translating English into major Indian languages is comparatively easier than translating many other European languages. This is due to the obvious fact that the British ruled over India for nearly two hundred years and it was during the colonial era that our language not only adopted various English expressions but also was redefined by the standards of British culture, and we must remember here that these cultural interchanges were mutual. Moreover, English (along with Hindi) has till date remained the official language of administration in India and therefore access to the English language is made more available through education since the colonial time. Today, English is barely considered a foreign tongue within the Indian subcontinent, at least by those who have access to education. On the other hand, it can also be argued that various English terms have permeated so intricately into the linguistic framework of our day to day discourse—for instance, as loan words, or use of acronymy, abbreviation and so forth—that a native speaker does not require any formal education or training in English to use these terms.

It is within this context that I would like to think about the possibilities of translating a writer like Samuel Beckett into Indian languages, a writer who openly declared his lack of enthusiasm at writing in English—a language that he apparently called his own—but continued writing in at least two other European languages, primarily in French, despite feeling, what he called, ill-equipped. Therefore, translating Beckett into Indian languages is difficult precisely because he did not write merely in English but repeatedly in French and German, often, as pointed out already, rewriting the same text twice through self-translation. As discussed earlier, it is impossible to grasp the entire Beckettian oeuvre without reading and comparing the existing versions of the texts in at least two different languages in which it was translated by Beckett. Therefore, an adequate translation into Indian languages (or in that case any other language) can take place only if the text that shall be subject to translation is brought together along with other existing versions of the text in a different language, under close and comparative linguistic analysis.

On the other hand, in order to maintain the uncertainty and the precariousness of language that Beckett attempted to disclose in his works—through continuously shifting from one language to the other—the method of translation concerned might consider involving various Indian languages, which belong to at least five language families (Indo-Aryan, Dravidian, Tibeto-Burman, Austro-Asiatic, Andamanese) that are arguably in absolute unfamiliarity (in terms of morphology and syntax) with one another. Hypothetically speaking, if we consider constructing a text with languages belonging to these different families brought together, in a discorded-togetherness with regard to morphological and syntactical familiarity, what results in the end is an impossibility of creating any coherent linguistic structure. In other words, we end up destroying language. In the famous letter that Beckett wrote to Axel Kaun in 1937, where he conceptualised, as mentioned earlier, what he called literature of the 'unword', Beckett exactly anticipated this eventual disruption and dissolution of language: 'To drill one hole after another into it until that which lurks behind, be it something or nothing, starts seeping through…' (Beckett 2009, 518). Thus, we can argue that translating Beckett into Indian languages, despite the apparent difficulty, can actually get him even closer to put language into disrepute and abuse.

Avikunthak's Translation of Beckett's 'Come and Go'

I shall now like to turn to Ashish Avikunthak's adaptation of Beckett's 'Come and Go' into a Hindi film called *Antaral/Endnote* (2005) as textual evidence to back my argument. While I am not willing to discuss at length the various subversions present in Avikunthak's film that are peculiar to any adaptation, my purpose is to mainly focus on how Avinkunthak's script, which is a very interesting and close translation of the original text into two Indian languages—Hindi and Bengali—brought together, retains not only the Beckettian intention of unsettling the structure of language and its expressivity but also, as I intend to argue in the end, its ethical relevance.[7]

Avikunthak has translated 'Come and Go' as *Antaral/Endnote* primarily in Hindi with occasional splattering of Bengali gibberish

7 For a detailed analysis of Avikunthak's adaptation, see Arka Chattopadhyay's essay on the film, 'Exhausting the inexhaustible: Reading the structure of Samuel Beckett's *Come and Go* through Ashish Avikunthak's *Endnote*' (2016).

rhymes and song. This translation stays very close to the original text which was actually written in English in 1965. Beckett's play also has an interesting history of publication and production—revealing the winding trajectory of translation it went through. Although it was initially written in English, it was first published in French and then in English. On the other hand, it was first produced in German, translated as 'Kommen und Gehen' by Elmar Tophoven, and then subsequently in English.[8]

Avikunthak's translation has used Hindi and Bengali, brought together, as we will see, in a discorded-togetherness. Although both the languages belong to the same family, that is the Indo-Aryan family, there are obvious differences in their syntactic construction, grammar, phonology and lexicon. Many Bengali speakers, for instance, may not speak or properly understand Hindi and vice versa. And since Hindi has occupied, problematically enough, the position of lingua franca in our country, the language is still spoken and used by native Bengali speakers. However, many Hindi speakers do not know Bengali at all. This only shows that the question of unfamiliarity is present even within languages belonging to the same family. Hence bringing them together only disrupts the comprehensibility of the text by exposing the differences and unfamiliarity present within the prescribed form and features peculiar to these two languages. Here, as Beckett would himself have anticipated, both grammar and style are brought under conflict and violation. Therefore, through his translation, Avikunthak arrives at a language which resembles in many ways the Beckettian anti-language. This method also provides Avikunthak with a more appropriate form in which to depict the content of the text.

The plot of 'Come and Go' is woven around three women, FLO, VI, and RU (Ashwini, Kuheli and Aditi in the film) who interchangeably

8 See the publication and production history provided in *The Complete Dramatic Works* by Samuel Beckett (2006, 352).

sit in alignment until the one in the middle has to take a brief exit when the remaining two share a secret about her (never disclosed to the audience) on stage. I would like to suggest that the inaudible murmurs shared between the three characters—that are recognised as 'impasse'[9] in the text by Arka Chattopadhyay—are founded on what can be called the Beckettian anti-language that freezes their sayability and audibility. These inaudible murmurs exchanged between the three women arguably pose the very limits of language—they are the Freudian *unheimlich* or the 'unfamiliar' erupting as perforations or gaps developing on the surface of language through which 'that which lurks behind, be it something or nothing, starts seeping through' (Beckett 2009, 518).

Avikunthak, on the other hand, by deploying two Indian languages with syntactical, grammatical, phonological and lexical differences, brings out the *unheimlich* or unfamiliarity even at the level of what is said and heard to further unsettle the structures of language with these differences that resist what I have earlier suggested as the comprehensibility of the text.

For once, even if we take for granted that the audience knows either of the languages, it is impossible to escape, in auditory terms, the conflict this juxtaposition creates due to the obvious differences that exist between the two languages. The Bengali gibberish rhyme comes (as a flashback scene) precisely after the women wonder (the exchange takes place in Hindi) if they could sit hand in hand like before. While, on the one hand, this sudden shift in language disturbs the auditory perception of the audience, on the other, the alienation that has settled down in the familial relationship among the three women, as hinted in the source text, is ultimately mirrored in the adaptation. This alienation is further reflected by the conflict that is created through the form in which the script is written that reveals the unfamiliarity present between the two languages of the same

9 See Arka Chattopadhyay's essay, 'Exhausting the Inexhaustible' (2016).

family. Thus, in Avikunthak's translation, the form coincides with the content.

Hence, it can be said that Avikunthak's method of translation achieves two very important accomplishments: (*a*) While translating Beckett into Indian languages, the method of translation reveals great possibilities of translating what is Beckettian—the concept of an anti-language, by putting into use the so-called unfamiliarity that exists within Indian languages, and (*b*) an indiscernibility between form and content that in itself is an essentially Beckettian principle.[10] And these further inform and are informed by the cinematographical pattern of the film that includes experimental jump cuts and out of focus frames challenging both visual and temporal linearity to problematise the language of cinema and resist the formation of any comprehensible narrative. We are instead left with disjunctive scenes and frames that attempt to fall in place together—like the three women and the two different languages they speak in—but largely fail. The use of black and white and sepia tones invokes a certain nostalgia for the films of the past when the narrative was important and each film had a story to tell. Even in the days of silent cinema, scenes were accompanied with words that connected them together. However, this nostalgia is shattered by the impossibility to speak any more or to connect the cinematic frames. The cinematic frames, like the words in Beckett's novella *Company*, are coming to an incorrigible end. Hence in the cinematic context, 'May we not speak of the old days?' (Beckett 2006, 355),. as asked by one of the characters, rendered in Hindi, becomes a failed attempt to revert to the older era of cinema when films spoke their stories, as unlike now, when films must begin on the imperative 'Let us not speak' (Beckett 2006, 354).

10 Beckett's famous analysis of Joycean style 'Here form *is* content, content *is* form' is to become his own stylistic principle despite his disagreements with the Joycean way. See Beckett's essay 'Dante…Bruno. Vico... Joyce' on Joyce's *Work in Progress*, collected in *Disjecta*.

Cinema like any other art form has to go through various compromises under the threat of censorship, popular demand, commercial profit and political correctness—to mention only a few. It is only allowed as an interlocutor of entertainment in popular imagination that cannot have the right to explicitly impart their critique of society and time. Of course, it is absurd to say that we have not come across many important critiques through films if we look at the history of world cinema. However, in all these instances they have either had to pacify their critical opinion through use of implications and suggestiveness, or had to struggle with various forces that governed and determined the releasable prospects of these films. To voluntarily not speak, therefore, would be an open strike against these odds that cinema has to confront and this strike can only be carried out through the cinematic medium itself just as words can be abused with words alone as envisioned by Beckett.

Thus, the Beckettian concept of an anti-language in literature, exemplified by the text of *Come and Go*, amply provides Avikunthak with possibilities of imagining an anti-language in cinema that comes out rather successfully through the latter's translation of the text into Indian languages.

Conclusion: Towards World-building

Now that we have tried to establish and deliberate upon the possible methodology of translating Beckett into Indian languages, let us draw our attention to what it reveals—as shown by Avikunthak's translation, the huge gap that persists between Indian languages belonging to different families as well as within the same family. In a country as diverse as India, that has 121 major languages and 270 mother tongues recorded in the 2011 census data[11] each belonging to either of the five language families listed previously, it

11 'The Linguistic Survey 2011 Report' can be accessed online at http://censusindia.gov.in/2011Census/C-16_25062018_NEW.pdf (accessed 31 October 2018).

is perhaps imperative to think about carrying out more intranational translation of texts, both indigenous and imported. However, so far as we Indians are concerned we are alien to most of the languages spoken within the country, although most of us speak at least two Indian languages (English included)—often in an ill-equipped sense. We not only feel at a loss when we confront people residing in different Indian states speaking in different Indian languages but also when we meet people from our own state, who may share our language but possess a very different dialect. It is only through more and more sincere attempts at intranational translation that the unfamiliarity that exists between the languages belonging from different families as well as within the same family can be reduced. These translations would not be to homogenise these languages but to open up possibilities of understanding, appreciating and relating to the voice of the neighbour while acknowledging the differences. For instance, each language shall pose a challenge to the translator in translating culturally charged words into the target language which may not offer an equivalent. These words are untranslatable words and they must be retained in the translated text with footnotes elaborating their meaning. This is how the voice of a neighbour is not appropriated but brought into familiar proximity. This is what I have referred to as opening up to the voice of the neighbour which should be seen as an ethical possibility facilitating a world of belongingness to emerge instead of turning translation into a nationalist project to promote mere communication between nation states. The world of belongingness is achieved when we refrain from coercing the voice of the neighbour into ours and accept its difference and variation by retaining what is untranslatable as untranslatable—the ethics of translation, after all, is predicated upon untranslatability.

That brings me to the last point which I would like to summarise as briefly as I can. Pheng Cheah says that the discourse of 'World literature is an important aspect of cosmopolitanism because it is a type of world-making activity that enables us to imagine a world' (2008, 26). Cheah is very clear about his conception of the world as opposed to the conception of the globe as perceived by the discourse of globalisation that merely attempts to bring about 'spatial diffusion and extensiveness achieved through global media and markets' (2008, 30). Contrarily, World literature contributes to an intellectual intercourse, cultural transaction and exchange 'aimed at bringing out universal humanity. It does not abolish national differences but takes place and is to be found in the intervals, mediations, passages, and crossings between national borders' (Cheah 2008, 30). This is only possible through a translation that does not attempt to domesticate the foreign text into the receiving language and culture, although one is always running the risk of doing so, but rather acknowledges that which is untranslatable and let it remain so in order to resist appropriation and uniformity, but promote, in Goethean sense, 'mutual understanding and tolerance between nations through the revelation of universal humanity across particular differences even as such differences are valued' (Cheah 2008, 28). This is possible within the geopolitical space of a particular nation too, and today when we engage with Goethe's understanding of world-building—'The idea is not that nations shall think alike, but that they shall learn how to understand each other' (quoted in Cheah 2008, 28)—we can adopt this idea to learn how to understand the different voices of our neighbours, living in either harmony or conflict within the premises of the same nation. These voices may not think or speak alike, may have different systems of faith and may not desire alike but it is only through translation that possibilitates understanding so that we can begin to accept and make space for the differences to exist and thereby build our world of belongingness.

Let us go back to Avikunthak's film once more. In the cinematic adaptation, the whispers shared between the three women that act as an impasse in Beckett's text posing limits to language and its communicability turn into metaphors of translation grounded on ethics of untranslatability. While it is possible to trace the Beckettian concept of anti-language in the disjunctive impact on the auditory perception of the audience posed by the two Indian languages used in the translation, it is also possible to locate an intermediary space of coming together in the subsequent murmurs shared by the women. While in Beckett's text these murmurs are gaps through which language exposes what it conceals—the nothingness that lurks behind its screen—in Avikunthak's translation the murmurs turn into gaps that translation should retain—the untranslatability.

Although the three women in Avikunthak's film reach their final moment of holding each other's hands, they do not form a ring as opposed to what happens at the end of Beckett's play. The open-endedness of the image suggests a future to come, a future of belongingness, unlike in Beckett's play where the characters intend to turn towards an impossible past where they can never belong. Thus, Avikunthak's translation also attempts to turn around the unfamiliarity that disrupts language to arrive at a more tolerant situation where languages, and people who embody them, may begin to understand one another despite their differences.

I shall not read this necessarily as a subversion in so far as the ethical intention revealed by the translation can be traced back to Beckett himself. Many critics have been of the opinion that Beckett's writings, particularly his post-war works, were deeply informed by the traumas and experiences of the war that defined what he called 'humanity in ruins' (Beckett 1995, 278). It can be argued that the concept of literature of the unword was born as a consequence of experiencing the gradual ruin of humanity—the letter to Axel Kaun was actually written on Beckett's return from Nazi Germany in 1937. In context of the world today, this experience is no less relevant than what it must have been during Beckett's time. Hence, to translate only the style that Beckett devised would not be enough;

one has to think of translating relevance too, the political as well as philosophical. It can be suggested, therefore, that Avikunthak's adaptation or translation not only retains the Beckettian concept of unsettling language in terms of expression but also retains its ethical relevance in response to time. This is also how one world is passed into another—Beckett's world into our world—and the world of belongingness is created.

I have tried to suggest the relevance of ethics in my understanding of world-building through translation which can also be contested by various political discourses surrounding the whole question of translation today. For instance, in the post-colonial context domestication or disruption of the text belonging to the dominating/colonising culture through translation can be seen as an act of resistance and reclamation. I have always found it difficult to reconcile ethics with radical politics but perhaps that is possible too and requires further thought. However, it can still be insisted that it is important today to be more understanding or tolerant towards the other (that should, of course, begin with those who have historically occupied more power, more privilege, more space, 'from the scratch' as Coetzee has reminded us in his novel *Disgrace*) so that as Pheng Cheah suggests 'we can belong in many ways' (2008, 38).

References

Beckett, Samuel, 'Three Dialogues', *Disjecta: Miscellaneous Writings and a Dramatic Fragment*, edited by Ruby Cohn, New York, Grove Press, 1984, pp. 138–45.

———, 'Dante…Bruno. Vico ... Joyce.', *Disjecta: Miscellaneous Writings and a Dramatic Fragment*, edited by Ruby Cohn, New York, Grove Press, 1984, pp. 19–33.

———, *The Capital of the Ruins, The Complete Short Prose 1929–1989*, edited by S.E. Gontarsky, New York, Grove Press, 1995, pp. 275–78.

———, *Come and Go, The Complete Dramatic Works*, London, Faber and Faber, 2006, pp. 351–57.

———, Beckett, Samuel, *The Letters of Samuel Beckett 1929–1940*, edited by Martha Dow Fehsenfeld and Lois More Overbeck, United Kingdom, Cambridge University Press, 2009.

———, *The Letters of Samuel Beckett 1941–1956*, edited by Martha Dow Fehsenfeld, Lois More Overbeck, Dan Gunn, and George Criag, United Kingdom, Cambridge University Press, 2011.

Chakraborty, Thirthankar, 'World Literature: From the Politics to a Poetics', *Sanglap: Journal of Literary and Cultural Inquiry*, Vol. 4, No. 1, 2017, pp. 43–54. Available at: http://sanglap-journal.in/index.php/sanglap/article/view/158 (accessed 04-02-2018).

Chattopadhyay, Arka, 'Exhausting the Inexhaustible: Reading the Structure of Samuel Beckett's *Come and Go* through Ashish Avikunthak's *Endnote*', *Textual Practice*, Vol. 31, No. 2, 2016, pp. 399–415. Available at: www.tandfonline.com/doi/full/10.1080/0950236X.2016.1187667 (accessed 04-02-2019).

Cheah, Pheng, 'What Is a World? On World Literature as World-Making Activity', *Daedalus*, Vol. 137, No. 3, 2008, pp. 26–38. Available at: www.jstor.org/stable/40543795 (accessed 4 February 2019).

Cohn, Ruby, 'Samuel Beckett Self-Translator', *PMLA*, Vol. 76, No. 5, 1961, pp. 613–21. Available at: www.jstor.org/stable/460556 (accessed 4 February 2019).

Derrida, Jacques, *Monolingualism of the Other or the Prosthesis of Origin*, translated by Patrick Mensah, Stanford, California, Stanford University Press, 1998.

McGuire, James. 'Beckett, the Translator, and the Metapoem.' *World Literature Today*, Vol. 64, No. 2, 1990, pp. 258–63. Available at: www.jstor.org/stable/40146405 (accessed 04-02-2019).

Venuti, Lawrence, 'Translation, Community, Utopia'. *The Translation Studies Reader*, edited by Lawrence Venuti, London and New York, Routledge, 2004, pp. 468–88.

16

Making Trans Experiences Visible through Translations

Regiane Corrêa de Oliveira Ramos

Beneath my colourful exterior lies a curled up, bruised individual that yearns for freedom—freedom to live life on her own and freedom to come across as the person she is. Acceptance is what I seek. My tough exterior and nonchalance is an armour that I have learned to wear to protect my vulnerability.

—Manobi Bandyopadhyay

The academic journal *TSQ: Transgender Studies Quarterly* is the first non-medical journal devoted to transgender studies.[1] It was founded by Paisley Currah and Susan Stryker whose aim was to create a platform for innovative research and scholarship that challenges the objectification, pathologisation, and exoticisation of transgender lives.[2] It is a space for transgender critique. Its mission, as Currah and Stryker point out, is:

1 For a detailed reading of the history of this academic field, see Stryker and Whittle (2006).

2 In the introduction to the first issue, Paisley Currah and Susan Stryker explain that since the beginning the category transgender represents 'a resistance to medicalization, to pathologization, and to the many mechanisms whereby the administrative state and its associated medico-legal-psychiatric institutions sought to contain and delimit the socially disruptive potentials of sex/gender atypicality, incongruence, and nonnormativity' (Stryker and Currah 2014, 5). In the article '(De)Subjugated Knowledges: An Introduction to Transgender Studies,' Susan Stryker defines transgender as 'someone who permanently changed social gender through the public presentation of self, without recourse to genital transformation' and transsexual as 'somebody who permanently changed genitals in order to claim membership in a gender other than the one assigned at birth' (Stryker 2015, 4).

> to foster a vigorous conversation among scholars, artists, activists, and others that examines how 'transgender' comes into play as a category, a process, a social assemblage, an increasingly intelligible gender identity, an identifiable threat to gender normativity, and a rubric for understanding the variability and contingency of gender across time, space, and cultures. (*TSQ: Transgender Studies Quarterly*)[3]

The first edition edited by Paisley Currah and Susan Stryker came out in May 2014 with Chelsea Elizabeth Manning on the cover and 'Postposttranssexual: Key Concepts for a Twenty-First-Century Transgender Studies *(TSQ: Transgender Studies Quarterly)*' as its title.[4] There are eighty-six key entries for this inaugural issue, that became a book, which shed light on a conceptual vocabulary for transgender studies. Among them we find the entry 'translation' (to carry or bring across) by A. Finn Enke. The applicability of translation within transgender studies is for Enke

> a necessary and profoundly hopeful act for those who trans gender, for we have been taught that transgender is marked by dysphoria, a word from Greek that means difficult to bear, difficult to carry. In order to carry or bring across, we [transgenders] become poets, storytellers, and artists. (Enke 2014, 241)

---

3 This information is freely available to anyone visiting the journal webpage at: https://read.dukeupress.edu/tsq/pages/About

4 Chelsea Elizabeth Manning is an American trans activist, politician and former United States Army soldier. Manning became famous for disclosing to WikiLeaks nearly 750,000 classified, or unclassified, military and diplomatic documents. Allucquére Rosanne Sandy Stone is a transgender who is considered a founder of the academic discipline of transgender studies in the United States. In 1987, Stone wrote the essay 'The Empire Strikes Back: A Posttranssexual Manifesto' (2006) which is considered, in Susan Stryker's words,

> the protean text from which contemporary transgender studies emerged. It developed a poststructuralist analysis of gender identity that opened up new possibilities for transsexuals—and, by extension, for other types of people who feel themselves to be 'differently gendered'—to escape the powerful effects of both medical and feminist discourses that have worked to efface and invalidate their life experiences. (Stryker and Whittle 2006, 221)

The issues of *TSQ* include a brief foreword by the general editors, the guest editorial team's introduction to the issue, several feature articles, and a few of several recurring sections: book, arts and culture and new media reviews; documents and images; opinion pieces; interviews; annotated bibliographies; translations; and fashion.

The 'Translation' section, that interests us here, aims to expand the scope of transgender studies 'beyond its Anglophone roots, by highlighting texts originating in languages other than English and by making visible the work of translation necessary to bring to English-reading audiences the work of researchers, writers, thinkers, and activists from around the world' (Stryker 2015, 525). It welcomes not only 'historical documents and contemporary voices that simultaneously challenge the Anglocentric bias of the transgender studies field while expanding the field's breadth and reach', but also 'translated fiction, nonfiction, poetry, and research texts' (Stryker 2015, 525).

The first 'Translation' section came out in Volume 2, Number 3 (1 August 2015) as 'Trans*formational Pedagogies'. It included the work of S.P.F. Dale who translated Ray Tanaka's article, 'Queers and the Issue of 'Priority', and the work of Fabian Alfie, who translated a passage describing cross-dressing in a fourteenth-century Italian text by Giovanni Sercambi. The second 'Translation' section became the main theme of Volume 3, Numbers 3–4 (1 November 2016), 'Translating Transgender'. This special issue, entirely on translation, makes transgender studies, as a field of critical theory, investigate interesting points such as: ethnographic studies of multilingual transgender spaces and communities; ethnographic studies of medical, legal, penal, or educational contexts in which transgender positionality or existence is negotiated translingually; reflections on the craft and practice of translation, broadly conceived; studies that model a 'multilingual transgender studies' or a multilingual trans futurity more broadly; reflections on the process of translating texts dealing with transgender and gender variance; essays on what transgender methodology in translation theory or practice might look like; essays exploring what the practices of working interpreters and translators (literary, poetic, technical, diplomatic) may reveal about transgender epistemology; historical studies linking multilingual, code switching, and translingual practice with transgender embodiment; historical studies linking the genealogy of monolingualism with various strains of gender normativity; and a metacriticism of the emergent field of transgender studies, its terms, and its methodologies from a multilingual point of view, just to mention some as the list is long (Gramling and Dutta 2016, 345–46).[5] The articles compiled in this edition 'proceed as a loose critical sojourn through a range of problematics that, together, test the heuristic and political capacities of the words translation and transgender in various contexts' (Gramling and Dutta 2016, 346). They induce thought-provoking questions which range from how have transgender persons participated in the vocation of translation, and how are they either accounted

5 For the entire list raised by them, see Gramling and Dutta (2016). Here are the articles included in the first issue 'Untranslatable Subjects: Travesti Access to Public Health Care in Brazil' by Alvaro Jarrín; 'Language Purism and Gender: Icelandic Trans* Activists and the Icelandic Linguistic Gender Binary' by Jyl Josephson; 'Þorgerður Einarsdóttir; From Representation to Corposubjectivation: The Configuration of Transgender in Mexico City' by Alba Pons Rabasa; 'Translating *Hijra* into Transgender: Performance and *Pehchān* in India's Trans-*Hijra* Communities' by Jeff Roy; 'Always in Translation: Trans Cinema across Languages' by Helen Hok-Sze Leung; 'Conceptualizing Sex, Gender, and Trans: An Anglo-Finnish Perspective' by Unni Leino; 'Pedro Lemebel and the Translatxrsation: On a Genderqueer Translation Praxis' by Arielle A. Concilio; 'Keeping the Trans in Translation: Queering Early Modern Transgender Memoirs' by Emily Rose; 'Translation, Transition, Transgender: Framing the Life of Charlotte von Mahlsdorf' by Brian James Baer; 'Untranslating Gender in Trish Salah's *Lyric Sexology Vol. 1*' by Kay Gabriel; 'Plus the Swinging of the Door' by Nathanaël; 'Flows of Trans-Language: Translating Transgender in the *Paraguayan Sea*' by Christopher Larkosh; 'In Memoriam to Identity: Transgender as Strategy in Qiu Miaojin's *Last Words from Montmartre*' by Ari Larissa Heinrich and Eloise Dowd; '"You Have Made Her a Man among Men": Translating the *Khuntha's* Anatomy in Fatimid Jurisprudence' by Saqer A. Almarri; and 'Translating the Human: The *Androginos* in Tosefta Bikurim' by Max Strassfeld.

for or discounted in a general history of translation to what do the fields of translation studies and transgender studies have to tell each other—in terms of their methodological and political constraints, their claims to interdisciplinary relevance and their relationship to university structures and discourses (Gramling and Dutta 2016, 347).[6] The third 'Translation' section is in Volume 4, Number 2 (1 May 2017), 'The Issue of Blackness'. The 'Translation Section: The Issue of Blackness' edited by David Gramling, Patrick Ploschnitzki and Tara Taylor, contains three short pieces, translated from German, which reflect upon the black queer person within the Black community in Germany. The fourth 'Translation' section appears in Volume 5, Number 1 (1 February 2018) with Emrah Karakus translating trans voices from Turkey. Thus, *TSQ: Transgender Studies Quarterly* journal points out that translation not only makes the trans narrative circulate globally but also emphasises the importance of building a bridge of solidarity for trans people worldwide. It provides comparative data and analysis regarding significant aspects of the human rights situation of trans and gender variant people and advocates for their protection.

The last couple of years in India have seen a surge of interest in translating hijras' autobiographies into English and into other Indian languages. The relationship between translation and minorities cannot, at first, be easily seen. However, it is one of the most important themes in this field of research in the past years, as *TSQ* highlights.

---

6 The other questions raised by the essays are: How has a pressure to 'be translatable' affected the lives, stories, and experiences of transgender persons, and what is the political consequence of this pressure? How has the rapid, monetised translation of certain discourses in the age of institutional transnationalisation—including medical pathological, juridical, human rights, sexual health, feminist, surgical, psychological, legislative, and activist discourses—impacted the ability of trans-identified persons or communities to thrive? What particular contingencies attend the task of translating texts that themselves narrate transgender subjectivities? How has transgender life in gender-segregative historical contexts prompted new practices of translational textualisation—that is, ways of rendering the body meaningful as human persona or civic subject? (Gramling and Dutta 2016, 347).

People who belong to minority groups in a given society, such as speakers of a certain non-official or regional language, people with special needs, and trans communities, all of them can share their experiences and try to connect with each other by means of translators and interpreters. They help trans people spread their points of view and their claims to legitimate place in their countries or society. This holds true especially in India, where 22 major languages and 22,000 distinct dialects coexist. This cultural linguistic diversity means that huge barriers have to be crossed all over the country, and language then plays a significant role in people's everyday life. However, more than different languages, the subcontinent presents a variety of local cultures that, but for translation, would remain unknown outside their original—and sometimes limited—space. Indian literature, in vernacular languages or in English, has been spread all over the world; contemporary Indian writers, whose works are originally published in one of the local languages, such as Sanskrit, Bengali, Hindi, Urdu, and among others, are translated into English, thus finding a broader audience at home and abroad. And, above all, Indian minorities can express their needs and hopes in texts which will be translated and be known in distant countries such as Brazil.

The voice of the hijra[7] community is being heard in Brazil thanks to the English translations of their (auto)biographies, a language which provides greater visibility and international reach. *I am Vidya: A Transgender's Journey* (2013) by Living Smile Vidya, *The Truth About Me: A Hijra Life Story* (2010) by A. Revathi, *Me Hijra, Me Laxmi* (2015) by Laxmi Narayan Tripathi, and *Gift of Goddess Lakshmi* (2017) by Manobi Bandyopadhyay have good reception among the local trans communities. When presented in congresses either in

7 Trans community in India, as Gee Imaan Semmalar points out, is diverse and includes *hijra, thirunangai, kinnar, mangalamukhi, Aravani, kothi, jogappas, shiv shaktis, thirunambis, bhaiyya,* and *paiyyan* (Semmalar 2014, 286). The hijra, as Laxmi Narayan Tripathi explains, is 'the oldest ethnic transgender community' of feminine-identified persons (Tripathi quoted in Lizzie Crocker 2017).

English or translation of excerpts into Portuguese, their narratives of intense stigma, discrimination and violation of human rights create a sense of, to use Benedict Anderson's words, 'imagined community' among the Brazilian trans people who also experience multiple forms of oppression and human violation.

As I have pointed out in 'The Voice of an Indian Trans Woman: A *Hijra* Autobiography', hijra literature, a new and evolving literary genre in India, is trying to make the reader/society aware that 'hijras are capable of more than just begging and sex work' (Revathi 2010, v). It is a compilation of the trans experiences and the culture of the hijras and their resistance to heteronormativity,[8] which create insidious processes of stigmatisation, discrimination, marginalisation, pathologisation, and confinement, operating at the level of social perception, social space, social institutions, common sense, judicial system, family, state, and the medical system (Foucault 1988, 80–81). These autobiographies discuss issues of human rights, democracy, caste system, laws and gender equality in India. They also describe the Indian trans activism that looks for respectability and representativeness for trans identity. Their social concerns are being circulated in India through translations.

In 2007, the first autobiography to be written by a *hijra* was Living Smile Vidya's. Originally written in Tamil, the book has been translated into Assamese, English, Kannada, Malayalam, Marathi, and other languages. In 2011, Sahitya Akademi Award granted Tamil Selvi an award for the best translation of Vidya's book. Selvi translated *Naan Sharavanan Illai. Vidya* (2007) from Tamil into *Naanu Avanalla ... Avalu ...!* (2015) in Kannada. From the Kannada translation, B. S. Lingadevaru produced the film Naanu Avanalla ... Avalu ...! (2015), portraying Vidya's life on the screen and making the hijra community visible. In the passage from the word (literary text) to the audiovisual

8 It is the sexual order of the present based on the heterosexual, familial and reproductive model. It is imposed by means of symbolic and physical violence, mainly at those who break gender norms.

(film and theatre),[9] the first autobiography of a hijra gains new records, new spaces and new audience. Through these different artistic expressions (literature, cinema, translations and theatre), Vidya makes her story circulate, rebelling against the 'cis-tem'. The abject body, therefore, is present and resistant in the (re)writing.

In 2010, A. Revathi publishes *The Truth About Me: A Hijra Life Story*. Although it was originally written in Tamil, it was first published in English with the translation of V. Geetha. It has been translated into Kannada, Malayalam, Tamil and Telugu. As Revathi explains,

> these books have been stocked in libraries of more than 300 colleges and universities in the country. Together the books create awareness among students about gender and sexuality. As far as I know, the books form part of the prescribed syllabus in 20 universities and colleges. (Revathi 2016, xiii)

She also emphasises the importance of the autobiographies of trans people and argues that ten years back there was not much discussion among students about the transgender community. These autobiographies were, in her own words, 'an eye opener' for people to know about the *hijra* community (Revathi 2016, xiii). Writing, she asserts, 'was powerful to herald social change. Yet I wondered how many more Revathis, if they had such opportunities, would have emerged? Certainly, they would not have been forced into sex work. Perhaps they too could have blossomed as writers, artists and other professionals' (Revathi 2016, 87). We could also question, Why not translators?

---

9 In August 2014, Living Smile Vidya, Gee Imman Semmalar and Angel Glady founded Panmmai Theater. It is the first theater company run by trans people whose goal is to use theater as a platform for, as Vidya explains, 'Panmai started out as a platform for us to tell our stories. But in the long term, we hope to turn it into space for other marginalized people to tell theirs' (Vidya quoted in Ranjani Rajendra 2015). According to Semmalar, in the play Color of Trans 'our focus has been to present the story of our lives, people's perception of us and the problems we face [...] Color of Trans is an attempt to shake people up and make them realize that we are individuals too' (Semmalar quoted in Ranjani Rajendra 2015).

The *Truth about Me: A Hijra Life Story* (2010) has forged 'a new grammar of writing', and Revathi, like other *hijras*, broke the established literary canons, introducing an intensely personal and direct language to talk about transsexuality. For her, writing was 'deeply cathartic and healing' process where her 'pain had been transformed into art' (Revathi 2010, 87). Revathi inscribes not only herself in the world but also her community. Writing (autobiography) about trauma is a powerful device to turn pain and loss into political action.

In 2015, *Me Hijra, Me Laxmi* came out. The original text was written in Marathi by the journalist Vaishali Rode who gave shape to Laxmi's life. The English version was translated by R. Raj Rao and P.G. Joshi and has, I consider, a peculiar process of translation or 'literary creation'.[10] In the Foreword of the book, Rao explains the linguistic process involved in translating Laxmi's story:

> It is a collaborative translation, with one of us (P.G. Joshi) working with the Marathi original (the source language) and the other (me) 'Englishing' the narrative (putting it into the target language). However, neither Joshi nor I are completely oblivious of the other's language: Joshi was, till recently, professor of English at a college affiliated to the University of Pune, and I am a domiciled Maharashtrian. What complicates the work is that it was not authored by Laxmi herself, who is not a Marathi speaker, though she has lived in Mumbai for long, but was written by Vaishali Rode, a Marathi journalist to whom Laxmi spoke. (Rao 2015, 212)

---

10 R. Raj Rao is the first person to recognise hijra literature. As Rao asserts in the Afterword of *Me Hijra, Me Laxmi* (2015),

> Laxmi's autobiography is one of the earliest works that belong to the genre of hijra literature. It seeks to make readers aware of who the hijras really are, and what goes into the shaping their personalities—yes, they do have personalities. It seeks to dispel myths about the hijras and help us shed our prejudices. (Rao 2015, 183)

The most relevant aspect of this narrative is that it generates a counterdiscourse and the hijras occupy a place, to borrow Sandy Stone's word, 'as speaking subject within the traditional gender frame to become complicit in the discourse which one wishes to deconstruct' (Stone 2006, 12).

Rao's description above presents the Indian linguistic diversity and the role that translation plays to make the trans stories circulate. It is interesting to note that Laxmi's story is first legitimised by Rode's curiosity to know more about the hijras. Later, she received another boost as well as greater exposure when Rao and Joshi's translation of excerpts of her book appeared in the magazine *Words without Borders*, The Queer Issue IV 2013. These excerpts, as Rao points out, had a good reception and this encouraged them to translate the entire book.

Laxmi's (auto)biography, as Vaishali Rode affirms, 'may shock the conservative society, which has preconceived notions about hijras, about their way of walking, talking, dressing, and clapping. But Laxmi's own language and demeanour contest it. She is cultured to her fingertips' (Rode 2015, 235–36). Empowered, she became critical not only of society but also of her own community:

> I observed all the rules because the decision to become a hijra was, after all, mine. But soon there came a time when I rebelled. I could not stand the restrictions on my freedom. [...] It is tiresome to swim against the current. I have been swimming against two currents—one society and the other community. Both need to change their attitude. Whereas society needs to confront its biases towards the hijras, the hijras themselves must be forthright. (Tripathi 2015, p. 160)

Her activism arises when she observes the precarious life of the prostitutes of Kamatipura, prostitution area of Mumbai. While working for DWS and Astitva, non-governmental organizations, Laxmi seeks to improve the living conditions of hijras and prostitutes. Her social work gained national and international repercussions and in 2017 she received an award for the Indian of the Year from Brands Academy. She strongly fought against Section 377 of the Indian Penal Code. After National Legal Services Authority and Poojya Mata Nasib Kaur Ji (Women welfare society), Laxmi also filed a writ petition. Her efforts, and also the LGBTQIA+ community's, got rewarded when the Supreme Court decriminalised homosexuality on 6 September 2018.

The colonial law criminalised homosexual relations in India for more than a century. It was used against vulnerable communities, mainly, hijras and sex workers. Section 377 denied dignity and self respect that the Constitution of India guarantees them.

In *Gift of Goddess Lakshmi* (2017), Jhimli Mukherjee Pandey translates Manobi Bandyopadhyay's story and hopes that 'as Manobi Di's "soul", who speaks to the reader through the book, I have been able to do justice to her' (Pandey 2017, 186). Bandyopadhyay, the bruised individual that yearns for freedom, has to be self-translated, explaining the trans body, as 'it would help society understand people like me better. We are slightly different outwardly, but we are humans just as you are and have the same needs—physical and emotional—just as you have' (Bandyopadhyay 2017, ix). Manobi, as she likes to be called, never let bullying affect her studies, always getting good grades in school. She believed that this would be the only way to overcome prejudice. As in other trans autobiographies, Manobi presents the school years as being marked by infinite abuses and discriminations, since her feminine features could be identified in her early life. The mechanism that schools develop in excluding those who live femininities and/or masculinities differently from the norms also reaches the undergraduate level: 'College usually comes as a relief in the lives of most students. They finally find freedom after fourteen years of regimented school life. But this didn't happen for me. I found college to be yet another place where I would have to fight for my identity and respect' (Bandyopadhyay 2017, 39–40). Discrimination against her (jokes, giggles, cursing, and other violence) runs through all school levels. Her professional life as a Bengali literature teacher is also marked by discrimination and violence. In 1995, she began teaching at Vivekananada Satavarshiki College in Jhargram and recalls her first day at the institution being ridiculed by teachers, students and staff:

> No one as lowly as a hijra should be allowed to teach in a college, share the same staffroom, toilet and facilities. Initially they thought

> that if they made me feel miserable, I would leave of my own volition. But when they realized that I won't give in so easily, they got together to assault me every now and then. (Bandyopadhyay 2017, 93)

Although physical and verbal violence has been a constant in her academic life, education for Manobi has always been synonymous with resistance. In her literature classes, she teaches the students to read Bengali literary texts critically, exposing them to every form of diversity and social injustice. She created the first transsexual magazine in India. The name of the magazine, Abomanob/ Subhuman, refers to the status given to transgender people by society. According to Manobi, 'it was my protest against our society which pretends to be magnanimous and inclusive while being nakedly brutal beneath its mask' (Bandyopadhyay, 2017, 112). In 2005, she defended her doctoral thesis on transsexuality at Kalyani University. The degree does not make her life easier, on the contrary, it turned out a nightmare. The academic certificates bear the male name Somnath Bandyopadhyay and the doctoral degree bears the female name Manabi Bandyopadhyay. As a result, she loses the right for a promotion to the position of reader. However, that does not stop her from applying for the position of principal. With a good academic curriculum (good grades, undergraduate experience, lectures, conferences, publications and books), she is selected to be the principal of Krishnagar Women's College in 2015, becoming India's first transsexual principal.

Revathi's and Manobi's books are published by Penguin Books India and Laxmi's by Oxford University Press, Penguin Random House India, and Viking, considered some of the most prestigious international publishers. In an interview, the Executive Editor of Penguin Random House India, Vaishali Mathur, argues that 'exploitation and ostracism they face makes them who they are—inspirational and examples of what determination can do in the face of odds. That's what makes their stories so special' (Mathur quoted in Kanishka Gupta 2017).

Vidya, Revathi, Laxmi and Manobi present in their books the importance of considering issues of representation in literary work. Hijra literature moves beyond the queer umbrella. It is the worldview of a transsexual. These writers are examples of sexual minority voices that literary studies should no longer ignore. For years, their right to speak or write were denied. Not only Vidya but also Revathi, Laxmi and Manobi first had to translate themselves (explain who they are) in order to make society perceive them as human beings. Now they have made space to write themselves into intelligibility and existence, against the social violence, institutional erasure, incarceration and homicide. Literature for them, thus, becomes a social transformation device. Legal change, as Revathi reminds us, 'without social freedom is meaningless' and 'true equality emerges only when women are treated with respect; as equals in the true sense of the term. Only when this happens, will trans people also be truly respected as humans' (Revathi 2016, 237).

Would translation studies be ready to treat trans narrative or hijra narrative as an object of analysis? What about literary studies? Would they be ready to join hands with transgender studies to make trans narrative or hijra narrative researchable? This would only happen when literature is not seen as an aesthetic object detached from any context, but seen through intersectionality (various forms of social stratification—such as class, caste, religion, race, sexual orientation, age, disability, and gender—do not exist separately from each other but are interwoven together) (Crenshaw 1989, 150). Also when the trans characters, as Casey Plett contends, are not written as 'tortured heroes'. In her critique of the rise gender novel, Plett asserts that

> trans people have historically always been written in certain ways to serve certain interests by cis people. And I think that's boring and dumb. Basically my argument is that a lot of these novels which have storylines written by cis people tend to put trans people on pedestals and make them like one-dimensional Disney heroes. When they put a trans character in, they're always alone, there's only one of them. Sure, trans people are alone a lot of the time and it sucks, but I'm really interested in what happens when you have lots of transpeople

> together … what happens when trans people talk to each other? When there's only one of us we can only be presented as an anomaly. (Plett quoted in Hans Rollmann 2015)

Only then, I would affirm, literature can truly become humanising. We should not ignore complexity of hijra literature/trans literature, either through autobiographies and novels or poetry. It aims not only visibility but also representativeness. It depicts trans lives and characters historically and culturally situated. I conclude my reflections upon hijra literature, which are still in an early stage, with my Portuguese translation of Revathi's poem.[11] Her words reverberate the trans struggle for rights and respect. The poem, for me, is a bridge of solidarity among trans people worldwide.

Meus direitos de Mulher Trans	**My Rights as a Trans Woman**
Rejeitada pelos pais Rejeitada pela sociedade Rejeitada pelo mundo Eu me manifesto hoje. Fui deixada sem herança sem prazer sem lar sem emprego. Nasci homem luto para ser como qualquer mulher ser filha, irmã mãe, avó neta.	Rejected by parents Rejected by society Rejected by the world I sing today. I am left with neither property nor pleasure I am left with neither home nor a job. I was born a man I have struggled to be as any woman to be a daughter, a sister a mother, a grandmother a granddaughter.

11 I translated this poem for the book *Corpos Transgressores: Políticas de Resistências* (2018) edited by Dánie Marcelo de Jesus, Glenda Cristina Valim de Melo, Vicente Tchalian and Sara Wagner Pimenta Gonçalves Júnior. The original poem can be found in A. Revathi's book, *A Life in Trans Activism* (2016, 67–68).

Meus direitos de Mulher Trans	**My Rights as a Trans Woman**
Nossa comunidade é excluída exilada somos *hijras/aravanis* somos pessoas trans. Violentadas pelos *goondas* e pela polícia criminalizadas pela lei que não consegue compreender nosso desespero para viver, para existir. Xingadas de prostitutas e mendigas o mundo nos dá alguma escolha? Ansiamos por amor precisamos amar também como todos os seres humanos. Continuaremos a lutar não pedimos sua piedade somente sua compreensão. Exigimos aceitação dos pais da sociedade do mundo para sermos vistas como seres humanos para viver como escolhemos.	Ours is an excluded and exiled community we are the aravanis the transgender people. Violated by goondas and the police criminalized by the law that fails to understand our desperation to live, to exist. We are called beggars and sex workers has this world left us any choice? We crave for love we need to love too as do all human beings. We will continue to struggle we ask not for your pity only your understanding. We demand acceptance from parents from society from the world to be human to live as we have chosen.

References

Bandyopadhyay, Manobi, *A Gift of Goddess Lakshmi*, New Delhi, Penguin Books, 2017.

Crenshaw, Kimberlé, 'Demarginalising the Intersection of Race and Sex: A Black Feminist Critique of Antidiscrimination Doctrine, Feminist Theory and Antiracist Politics', *University of Chicago Legal Forum*, Vol. 1989, No. 1, 1989, pp. 139–67.

Crocker, Lizzie, 'How India Embraces the "Third Gender": Laxmi Narayan Tripathi at Women in the World.' *Daily Beast,* 4 July 2017. Available at: https://www.thedailybeast.com/how-india-embraces-the-third-gender-laxmi-narayan-tripathi-at-women-in-the-world?ref=scroll (accessed 15 November 2017).

Currah, Paisley and Susan Stryker, *Postposttranssexual: Key Concepts for a 21st Century Transgender Studies (TSQ: Transgender Studies Quarterly)*, Durham, Duke University Press, 2014.

Enke, A. Finn, 'Translation', In Currah and Stryker, *Postposttranssexual: Key Concepts for a 21st Century Transgender Studies (TSQ: Transgender Studies Quarterly)*, Durham, Duke University Press, 2014, pp. 241–44.

Foucault, Michel, *História da Sexualidade I: A Vontade de Saber*, Rio de Janeiro, Graal, 1988.

Gramling, David and Aniruddha Dutta, 'Introduction', *TSQ: Transgender Studies Quarterly*, Vol. 3, No. 3–4, November 2016, pp. 333–56.

Gupta,Kanishka. 'These books are (not) lost in transgender.' *DNA,* 15 March 2017. Available at: http://www.dnaindia.com/lifestyle/report-these-books-are-not-lost-in-transgender-2352793 (accessed 18 December 2017).

Pandey, Jhimli Mukherjee, Acknowledgements. *A Gift of Goddess Lakshmi.* By Manobi Bandyopadhyay. New Delhi, Penguin Books, 2017.

Rajendra, Ranjani, 'Panmai, the first transgender theatre group in Tamil Nadu, on the need to have a space to tell their stories.' *The Hindu*, 3 August 2015, Metroplus. Web. 15 March 2017. Available at: https://www.thehindu.com/features/metroplus/a-chat-with-panmai-the-first-transgender-theatre-group-in-tamil-nadu/article7495717.ece Web (accessed 18 December 2017).

Ramos, Regiane Corrêa de Oliveira, 'The Voice of an Indian Trans Woman: A Hijra Autobiography', *Indi@log*, Vol. 5, 2018, pp. 71–88.

Rao, R. Raj, Foreword. *Me Hijra, Me Laxmi.* By Laxmi Narayan Tripathi. New Delhi, Oxford University Press, 2015, pp. 181–213.

Revathi, A., *The Truth about Me: A Hijra Life Story*, translated by V. Geetha, New Delhi, Penguin Books, 2010.

———, *A Life in Trans Activism*, translated by Nandini Murali, New Delhi, Zubaan, 2016.

Rode, Vaishali, Preface to the Marathi Edition. *Me Hijra, Me Laxmi*. By Laxmi Narayan Tripathi. New Delhi, Oxford University Press, 2015, pp. 221–37.

Rollmann, Hans, 'How Do You Define the Genre of Trans Literature?' Popmatters, 27 September 2015. Web 18 December 2017. Available at: https://www.popmatters.com/how-do-you-define-the-genre-of-trans-literature-2495490457.html (accessed 18 December 2018).

Semmalar, Gee Imaan, 'Unpacking Solidarities of the Oppressed: Notes on Trans Struggles', *Women's Studies Quarterly*, Vol. 42, No. 3–4, Fall/Winter 2014, pp. 286–91.

Stone, Sandy, 'The "Empire" Strikes Back: A Posttranssexual Manifesto', in Susan Stryker and Stephen Whittle, *Transgender Studies Reader*, New York, Routledge, 2006.

Stryker, Susan and Stephen Whittle, *The Transgender Studies Reader*, New York, Routledge, 2006.

Stryker, Susan 'Introduction to "Translation"'. *TSQ: Transgender Studies Quarterly*, Vol. 2, No. 3, August 2015, p. 525.

Stryker, Susan, and Paisley Currah, 'Introduction'. *TSQ: Transgender Studies Quarterly*, Vol. 1, No. 1–2, May 2014, p. 5.

Tripathi, Laxmi Narayan, *Me Hijra, Me Laxmi*, translated by R. Raj Rao and P.G. Joshi, New Delhi, Oxford University Press, 2015.

Vidya, Living Smile, *I am Vidya: A Transgender's Journey*, New Delhi, Rupa Publications, 2013.

17

Enabling Translation: Carrying Disability across Cultures

Someshwar Sati

When we first announced our intention of organising a workshop on translating disability short stories from various Indian languages into English, even the most liberal of our colleagues—who are never tired of flagging racial, feminist and Dalit concerns—met our announcement with puzzled looks—looks that seemed to interrogate the state of our sanity. What is the point they seemed to ask? Would such an academic exercise be academically viable? Do we have enough disability short stories within the canon of Indian literature to merit such a workshop?

These questions made us approach the organisation of the workshop with a great deal of caution. But to our pleasant surprise within a week of the above announcement our inbox was flooded with abstracts from academics wanting to be a part of the workshop. Soon, we had a list of over 80 disability short stories across 12 different Indian languages. The overwhelming response to our call for papers and the sheer number of disability texts that these responses uncovered were enough to put our worst fears to rest and silence the sceptics. However, despite the success of the workshop, the troubling question, 'What is the point?' continues to haunt us even today. What follows is an attempt to address this query through a retrospective reflection on the academic deliberations carried out at the workshop.

During the course of the academic deliberations, it slowly dawned upon us that there existed a curious though obvious parallel between the status of disabled people in society and that of a translated text within the disciplinary domain of translation studies. Both of them are discriminated against on grounds of their so-called difference from a standard norm. On the one hand, disabled people have been ostracised and marginalised in society for quite some time now. Their disability has been understood down the ages as a medical problem: a clinically diagnosed condition of the human body gone wrong which incapacitates the individual, rendering him or her dysfunctional. This association of disability with deformity and dysfunctionality renders disabled people as less than human, setting them apart from the rest of the non-disabled world. A similar trope of lack also structures the way a translated text was perceived by conventional translation studies. Within the academic domain of this discipline, the relationship between the original/source text and its translated version was placed and understood within a kind of hierarchical thinking that celebrated the supremacy of the former, denigrating the latter to being an inferior copy. The focus of this discipline, in other words, was on the delineation of the losses that occurred during translation; ultimately relegating the process itself as something that deforms and mutilates the original by either causing irreparable damage to it or completely destroying it.

Recent work in translation studies, however, tends to challenge the mode of hierarchical thinking that had hitherto governed the discipline. Carlos Fuentes even goes to the extent of saying that 'originality is a sickness', a sickness that stems from a modernity which always seeks to see itself as new (1990, 70). But it is in the writings of Octavio Paz that we find the most explicit expression of this shift of emphasis in conceptualising the relationship between the original and their translated texts. According to him,

> each [text is] slightly different from the one that came before it: translations of translations of translations. Each text is unique, yet

> at the same time it is the translation of another text. No text can be completely original because language itself, in its very essence, is already a translation—first from the nonverbal world, and then, because each sign and each phrase is a translation of another sign, another phrase. (1992, 154)

Such a radical view has enabled translation studies to follow the ideological orientations of other right-based literary and cultural movements and question various structures of power. In a similar vein, disability studies, as a rapidly emerging discipline, attempts to affect a paradigm shift in the way we understand and respond to disability and disabled people. According to Dan Goodley, 'disability studies are a broad area of theory, research and practice that are antagonistic to the popular view that disability equates with personal tragedy. While we may identify people as having physical, sensory, cognitive or mental health impairments, disability studies place the problems of disability in society' (2011, xi). 'If we locate disability in the person', Goodley adds,

> then we maintain a disabling status quo. In contrast, by viewing disability as a cultural and political phenomenon, we ask serious questions about the social world. Undoubtedly, societies subject people with impairments to discrimination. Disabled people have been hated, made exotic, pitied, patronised and ignored. Disability also evokes admiration, curiosity, fascination and sympathy. Disability studies respond to these acts of political and cultural life. (2011, xi)

The present chapter is a meditation on how translation can be appropriated as a disruptive inter-linguistic literary activity to challenge what disability is and what it signifies within the normative structures of power.

What follows here, then, is the critical examination of the role that translation studies plays in destabilising the understanding of normalcy in relation to which disability has been traditionally defined as an inevitable locus of lack and inadequacy. This examination will inevitably throw up a set of troubling questions: What are the emancipatory potentials inherent in the act of translating disability texts? How can translation be effectively used to disturb the form of hierarchical thinking implicit in the binary opposition of ability and disability? How can this form of literary practice be strategically deployed to recognise, interrogate and even unmask various forms of oppression inflicted by an able-ist society on disabled people?

In addressing the questions mentioned previously, this chapter would obviously be presenting translation as a form of social activism that can help us affect a radical epistemological shift in the way we perceive and respond to disability and disabled people. In this sense, translation can also help us redefine the egalitarian contours of our democratic society.

Translation as a literary practice draws attention to the role that language plays in shaping the world we live in, and, by extension, underscores the linguistic organisation of social relations. For this reason, it can play an effective role in bringing about an affective attitudinal change in the way we understand and conceptualise the experience of disablement. This argument was repeatedly discussed at the workshop by a number of participants who laid emphasis on the need to use politically correct language to evoke the experience of disablement while translating a disability text. The most cited story in this context was Rabindranath Tagore's 'Shubha'—the touching story of a young girl who could not speak.

Tagore, in his Bengali version of the story, uses the word '*boba*' to refer to the young girl's impairment. Supriya Chaudhuri in her translation of the story (2000) uses the word 'dumb' as the English version of 'boba'. But unlike its Bengali counterpart, the word 'dumb' has a pejorative connotation. A casual look at the Webster Dictionary for the entry on 'dumb' is quite revealing. In addition to being used to refer to deaf or hard of hearing people, people with speech-related disabilities, or people with linguistic or communication disorders or disabilities, the word also denotes a person who lacks intelligence and/ or is stupid. The result is disastrous. The two meanings of the word fuse into one and equate a person with hearing and speech disability with one who is stupid. Therefore, a translator while translating a text needs to unlearn the patterns of linguistic able-ism in their choice of words. At the workshop, Banibrata Mahanta, Somrita Ganguly and Ananya Ghoshal preferred to use a more value neutral term like 'mute' in place of the derogative 'dumb'.

This leads us to the question of ethics. What kind of idiom should we use when translating a disability text referring to the said phenomenon? After all, a reformation in language is supposed to bring an attitudinal shift in people and in the way they perceive and respond to disability and disabled people. A disabled friendly translator, in the course of translating a disability text, is not only fixing language but fixing attitude. The translator's role, therefore, is 'not simply aesthetic, cultural and political, but one that involves an attitude of praxis' (Kothari 2007, 47).

We therefore can safely conclude that disability is not a clinically diagnosed medical condition but a socially constituted pathology that needs to be problematised. Translation can play an important role in this process by opening up a space for a transformative discursive radicalism. As Radha Chakravarty says, 'the idiom in which we speak or write determines the way we perceive and represent our world. To change the idiom therefore is to transform our perspective on the world, in our representations as well as social relations' (2016). Chakravarty's argument effectively shifts the focus of the experience of disablement from the human body to the normative linguistic conceptions of the phenomenon. The problem then, as Lennard Davis says in *Enforcing Normalcy*, 'is not the persons with disability; the problem is the way normalcy has been constructed to create the problem of the disabled person' (1995, 24). He, therefore, believes that the primary task of developing the consciousness of disability issues is to 'reverse the hegemony of normalcy and institute alternative ways of thinking' (1995, 49). This chapter is an attempt to demonstrate how translation as a form of interlingual and intercultural academic practice can help us reverse the hegemony of normalcy and institute alternative ways of thinking about the experience of disablement.

Let us continue with our discussion by referring to an Urdu short story by Suraj Sanim and its translation into English by Shefali Jain. This narrative, however, is not about disability. There are no physically or cognitively disabled characters in it, nor does its plot directly refer to the materially embodied experience of disablement. Yet, the story is titled 'Viklang' in its Hindi translation.

Set in the India of 1960s and 1970s with its promise of universal progress and the hope of establishing an egalitarian society, the plot of the story chronicles the friendship between the narrator—who comes from a well-to-do family—and his friend Bhushan—a bright and talented young boy from the working class who has to sell newspapers and magazines to support his studies. He braves the adversities arising out of his underprivileged economic background in the hope that his education will one day help him overcome his poverty. However, Bhushan's dream of making it big in life fails to materialise as he is unable to pay the fee for his matriculation examination. The promise of an egalitarian society thus remains unfulfilled for the protagonist. He ultimately becomes a waiter in a club. 'Apaahij' is thus a story about the fraught relationship between socially and economically underprivileged subjects and the promise of universal progress. The narrator despite having an inferior intellect grows up to become an IAS (Indian Administrative Service) officer. Sanim's story and the pitying gaze of the narrator suggests that the poor boy was destined to become what he became because of his underprivileged social and economic background and it is this background that turns Bhushan into an '*apaahij*'. This is indeed a striking story that invites the reader to read disability metaphorically as analogous to poverty. The ease with which the author establishes the association between poverty and disability and the uncritical acceptance of this association by the reader is indeed troubling as it speaks volumes about the way the phenomena is lodged in our collective conscience. Using Gayatri Chakraborty Spivak's notion of reading as translation, Shefali Jain strategically deploys translation as an effective means to deconstruct the naturalness of such an arbitrary association and opens up new spaces of interpretation.

While dwelling on the two aspects of language, 'logic' and 'rhetoricity', Spivak writes that although every act of reading or communication carries a bit of the risk of fraying, or 'disruptive rhetoricity', 'our stake in agency' (1993, 180) keeps this down to a minimum. She writes that the translator's task is to facilitate this fraying and pry open the gaps already present in the text rather than to follow the mere logic of language. Shefali Jain in her translation of the story 'Apaahij', locates and widens several moments in the text when the authorial voice seems to detach itself from the pitying gaze of the narrator thereby problematising any direct equation constructed between poverty and impairment. Her translation underscores the fact that though Bhushan is represented throughout the narrative from a sympathetic lens, he is not entirely without agency. Jain's translation focuses on moments that lie submerged within the narrative surface of the original—moments which see the narrator constantly snubbing Bhushan. Her translation reads these constant snubs as defensive gestures of an omniscient narrator who constantly feels threatened and insulted by the poor man's superior intellect. Such a translational gesture not only disrupts the stable assurance of an omniscient narrator and his attempt at the equation of disability and poverty, but also problematises the attempts to deny agency to the subalterns—be it the poor or the disabled.

For an able-ist consciousness, the process of narrativising the experience of disablement has always been a matter of reducing the alterity of the disabled world into an accessible domain for able-ist intervention. But, for a disabled friendly critical intellect, the translation of such narratives is less a process of internalising normative assumptions about disability and more of disrupting their totalising grip and imparting to the original narrative a completely different meaning. Borrowing from the great Brazilian translator Haraldo de Campos, Susan Bassnett and Harish Trivedi poignantly observe that 'translation may be likened to a blood transfusion, where the emphasis is on the health and nourishment of the translator. This is a far cry from the notion of faithfulness to an original, of the translator as servant of the source text. Translation... is a dialogue, the translator is an all-powerful reader and a free agent as a writer' (1999, 5). Jain's translation, true to Bassnett and Trivedi's observation, demonstrates what a translator can do to a text and opens up new realms of signification that destabilises existing modes of hierarchical thinking.

Many of the texts translated at the workshop had been previously translated. However, earlier these translated narratives had not been presented as disability texts. The workshop had provided a number of participants with the unique opportunity of revisiting these short stories and resituating them within a new frame of reference—that of disability.

The Urdu short story '*Woh*' by Rashid Jahan, for example, has been canonised in the Indian academia for reasons other than disability. This story, which opens the second volume of the now well-known and institutionalized *Women Writing in India* edited by Suzie Tharu and K. Lalitha, figures prominently in most women writing courses throughout the country. 'Woh' is the story of its narrator protagonist, Sufia, and her encounter with an unnamed prostitute whose profession instinctively invites social revulsion. The compounder who distributes medicines at the hospital describes her as 'a wicked woman ... a prostitute' (Jahan 2014, 117) and even expresses his disdain for the doctor who pays little regard for her fallen ways and treats her like any other patient. Naseeba, the maid-servant who works at the school where Sufia teaches, refuses to touch the chair on which the prostitute sits. She even hits her with a slate and accuses her of being a 'a bitch and a whore' (Jahan 2014, 120). This sense of disgust is normalised throughout the narrative as the revulsion to the woman's so-called immoral profession is shared by most of the characters within the story. Sufia, however, controls her disgust, smiles at her, and is most willing to share social spaces and be sociable with the prostitute. The readers of the story are supposed to identify themselves with the narrator opening up new spaces of social interactions.

It is from this feminist perspective that 'Woh' has been often read and repeatedly translated. Two such translations immediately come to mind—one by M.T. Khan and the other by Rakhshanda Jalil. Both translations uncover and problematise the dominant social reactions to prostitutes. Both translations also clearly mention that the prostitute has a facial disfigurement: 'I was repulsed by the sight of her but, somehow, I managed to look at her and smile. She smiled too; or at least, she attempted to. Her nose had completely disappeared; in its place were two large, red gaping holes. An eye was missing, and with the other, she could barely see without craning her neck' (Jahan 2014, 117).

But in the hands of both Khan and Jalil, the reference to the woman's disablement is reduced to its metaphorical signification. This effectively erases the materially embodied experience of disablement from the story and precludes its analysis as a socially significant aspect of identity. Both Khan's and Jalil's translations seem to impart an evaluative moral connotation to the prostitute's profession and use the prostitute's facial disfigurement as a euphemism for the profession to which she belongs, reducing the experience of disablement to its metaphorical signification. In their hands, the facial disfigurement becomes a narrative device to underscore the fact that the prostitute is bearing the fruit of her profession.

Both translations tend to overlook the fact that the response of social revulsion exhibited by the various characters in the story can also be read as an instinctive response to the prostitute's facial disfigurement rather than to her profession. At the workshop, Shilpaa Anand drew our attention to the above and we realised that her translation focuses primarily on the woman's facial disfigurement and the social reaction to her deformed face. The experience of disablement within the text is constituted by the widespread social response to the disabled individual. Disability in this sense is primarily formulated within the visual gaze of the onlooker. Significantly, Anand's translation underscores Sufia's struggle to know the prostitute's medical diagnosis and focuses on the latter's diseased condition. Anand's translation of Rashid Jahan's '*Woh*', thus affects an epistemic shift in the way the story is read, pushing the narrative beyond the discourse of feminism within which '*Woh*' has been canonised for some time now.

While translations like the one carried out by Anand are a source of great joy for us and have provided us with a great deal of satisfaction, they have also simultaneously raised a troubling question: Why was a workshop required to make these translators recognise disability as a conceptual framework for reading and translating texts? This becomes even more interesting when we remind ourselves that translation studies of late have been obsessed with the articulation of marginalised subjectivities and the resistance they offer to dominant structures of power. The cry for disability appears to be lost amidst the lightning of marginalised articulations particularly those along the lines of race, gender and caste. If disability as a conceptual paradigm is to make an entry into the highly competitive field of translation studies, it must first argue its case and legitimise its inclusion. This chapter, in fact, is an effort in this direction.

References

Bassnett, Susan and Harish Trivedi, ed. *Postcolonial Translation: Theory and Practice*, London and New York, Routledge, 1999.

Chakravarty, Radha, 'A Different Idiom: Translation and Disability', *Disability In Translation: An Indian Experience,* edited by G.J.V. Prasad and Someshwar Sati. New Delhi: Routledge, 2016.

Davis, Lennard, *Enforcing Normalcy: Disability, Deafness and the Body*, London and New York, Verso, 1995.

Fuentes, Carlos, *Aura*, London, Andre Deutsch, 1990.

Goodley, Dan, *Disability Studies: An Interdisciplinary Studies*, Los Angeles, London, New Delhi, Singapore and Washington DC, Sage Publications, 2011.

Jahan, Rashid. 'That One', translated by Rakhshanda Jalil, *A Rebel and Her Cause: The Life and Work of Rashid Jahan*, edited by Rakshanda Jalil, New Delhi, Women Unlimited, 2014, pp. 117–20.

Kothari, Rita, 'The Translation of Dalit Literature into English', in *Translation as Intervention*, edited by Jeremy Munday, London, Continuum International Publishing Group, 2007, pp. 38–53.

Paz, Octavio, 'Translations of Literatures and Letters', translated by Irene del Corral, *Theories of Translation from Dryden to Derrida*, edited by R. Schulte and J. Biguenet, Chicago, University of Chicago Press, 1992, pp. 152–63.

Shahbaz, M., 'Viklang', *Urdu Ki Nayi Kahaniyan*, edited by Ramlal and Usmani, New Delhi, National Book Trust, 2011.

Spivak, Gayatri Chakravorty, *Outside in the Teaching Machine*, New York, Routledge, 1993.

Tagore, Rabindranath,'Subha', translated by Supriya Chaudhuri, in *Rabindranath Tagore: Selected Short Stories*, edited by Sukanta Chaudhuri, New Delhi, Oxford University Press, 2000, pp. 104–09.

18

Money, Work and Family in Ghachar Ghochar: *A Translational Economy of India*

Amrapali Saha

Translation, writes Rita Kothari in her Introduction to *Translating India* (2014), is a site of a community's unspoken desires and anxieties, and different languages in India, including English, have different narratives of translation to tell. One such narrative is that of Vivek Shanbhag's *Ghachar Ghochar*, originally published in Kannada in 2013, and translated into English by Srinath Perur in 2016. The novel is an insightful translation of the idea of India in its consummate disparateness, articulated with a surprising depth of meaning. To translate is to unravel the skeins of meanings, social and cultural, and behold the tenuousness of the world that we have spun around us through language. 'Words after all are nothing by themselves', as the unnamed narrator of the novel observes fittingly, 'They burst into meaning only in the minds they've entered' (Shanbhag 2016, 5). Thus, as David Damrosch suggests, translation is at once a linguistic and a cultural project (2009, 66), which makes the acts of producing and reading translations necessary for fruitful discursive engagements in the domain of Indian literatures in English.

Through this study of the networks of and changing relations between money, work and family in the novel, my objective will be to piece together a translational economy of India as presented in Shanbhag's work. In its intimate portrayal of a close-knit Kannadiga family as it rises from the bounds of urban poverty to the newly discovered freedom of sudden affluence, *Ghachar Ghochar* maps the story of an India 'shining', its middle class rising and, more importantly, the undertow of its concomitant desires and anxieties. Shanbhag's work is not only an incisive scrutiny of the micropolitics of familial relationships and the disparate parts that constitute his fictional family, but also a demonstration of how critical it is to grasp these parts and their internal complexities, located as they are within the broader narrative of socio-economic development in modern India.

Money, Work and Family in *Ghachar Ghochar*

The Indian family, writes Patricia Uberoi, has an iconic status in national self-representation, that of an 'imagined' tradition, which indexes the moral and spiritual superiority of India vis-à-vis a 'degenerate West' (1996, 144). Even so, there is a dichotomy inherent in this self-aggrandising socio-cultural representation of the family in India. To put it differently, the enduring image of the family as *the* source of love, support and nurture in an individual's life often glosses over the concomitant reality of the family as a site of contestation and struggle over values and resources for many. Under these circumstances, one must examine the family as a site of inequality, exploitation and violence, argues Uberoi. Keeping this in mind, *Ghachar Ghochar* brings to life a family that is neither an idealised concept, nor a homogenous entity. On the contrary, the novel is a perspicuous anatomy of the set of affective relationships that constitute its particular familial world, a dysfunctional unit suffering a credibility crisis. More often than not in the novel, the mere mention of the 'family' evokes a sense of menace and violence characteristic of a mafia syndicate, which demands strict allegiance from its members and turns ruthless when it comes to the matter of its own survival. Consider the introduction that the son of the family, the narrator of this novel, offers to his own family.

> Ours is a joint family. We live in the same house—my wife and I, my parents, my uncle and Malati. It's natural to ask, I suppose, why the six of us should live together. What can I say—it is one of the strengths of families to pretend that they desire what is inevitable. (Shanbhag 2016, 10)

Shanbhag, thus, begins his novel by puncturing the myth of a traditional Indian family sustaining itself on the unconditional love of its members. In fact, the family in *Ghachar Ghochar* is placed at the vortex of a liberalising economy marked by consumption. Set against the backdrop of the consumer revolution in India, this taut social satire works towards demystifying the internal workings and moral underpinnings of an Indian family 'from the inside'. Echoing the Anna Karenina principle that all happy families are alike, but every unhappy family is unhappy in its own way, Shanbhag's novel serves as a crucible for the tensions, dualities and paradoxes that Sanjukta Dasgupta and Malashri Lal outline as being integral to understanding family dynamics (2007, 15). The prevalent discourse surrounding the family in India has by and large projected the institution as a benevolent dictator, providing the security of group identity and fulfilling a deep emotional need, often for the purpose of reinforcing the familial power, trust and interdependence that is demanded from its constituent members. The family, as shown in the novel, thus ends up operating in direct contravention of democratic principles. As an illustration, the narrator of the novel remarks that 'the well-being' of a household often 'rests on selective acts of blindness and deafness' (Shanbhag 2016, 97). In giving us a behind-the-scenes look so to speak at the often idealised and all-powerful institution of the family in India, the novel presents itself as a site of tensions between the paradoxical need for translating and the simultaneous untranslatability of the desires and anxieties of Shanbhag's middle-class family in question.

Families in fiction, observes Ira Raja, represent a measure of continuity as well as an index of change (2016, 6). That is certainly true of *Ghachar Ghochar*, which depicts a lower-middle class family in Bangalore as it transitions from subsisting on the modest salary of the older brother 'Appa' (the narrator's father)—a salesman in the tea trade—to acquiring the status of the nouveau riche when the younger brother 'Chikkappa' (younger uncle) establishes Sona Masala—a successful business venture in the spice trade. The transition, however, is far from smooth, as the family battles class anxieties and irrepressible fears of an adverse turn in their fortunes. Coming in the wake of their increased purchasing power and a consequent drive for material consumption, there is a gradual attenuation of the family's cherished ideals of economic thrift and moral integrity. As the family is dismantled from its old home in a teeming lower-middle class neighbourhood in Bangalore and rebuilds itself in a larger house in an upmarket part of the city, something is no longer quite right with the family. The shared space of the new home becomes fraught with several kinds of tensions, as Shanbhag demonstrates, ranging from a clash of values between the old salaried middle-class typified by Appa and the new entrepreneurial middle-class as embodied in Chikkappa, a conflict that is exacerbated by the growing influence of money within an increasingly modernising economy. Their 'improved finances' result in the family metamorphosing into a sort of hybrid entity, an intra-class translation straddling two divergent modalities of middle-class life within one home. Since the security and survival of the family are privileged above all, the individual members unite and attempt to salvage as much of the wreckage as they can, which results in waging wars against any perceived enemy, whether it is a band of marauding ants, or a dissenting daughter-in-law. Money, however, outsmarts all of them, in spite of the family's preoccupation with it. As the narrator realises, perhaps too late at that,

> It's not we who control money, it's the money that controls us … Money had swept us up and flung us in the midst of a whirlwind. (Shanbhag 2016, 49)

The family that used to function in an intricate web of interdependence, 'walking like a single body across the tightrope of' (Shanbag 2016, 19) their circumstances, ends up participating in an 'orgy of lavishness' (Shanbhag 2016, 49) thanks to their freshly-minted affluence. Shanbhag, however, is not interested in ameliorating this 'difference of culture' as the narrator of the novel terms it; instead, his objective is to truthfully represent the antinomies of change. There is no suturing of those differences in the text. As a matter of fact, the writer's focus is on highlighting the tensions that arise from the juxtaposition of contradictions in mounting a kaleidoscopic view of the family's unique circumstances. The middle class, as Satish Deshpande points out, has often been thought of as the stable centre of polity (2003, 130), which, however, in the novel is exposed as a lost cosmopolitan ideal struggling with its Janus-faced realities. Merchant, Rose and Gour write that middle-class aspirations are accompanied by anxieties and insecurities associated with changing lifestyles that challenge traditional beliefs and class systems (2015, 162). These beliefs and class systems are challenged to such an extent that economic development is interpreted through the lens of traditional values. Appa, for instance, believes that wealth should not strike suddenly like a visitation, but instead grow gradually like a tree (Shanbhag 2016, 21). Chikkappa, on the other hand, is shown at ease with his burgeoning business, engaging in unscrupulous financial practices, maintaining an army of ruffians to work at his bidding and bribing government officials as and when required, yet he is as hardworking and committed to his work as Appa used to be.

Interestingly, the narrator neither condemns Chikkappa nor does he pronounce moral judgements on his uncle for his actions. The narrator's struggle lies in attempting to strike a balance between the polarised extremes of his family life in the 'cluttered mess' of economic progress and social development. The Coffee House, where he goes to seek refuge from domestic strife, becomes the ideal for him, an entity that is as much a thing of the past as it is comfortably situated in the present, at ease with its hybrid existence. However, not all stories take the same form. The push and pull between the past and the present manifests itself differently when it comes to the narrator's home. Although the narrator keeps reflecting upon the past when his father was a salaried professional and the family lived a hand-to-mouth existence, his nostalgia evoking a 'simpler time', he is simultaneously aware that those were also times of financial hardship and socio-economic deprivation. Thus, in light of the rapid transformations that have followed from the post-liberalisation era, with things becoming increasingly 'ghachar ghochar' (a nonsense word meaning 'hopelessly entangled'), the novel's fundamental concern is with the dialectics of change and the translation of their meanings within a particular contextual framework.

A Translational Economy of India

David Damrosch suggests that an excellent translation can be seen as an expansive transformation of the original, adding a new stage in the life of a work as it moves from its first home out into the world (2009, 66). For a novel like *Ghachar Ghochar* that is many texts at once, translation has a deeper implication, signifying more than the process of an interlingual transfer from Kannada to English. Translation in this instance does not operate as a synthesising, harmonising force, but is meant to recreate a disjunctive experience mirroring the contents of the novel. One finds many things in translation in the novel, a country, a city, a class, a family, and even the cast of characters, in as much as translation signifies a site of tension between the antinomies of change. The short, slender volume defies categorisation into the 'big, baggy, polyphonic, and crucially, written in English work' that has come to represent the category of the 'Great Indian Novel', writes Parul Sehgal (2017) in her review of the book in *The New York Times*. What the novel offers instead is a 'heterogeneous alterity', to quote Rajeswari Sunder Rajan (2011), which if the title of the book is anything to go by, remains paradoxically untranslatable and yet curiously intelligible in itself. Though Shanbhag's work resists being slotted as a putative nation-novel, 'the nation has not disappeared', rather 'it is worn more lightly than before' (Rajan 2011, 224). The translated novel emerges as a site of 'novelty, resistance, impurity, and hybridity', as is evidenced from the body of the text, examples being the untranslated title, or the appearance of Kannada words sans italicisation or a glossary in the English text. These are important choices, keeping in mind what Vimala C. Rao had pointed out in her essay, 'Translation Tensions' (2003, 137), that in a post-colonial, post-modern and post-structuralist world, translation must foster diversity, linguistic and cultural.

Translation, as Michael Cronin proposes, should seek to develop an eye for the myriad fractal complexities of the local while remaining aware of larger contexts (2006, 131). Attention to detail, he argues, will confront us with the limits of our understanding. Reading Shanbhag's novel in this instance is to become aware of the fact that writers like him, who might have been previously situated on the margins of the urban-centred, cosmopolitan and writing-in-English Indian literary scene, are gaining cultural currency and becoming increasingly vital to transnational conversations on the idea of India and its many translations. To recreate what lies under the surface of the original text in another language through translation, suggests Shanbhag (Author Q&A), one must understand what went into the making of the original, then consequently dismantle the text and rebuild it in another language. Moreover, it must be a collaborative process between the writer and the translator. Vimala Rao would have concurred with Shanbhag's view of what a translation should aspire to do, that is to take hybridity, rather than purity, as the organising principle, such that both the original and the translated text are recognised on their own, different as they are (2003, 141). Rao observes that more often than not there is a belief when it comes to the translation of regional writers into English that the 'honesty, originality, authenticity, and purity' (2003, 138) with which they write will be diluted, or distorted in the English translation. However, instead of framing the discourse on translation around principles of loss and gain, as Rao argues, is it not better to develop an increased awareness of the complexities of the process of translation.

Translation should neither offer the original text in a syncopated version, nor engender an obsessive effort towards achieving equivalence. Instead, translation is a process of unmaking and remaking like any other form of writing, an act of creation. The novel illustrates this hybridity at work, the untranslated title suggesting a fluidity of meanings, a situation when 'things get hopelessly entangled' (Shanbhag 2016, 75), and are allowed to remain so for the reader's own interpretation. In fact, during the translation process, Shanbhag even added passages to the English text of the novel, describing the couple's buying spree during their honeymoon and the narrator going through his wife's wardrobe (Author Q&A), additions which may be rightfully construed as producing a more nuanced picture of the relationships in the novel. As T.S. Satyanath puts forth, the issue at stake is not to look at how one gets consumed by another, but how does one perceive another and resist shallow homogenisation of one another (2009, 215). If the original text is not regarded as a pure and sanctified whole, the English translation, or for that matter its translation into any other language, can evolve in acknowledgement of its polysemy of otherness. The two texts can then in fact be regarded as concatenated identities, at once a measure of continuity, as well as an index of change.

References

Primary Text

Shanbhag, Vivek, *Ghachar Ghochar*, translated by Srinath Perur, New Delhi, Harper Perennial, 2016.

Secondary Texts

Cronin, Michael, *Translation and Identity*, London and New York, Routledge, 2006.

Damrosch, David, *How to Read World Literature*, UK, Wiley-Blackwell, 2009.

Dasgupta, Sanjukta and Malashri Lal, 'Introduction', *The Indian Family in Transition: Reading Literary and Cultural Texts*, edited by Sanjukta Dasgupta and Malashri Lal, New Delhi, Sage Publications, 2007, pp. 13–31.

Deshpande, Satish, *Contemporary India: A Sociological View*, New Delhi, Penguin Books India, 2003.

Kothari, Rita, *Translating India: The Cultural Politics of English*, London and New York, Routledge, 2014.

Merchant, Altaf, Gregory M. Rose and Mohit Gour, 'Meanings of Money Among Middle-Class Hindu Families in India,' *The Middle Class in Emerging Societies: Consumers, Lifestyles and Markets*, edited by Leslie L. Marsh and Hongmei Li, London and New York, Routledge, 2015, pp. 161–83.

Raja, Ira. 'Introduction.' *Security, Socialisation and Affect in Indian Families: Unfamiliar Ground*. London and New York: Routledge, 2016, pp. 1–6.

Rajan, Rajeswari Sunder, 'After "Midnight's Children": Some Notes on the New Indian Novel in English,' *Social Research*, Vol. 78, No. 1, 2011, pp. 203–30.

Rao, Vimala C., 'Translation Tensions,' *Indian Literature*, Vol. 47, No. 5, 2003, pp. 137–42.

Satyanath, T.S., 'Nadu(s) and Desa: On the Construction of Regional and National Identities in Modern Kannada Representations,' *Indian Literature*, Vol. 53, No. 1, 2009, pp. 209–19.

Sehgal, Parul, 'A Great Indian Novel Reaches American Shores,' *The New York Times*, 6 April 2017. Available at: https://www.nytimes.com/2017/04/06/books/review/ghachar-ghochar-vivek-shanbhag.html

Shanbhag, Vivek, 'Author Q&A,' Penguin Random House, 2007.

Uberoi, Patricia, 'The Family in Official Discourse,' *India International Centre Quarterly*, Vol. 23, No. 3/4, 1996, pp. 134–55.

About the Editor and Contributors

Editor

G.J.V. Prasad is Professor of English at Jawaharlal Nehru University (JNU). His major research interests are Indian English Literature, Contemporary Theatre, Dalit Writings, Australian Literature and Translation Theory. His latest work includes a forthcoming edited book on translation and disability. Prasad is also a poet and novelist. He is a recipient of the Katha award for translation from Tamil. He has co-edited with Sara Rai a collection of stories from Indian languages, *Imaging the Other*. His academic publications include the following books: *Continuities in Indian English Poetry: Nation language form* (1999), *Writing India Writing English: Literature, Language, Location* (2011) and four edited volumes of critical essays including *Translation and Culture: Indian Perspectives* (2010). He is the current editor of *The Journal of the School of Language, Literature & Culture Studies* (JSL), JNU and Chairperson of the Indian Association for Commonwealth Literature and Language Studies (IACLALS).

Contributors

Amitendu Bhattacharya is Assistant Professor of English in the Department of Humanities and Social Sciences at the Birla Institute of Technology and Science, Pilani, K.K. Birla Goa Campus.

Amrapali Saha is a PhD Research Scholar at the Centre for English Studies, JNU, New Delhi.

Fatima Rizvi is Associate Professor in the Department of English and Modern European Languages at the University of Lucknow. She specialises in Urdu literature in translation and adaptation. She translates Urdu and Hindi.

Gargi Bhattacharya works in the Department of Sanskrit, Pali & Prakrit, Visva-Bharati, Santiniketan. At present she is also Vice Principal of Bhasha-Bhavana (Institute of Language, Literature & Culture), Visva-Bharati. Dr Bhattacharya has translated seven minor Upanishads in Bengali that have been published by Ramakrishna Mission Institute of Golpark, Kolkata in 2017.

Hiren J. Patel is an Assistant Professor of English at V.S. Patel College of Arts and Science, Bilimora (Gujarat). He received his doctoral degree in Comparative Literature and Translation Studies from Central University of Gujarat, Gandhinagar in 2018. His research interests include nineteenth-century Gujarati literature, Shakespeare's translations into Gujarati, the Gujarati language, Translation Studies and Reception Theory.

Huzaifa Omair Siddiqi is a doctoral research scholar at the Centre for English Studies, JNU. His research is primarily on phenomenology and speculative materialism. He is also a contributor to *The Telegraph India* and *Scroll.in.*

Lav Kanoi was previously employed at Ashoka University as Senior Research Associate to the Vice-Chancellor, prior to which he worked with governments and large corporations as a strategy/management consultant. He is a Young India Fellow and holds an MA in English Literature (Jadavpur University), and has published translations from Latin to English and Bengali to Hindi. Lav is presently undertaking doctoral work at Yale University.

Nipun Nutan is currently working as Assistant Professor of French language at Amity School of Language, Amity University, Gurgaon. He has been pursuing his PhD from the Centre for French and Francophone Studies, JNU, New Delhi. His research interests include translation history, literary translation and post-colonial translation.

Priyada Shridhar Padhye is an Assistant Professor at the Centre for German Studies in JNU since 2015. She teaches courses related to German as a foreign language as well as Translation Studies. Her areas of interest are methodology of teaching German as a foreign language, methodology of teaching specialised translation and theory of translation.

Regiane Corrêa de Oliveira Ramos teaches English at the Universidade Estadual de Mato Grosso do Sul (UEMS), Brazil. She is the president of BrIndARC - Brasil-Índia Associação de Redes de Conhecimento (Brazil-India Knowledge Networks Association). She holds PhD from University of São Paulo and was a CAPES Fellow (2012–2013) in the English Department at JNU, Delhi. Her interest is in postcolonial studies, decolonial studies, multiliteracy studies and gender studies. Currently, she is researching on *hijra* autobiographies in English.

Runjhun Verma is a teacher of French at Alliance Française de Delhi and at Delhi School of Journalism. Her areas of interest include literary translation and her PhD thesis dealt with the politics of literary translation of Indian literary works into French.

Sachin C. Ketkar is a bilingual writer, translator, editor, blogger and researcher based in Baroda, Gujarat. He works as Professor in English, Faculty of Arts, The Maharaja Sayajirao University of Baroda, Vadodara. His books in English include *Skin, Spam and Other Fake Encounters: Selected Marathi Poems in translation* (2011), *(Trans)Migrating Words: Refractions on Indian Translation Studies*

(2010) and *A Dirge for the Dead Dog and Other Incantations* (2003). He has extensively translated present-day Marathi poetry, most of which is collected in the anthology *Live Update: An Anthology of Recent Marathi Poetry* (2005) edited by him. He has translated fiction by Jorge Luis Borges, Ted Hughes and Adam Thopre into Marathi. He won 'Indian Literature Poetry Translation Prize', given by *Indian Literature Journal*, Sahitya Akademi, New Delhi for translation of modern Gujarati poetry in 2000.

Samudranil Gupta is a research scholar at JNU. His area of interest lies in Beckett studies, literature, philosophy, modernism, post-war European fiction and world literature.

Shinjini Basu is Assistant Professor at Sir Gurudas Mahavidyalaya, Kolkata. Her doctoral work was on the relation between crime and colonial modernity. Her areas of interest are literary theories and colonial and post-colonial studies. She has published, both in Bengali and English, on translation, post-colonial novel, colonial and post-colonial political practices and gender discourse.

Soham Pain is Assistant Professor of English at Chopra Kamala Paul Smriti Mahavidyalaya, Chopra, West Bengal, India. Pain's doctoral thesis was on R.K. Narayan. He was a Fulbright-Nehru Doctoral Fellow (2014–2015) at UT, Austin.

Someshwar Sati is presently an Associate Professor at the Department of English, Kirori Mal College, University of Delhi. His doctoral research was on the Indian English Novel. His research areas include postcolonial theory, the Indian English novel: Midnight's Children and after, disability studies and theory, disability in translation, translation studies, the Victorian English novel and the twentieth century English novel. He has also been awarded the CDN Prize for the best paper presented at the IACLALS 2016 conference organised by IACLALS and the Department of English, Kakatiya University, Warangal.

Subhendu Mund has been teaching and has worked in the educational administration for 40 years. Now he is an independent writer and scholar living in Bhubaneswar (India). He has published 37 books of poems, short stories, travel writing, dictionaries, critical essays, monographs, translation and research work in Odia, English and Kannada. He has published 80 research papers on Indian English Literature and Odishan Studies.

Tara Menon is a PhD candidate in Comparative Literature at Yale University.

Index

Note—The letter '*n*' following locators refers to footnotes.

E

F

N

O

P